MORAL LUCK

SUNY Series in Ethical Theory

Robert B. Louden, Editor

MORAL LUCK

EDITED BY

DANIEL STATMAN

STATE UNIVERSITY OF NEW YORK PRESS

Published by
State University of New York Press, Albany

For information, address State University of New York Press,
State University Plaza, Albany, N.Y. 12246

Production by M. R. Mulholland
Marketing by Fran Keneston

Library of Congress Cataloging-in-Publication Data
Moral luck / edited by Daniel Statman.
        p.   cm. — (SUNY series in ethical theory)
    Includes bibliographical references.
    ISBN 0-7914-1539-2 (alk. paper). — ISBN 0-7914-1540-6 (pbk. :
alk. paper)
    1. Ethics. 2. Fortune—Moral and ethical aspects. I. Statman,
Daniel. II. Series.
BJ1275.M798   1993
170—dc20   92-31367
                                                          CIP

10 9 8 7 6 5 4 3 2 1

to my mother, with love

Contents

Acknowledgments

I thank the following for their generous permission to use copyrighted material:

American Philosophical Association, for permission to reprint a revised version of "Luck" by Nicholas Rescher, APA Proceedings, Vol. 64 (1990).

American Philosophical Quarterly, for permission to reprint "Crime and Moral Luck" by Steven Sverdlik, Vol. 25 (1988).

Cambridge University Press, for permission to reprint chapter two of Bernard Williams's *Moral Luck* (1981); chapter three of Thomas Nagel's *Mortal Questions* (1979); and extracts from Martha C. Nussbaum's *The Fragility of Goodness* (1986).

Ethics, for permission to reprint "Luck and Moral Responsibility" by Michael J. Zimmerman, Vol. 97 (1987).

Metaphilosophy, for permission to reprint "Morality and Bad Luck" by Judith Jarvis Thomson, Vol. 20 (1989); and "The Virtues of Impure Agency" by Margaret Walker, Vol. 22 (1991).

Mind, for permission to reprint "Luck and Desert" by Norvin Richards, Vol. 65 (1986).

Philosophical Investigations, for permission to reprint "What's Luck Got to Do With It?" by Don S. Levi, Vol. 12 (1989).

Philosophy, for permission to reprint "Morality and Luck" by Henning Jensen, Vol. 59 (1984).

Judith Andre for permission to reprint her article "Nagel, Williams and Moral Luck", first published in *Analysis* 43 (1983), pp. 202–207.

1

Introduction

Daniel Statman

I

Luck seems to be everywhere. It is a matter of luck who your neighbors are (or will be); it is pure luck that just as you finish your Ph.D. in philosophy, a new university is founded and you are invited to lecture there; it is (bad) luck that your life is ruined by a drunken driver who hits your son. To be sure, one could go on with this, giving more and more examples of luck in different areas and different dimensions of human existence. This widespread and profound effect of luck on human life hangs over us like a threat, generating the feeling that we have no real control over our lives. It undermines our sense of security and stability, promoting a sense of uncertainty with regard to our projects, relationships and aims. It makes our lives seem weak and fragile, always at the mercy of luck.[1]

However, there is at least one area where luck seems to be lacking or irrelevant, that is, the area of morality. The idea of one's moral status being subject to luck seems almost unintelligible to most of us, and the expression *moral luck* seems to be an impossible juxtaposition of two altogether different concepts. No doubt this is one of the reasons for our subject being so attractive and intriguing. As Margaret Coyne [Walker] puts it: "The very idea of 'moral luck' cannot fail to engage our interest, if only because some of us are astonished at the very idea" (1985, p. 319). While one can be lucky in one's business, in one's married life, and in one's health, one cannot, so it is commonly assumed, be subject to luck as far as one's moral worth is concerned.

This deeply rooted assumption of our moral thinking was attacked in 1976 by two leading figures in contemporary moral philosophy, Bernard Williams and Thomas Nagel.[2] Both of them challenged the alleged immunity of morality to luck, seeking to show that luck threatens morality no less than it threatens so many other dimensions of human life. They argued for the existence of what they called *moral luck*, thereby endowing philosophy with a new concept and a wide field of problems. These new ideas have aroused great interest and have invited numerous responses among philosophers, some of which are included in this book.

The fact that luck threatens our moral concepts does not imply that it threatens all of them equally. Axiological concepts, such as 'good' and 'bad', 'admirable,' and so on, are not threatened by luck in the same way as are the concepts of responsibility and justification. This point is made very clearly in Judith Thomson's paper. If David is arrogant, a bully, a coward, and full of envy, then, as Thomson puts it (p. 208), it would be crazy to think that, because his having these features is (supposedly) a matter of luck, he is, therefore, not a bad person. (If *he* is not, who is?) However, there seems to be a difference with regard to a different family of moral notions, including those of responsibility, blame, and others. We would usually withdraw our ascription of blame to somebody if we found out that the event for which we thought the person blameworthy was beyond his or her control and was only a matter of luck.[3] Thus, the debate around moral luck turns mainly around the question of whether and to what extent our moral notions of responsibility, justification, blame, and so forth, are subject to luck. If, indeed, they are, then very serious reflection over our moral concepts and our conception of morality is required. Williams seems to be right in arguing that "the involvement of morality with luck is not something that can simply be accepted *without calling our moral conceptions into question.*"[4]

Though Williams rejects the immunity of morality to luck, he explores the attraction of this idea very clearly. "Such a conception," he says, "has an ultimate form of justice at its heart . . . it offers an inducement, a solace to a sense of the world's unfairness" (p. 36). The nature of this justice is not fully explicated by Williams, but it would seem that immunity to luck might be considered just in at least two ways. First, justice as equality. If morality is immune to luck then the option of being moral is open to everybody everywhere and furthermore, it is open to everybody *equally.* Second, justice as desert. If morality depends on luck, then at least sometimes people are judged morally for things that are beyond their control. This seems to be unfair; one does not deserve to be held responsible for what is beyond one's control. Hence the importance and justice of immunity to luck.

However the mere possibility of a small island of justice in a sea of unfairness is not sufficient to offer this solace to one's sense of unfairness. Something more is required, namely, that moral value possesses "some special, indeed supreme, kind of dignity or importance" (ibid). If this special value is guaranteed then morality's immunity to luck would imply a more basic and general result concerning one's own (partial) immunity to luck. One would then be in control of the most important elements that constitute one's human value. One's worth as a human being in general would not be a matter of luck. Thus, argues Williams, there is a close connection between (a) the idea of the immunity of morality to luck and (b) the idea of the supreme value of morality—both of which are rejected by Williams.

The desire to make human life immune to luck is not new, as Williams rightly mentions (p. 35). In its ancient form the desire is expressed in an attempt to make one's happiness and perfection depend as much as possible on oneself and as little as possible on factors beyond one's control. Though one cannot make oneself immune to all diseases and physical pain, nor to all the annoyances and disappointments caused by friends and family, one can view these different kinds of misfortune with indifference, and seek one's happiness within one's internal world.[5] The more self-sufficient one is, the more free from luck one is. The ancient concept of immunity to luck also presupposes the preceding ideas (a and b), mutatis mutandis. It presupposes that a certain kind of human activity (usually the contemplative) is immune to luck[6] and also that this kind of activity is of a supreme value. The most famous classical doctrines that preached this idea were those of the Cynics, the Epicureans,[7] and the Stoics.[8] However it is also to be found in many other sources of Greek philosophy, such as Plato and Aristotle, as Martha Nussbaum (1986) nicely shows.

Nussbaum's thesis is that Plato, in most of his dialogues, tends to make the good life immune to luck, particularly through the ideal of the contemplative life, while Aristotle in most of his writings suggests an ideal of a more mixed life that, as such, is much more vulnerable to luck. According to Aristotle, though attaining *aretē* is, to a large extent, under one's control, this is not the case with *eudaimonia*. Whether one has a successful and a flourishing life depends on all kinds of luck. Aristotle's view is analyzed by Nussbaum in the extracts from her book included here.[9]

The attractiveness of the idea that the good life should be immune to luck is evident. What is less evident is why anybody should seek to reject this immunity or narrow it and the reason for this is again explored very well by Nussbaum.[10] Making life immune to luck means eliminating from a good life those ingredients that to some extent are affected by luck, such as physical health, social recognition, friends, and family. Because these ingredients are essential to humanity, any human life lacking them will be, or tend to be, poorer and duller. Therefore, one has to choose between a life open to many kinds of values and experiences, but more vulnerable to luck, and a life immune to luck, but focusing only on one kind of activity (usually contemplative) and neglecting other kinds of activities that would make life richer, more interesting, and more attractive.[11]

Ideas a and b are emphasized by Kant and, consequently, the objection to moral luck is usually regarded as a Kantian concept.[12] Kant's view on this is expressed well in the famous opening passage of the *Grundlegung*, where he praises the supreme value of "the good will," which is independent of all the contingencies of the world.[13]

Now because ideas a and b are essential to Kantian morality, and because our fundamental moral conception is Kantian,[14] it follows that acceptance of moral luck "cannot leave the concept of morality where it was" (Williams, p. 54). Morality contingent on luck would be ultimately different from morality immune to luck. Hence, eventually, the acceptance of the possibility of moral luck would have to be accompanied by a new approach to morality in general.

This last point is recognized very clearly by Williams, who welcomes it. A major philosophical aim in Williams's work in the last twenty years has been to explicate what he takes to be the mistakes and the weaknesses of common (Kantian) morality. Central to his view is an objection to the notion of a moral theory, at least in the modern meaning of this concept. Williams believes that the modern approach to morality is narrow and distorted, and therefore, we should abandon it and return to the Greek approach, which asked the right questions and pointed in the right direction for answers.[15] Thus, from Williams's point of view, rejecting the idea that morality is immune to luck is not only intrinsically interesting and important, but is another way of expressing the many defects of modern morality.

II

The fact that one's motives, intentions and personality are influenced by luck is taken by Williams to be a bitter truth. This is what he calls *constitutive luck*.[16] However, Williams does not elaborate on this kind of luck, which he seems to regard as quite obvious. Nor does he concentrate on other kinds of luck (to be explicated by Nagel) that concern judgment of other agents. Rather, Williams's main interest is in the influence luck may have on "the agent's reflective assessment of his own actions" (p. 36); that is, the agent's ability to justify rationally his or her own decisions and actions. It is very important to bear this point in mind when reading Williams's chapter. This is a salient difference between Williams's discussion on moral luck and that of Nagel and other writers. Whereas the latter tend to concentrate on questions concerning moral responsibility viewed from an 'objective' point of view, that is, viewed by a spectator judging another agent from the outside, Williams is concerned with judgments made, so to speak, from the inside, by an agent who reflectively wishes to assess his or her own actions.[17]

Williams, then, wishes to show that rational justification of oneself depends on luck. An example is put forward to demonstrate this point, the story of Gauguin.[18] Gauguin, a creative artist, abandoned his wife and children to live a life in which, so he supposed, he could pursue his art. He believed that only by going alone to Tahiti, turning away from his obligations to his family, could he realize his gifts as a painter. Now, according to Williams, whether this choice can be justified depends primarily on Gauguin's *success*. If he failed, it would become clear that he had no basis for thinking that he was justified in acting as he did. But, argues Williams, "whether he will succeed cannot, in the nature of the case, be foreseen" (p. 38). Therefore, at the time of the choice, Gauguin had to rely on factors that were beyond his control. Obviously one's will, strong as it might be, is not sufficient to make one a great artist. Much more is needed, in particular talent and inspiration. Hence, justification of Gauguin's decision depends on factors that are a matter of luck.[19]

However not all kinds of luck are equally relevant to the justification of Gauguin's decision. Williams distinguishes two different kinds of luck: luck intrinsic to the project and luck extrinsic to it. Gauguin's success in becoming a great painter is a

matter of intrinsic luck; his injury in a traffic accident on the way
to Tahiti is a matter of (bad) extrinsic luck. Though both kinds of
luck are necessary for success and hence for justification, only
the former, argues Williams, relates to *unjustification*. What
would prove him wrong and unjustified in his project would
not just be that the *project* failed (as a result of some extrinsic
cause) but that *he* failed.[20] Once again, it should be kept in mind
that Williams's main concern is "the agent's reflective assessment of his own actions." While extrinsic failure does not cause
the agent to see his or her decision as unjustified, intrinsic failure does.

A retrospective acknowledgment of an unjustified choice expresses itself in a special species of regret that is called by
Williams *agent-regret*. Agent-regret can be sensed by a person
only toward his or her own past actions, and it has a particular
kind of expression, that is, a desire to make some sort of reparation. Williams emphasizes that the sentiment of agent-regret is
not restricted to voluntary actions. A lorry driver who, through
no fault of his, runs over a child, will feel a different sense of
regret than that felt by any spectator; he will feel agent-regret
and will feel a pressing need to make some reparation or
compensation.[21]

Williams's account of agent-regret is not supposed to be
merely a descriptive or a conceptual one, but a normative one too.
That is to say, people not only feel what Williams calls *agent-
regret* but they *ought* to have these feelings, in the sense that is
would be irrational of them not to experience them. Williams is
very strict on this point, arguing that "it would be a kind of insanity [!] never to experience sentiments of this kind towards anyone, and it would be an insane concept of rationality which
insisted that a rational person never would." This alleged "insanity" is connected with the false assumption, "that we might . . .
entirely detach ourselves from the unintentional aspects of our
actions . . . and yet still retain our identity and character as
agents" (p. 44). As one's personal identity is constituted by the involuntary aspects of one's behavior too, one cannot detach oneself
from these aspects, without hurting severely (if not destroying altogether) one's identity and character as an agent. "[T]he idea of
the voluntary," argues Williams in chapter 14, "is essentially superficial" (p. 253).[22]

An interesting and quite common case of involuntary action
relevant to our matter is the case of moral dilemmas. In these sit-

uations, one must choose between two evils and, in this sense, one is not acting voluntarily. Nevertheless an agent faced with these choices will feel, and according to Williams, *should* feel, (agent-) regret, and a desire to make up in some way for the wrong action he or she committed.[23]

This brings us back to the case of Gauguin. Gauguin's success lies beyond his control, hence, whether or not he was justified is a matter of luck. If he had bad intrinsic luck and he failed he would be unjustified and sense feelings of agent-regret about his wrong decision. If he had bad extrinsic luck, then though he would regret the failure of the project, the regret would not take the particular form of *agent*-regret and would not be much different from the regret experienced by a spectator.

Central to Williams's argument is his contention that Gauguin's justification, if there is to be one, is not available to him at the time of the choice, in advance of knowing whether it would come out right. That is, his justification is essentially retrospective.[24] The reason for this necessarily retrospective perspective is not only the trivial fact that Gauguin's choice, as with many other human choices, is made under the conditions of uncertainty that result from limited human knowledge; it has a much deeper reason. The later Gauguin is, to some extent, a different *person*, a person who is the product of his earlier choices. That is, Gauguin's standpoint after his success in Tahiti differs from his standpoint at the time of the choice not only formally, in the direction, so to speak, of the perspective (retrospective or prospective) but also substantially; he is now a different man.

This, of course, is not the case in all choices. However some choices, such as Gauguin's, are such that their outcome is substantial in such a way that it "conditions the agent's sense of what is significant in his life and hence his standpoint of retrospective assessment" (p. 50). This explains again the importance of the distinction between intrinsic and extrinsic luck: "With an intrinsic failure, the project which generated the decision is revealed as an empty thing, incapable of grounding the agent's life. With extrinsic failure, it is not so revealed, and while he must acknowledge that it has failed, nevertheless it has not been discredited, and may, perhaps in the form of some new aspiration, contribute to making sense of what is left" (ibid.).

So, according to Williams, one's reflective justification is a matter of luck. But why *moral* luck? Williams argues that "even if Gauguin can be ultimately justified, that need not provide him with any way of justifying himself to others, at least to all others" (p. 38). But if that is so, it would be natural to raise the objection that this kind of luck has nothing to do with morality.[25] Moral judgments are universal and objective, at least in the sense that if action *a* is right for me, it is right for anybody in relevantly similar circumstances; and if I am morally justified in doing *a*, this is a justification from any (moral) point of view. Therefore, it might be argued, "[i]f success does not permit Gauguin to justify himself to others, but still determines his most basic feelings, that shows only that his most basic feelings need not be moral" (Nagel, p. 70, n. 3).[26]

In "Moral Luck," Williams offers two answers to this objection, neither of which is very convincing (pp. 51–4). However, irrespective of the validity of these answers, the very question we are discussing, namely, whether Gauguin's case was one of *moral* luck (as opposed to nonmoral luck), seems misplaced from Williams's point of view. The question presupposes a distinction between the moral and the nonmoral, that is, between questions, evaluations and judgments that reside within the domain of morality and those that reside without. This distinction is essential to modern ethics, yet it is rejected by Williams, as a mistaken narrowing of the area of ethics.[27]

Now it is important to notice that one of Williams's reasons for rejecting this distinction is the problem of moral luck itself. A basic motive for using the concept of the moral, argues Williams, is "the motive of establishing a dimension of decision and assessment which can hope to transcend luck" (p. 53). However, because the establishment of such a dimension has failed and luck seems to affect morality very significantly (constitutive luck, the relation of one's decisions to morality, luck in what one will turn out to have done), this basic motive, in effect, is seriously undermined.

All this is quite confusing. Indeed, in his "Postscript," Williams admits that his formulations in "Moral Luck" regarding these questions were somewhat misleading and in need of clarification. This clarification is Williams's main object in the Postscript, written especially for this book. Williams contends that the most important source of misunderstanding in "Moral Luck" was that he raised three different issues at once: "One was the question . . . how important is morality in the narrow sense as contrasted with a wider sense of the ethical? The second question concerns the importance, for a given agent and for our view of certain agents, of the ethical even in the wider sense. . . . The third question raised in the article is that of retrospective justification, and this is the widest, because it can arise beyond the ethical, in any application of practical rationality" (pp. 255–56).

The first question is dealt with through the example of the lorry driver. We have a strong temptation to say that though the driver might feel bad about what he did, this reaction is not a *moral* one nor, similarly, is the blame he suffers a *moral* blame. However, argues Williams, invoking the category of the 'moral' to make a distinction between different sorts of reactions "achieves absolutely nothing" (chapter 14, p. 254). Also, as mentioned previously, one of the characteristics of morality in the narrow sense is its pretension to be immune to luck, whereas, in fact, such immunity is an illusion. Hence, Williams's answer to the first question quoted earlier would be very simple: Morality in the narrow sense is not important "and we would be better off without it" (1985, p. 174).

The second question is illustrated through the story of Gauguin, a story that invites reflection on the placing of ethical concerns—even in the wider sense—among other values and, more broadly, among other human needs and projects. Granted that Gauguin offended a certain conception of the ethical in abandoning his family, it is still far from certain that we would like to condemn him for that when taking into account his great success as a painter. Gauguin encourages us to put a limit to the "imperialist" character of ethical concerns, which seek to invade the whole practical realm.

The third question, that of retrospective justification, is also exemplified in the case of Gauguin, who could not justify his decision in advance but only retrospectively. This question arises in any application of practical rationality, not just in ethics: Is rational self-criticism possible only to the extent that one might have avoided the outcome by taking thought or greater care in advance, or perhaps it is possible even when the unfortunate results could not have been prevented by any greater rationality? In other words, is self-criticism concerning the undesirable results of one's decision rational even when the results are a matter of luck? To this question Williams answers in the affirmative, and he believes the opposite view to be "very importantly wrong" (chapter 14, p. 256).

Thus the unclear distinction between these three questions in "Moral Luck" has generated some misunderstanding. However, argues Williams toward the end of chapter 14, the questions *are*, after all, interrelated, and in more than one way (pp. 256–57). This interrelation is again connected to the notion of luck. For instance, the idea of rational agency described previously "is itself formed by aspirations shared by morality, to escape as far as possible from contingency" (ibid., p. 257). That is, morality's aspiration for immunity to luck has inspired a similar aspiration in the domain of rational agency—both of which must be rejected.

Williams's "Postscript" is important, among other reasons, for it emphasizes how deeply the problem of luck penetrates into the practical realm; in morality, more broadly, in ethics, and, more broadly still, in rational agency—and in the interrelations between these three areas. Understanding the unavoidability of moral luck, is therefore, according to Williams, an essential step in gaining a better understanding of the entire practical domain.

III

Nagel's view on moral luck is at once more conservative and more radical than that of Williams.[28] It is conservative in its acceptance of at least two ideas of modern morality, which are rejected by Williams: (a) that there cannot be any moral justification that is not a justification of oneself to others, and (b) that one cannot be held morally responsible and blameworthy for results that occurred without one having contributed anything to their occurrence. Accepting (a) means that moral justification does not depend on one's subjective self-assessment, and it has a more objective nature. Hence, as opposed to Williams, Nagel argues that changes in the agent's perspective as a result of earlier choices would be irrelevant for moral justification, which is "objective and timeless" (Nagel, p. 63). Accepting (b) means assigning more importance to the voluntary aspect of one's actions in their moral evaluation.

In accordance with his acceptance of (a), Nagel objects, as we have already mentioned, to Williams's account of Gauguin's case as an example of *moral* luck.[29] Similarly, in accordance with his acceptance of (b), he argues, contra Williams, that the case of a truck driver who entirely without fault runs over a child (Williams, p. 43), is not a case of *moral* bad luck (Nagel, p. 61).

So much for the conservative aspect of Nagel's account.[30] He is also more radical in that he shows the wide extent to which luck affects morality with its various implications. According to

Nagel, luck affects morality in four ways (p. 60). The first way is *constitutive luck*, that is, "the kind of person you are, where this is not a question of what you deliberately do, but of your inclinations, capacities, and temperament." Because one's capacities, inclinations, and so forth depend, at least partially, on factors beyond one's control, (e.g., heredity, environment), so, to that extent, the kind of person one is is a matter of luck.[31] The second way is *circumstantial luck;* that is, "the kind of problems and situations one faces." The other two ways "have to do with the causes and effects of actions." One of them, which I shall call *causal luck*, is concerned with the way antecedent circumstances determine "the stripped-down acts of the will itself" (p. 66). The other, which I shall call *resultant luck*,[32] is luck "in the way one's actions and projects turn out."

Interesting logical interrelations exist among these four sorts of luck. I shall not endeavor to explore all of them here. However it is important to note the independence of each of them, an independence that might be shown in the following way. Even if the acts of the will itself are not determined by antecedent causes, it is still possible that the kind of person one is is so determined. And, even if it is not, one might still be vulnerable to luck with regard to the circumstances in which one finds oneself. And, finally, even if this sort of luck is overcome, one's moral status might still be at the mercy of luck due to the fact that the actual results of one's actions are not entirely within one's control. The fact that the different kinds of luck are independent of each other makes life more difficult for critics of moral luck. They have to show that each and all of these kinds of luck have no effect on morality.

This extensive, and on the face of it, inescapable entry of luck into the realm of morality leads Nagel to believe that we face a real paradox here (p. 66). On the one hand, we believe that one can be held responsible only for what is under one's control and thus not a matter of luck, whereas on the other hand, we have to recognize the bitter truth that luck is everywhere, so that "eventually nothing remains to be ascribed to the responsible self" (p. 68).

Note that the freedom of the will is strictly denied only by one sort of luck; namely, causal luck. This means that the problem of moral luck is much wider than the well-known and well-discussed problem of the relation between determinism and moral responsibility. Indeed, neither Williams nor Nagel presumes to make any substantial contribution to understanding the relationship between these two concepts, apart from classifying it as another case of moral luck.[33] Rather, their contribution lies in their analysis of resultant (Williams and Nagel) and circumstantial (Nagel) luck. These two sorts of luck have also received more attention in the debate around moral luck.[34] Hence, I too shall concentrate in what follows on these two types of luck. The next section will be devoted to a discussion of resultant luck, and Section V to circumstantial luck.

Before we turn to these discussions, however, I would like to make one comment regarding the idea of constitutive luck. There seems to be something odd about this idea. Suppose somebody says, "Oh, how lucky I am to have such parents!" The natural response to this seems to be, "Well, had you had different parents, you wouldn't have been the same person." That is, luck necessarily presupposes the existence of some subject who is affected by it. Because luck in the very constitution of an agent cannot be luck for anyone, the idea of one being lucky in the kind of person one is sounds incoherent.[35] This criticism of the notion of constitutive luck is pointed out briefly by Rescher (pp. 156–57), who argues that the concept of factors being within or without one's control does not apply to those such as personality and character. Though these factors might fail to be *within* one's control, they are not things that lie *outside* oneself either, but are part of what constitutes one's self as such. Therefore, concludes Rescher, the idea of constitutive luck involves a category mistake.

A different objection to the notion of constitutive luck can be developed on the basis of Harry Frankfurt's ideas regarding responsibility and character. According to Frankfurt, the responsibility of a person for his or her character has to do, not with the question of whether its *existence* is within the person's control, but rather "whether he has *taken responsibility for* his characteristics. It concerns whether the dispositions at issue . . . are characteristics with which he identifies and which he thus by his own will incorporates into himself as constitutive of what he is" (1988, pp. 171–172). So, on the one hand, though the existence of certain characteristics is not within the agent's control and is thus a matter of luck, this has no bearing on the agent's moral responsibility, which applies only to free acts. On the other hand, an agent can take responsibility for (some of) these characteristics by identifying with them, and as this is done freely, it raises no problem of luck. In other words, there is no problem of constitutive luck because it is the person who constitutes himself or herself, by identifying with certain of his desires.

IV

Resultant luck is luck, good or bad, in the way things turn out. It seems that immunity from this kind of luck was Kant's main object in his famous opening passages of the *Grundlegung*. Kant says that the value of the good will is not conditioned by any of the world's contingencies; therefore,

> Even if it should happen that, by a particularly unfortunate fate or by the niggardly provision of a stepmotherly nature, this will should be wholly lacking in power to accomplish its purpose, and if even the greatest effort should not avail it to achieve anything of its end, and if there remained only the good will (not as a mere will, but as the summoning of all the means in our power), it would sparkle like a jewel in its own right, as something that had its full worth in itself. Useful-ness or fruitlessness can neither diminish nor augment this worth. (Kant 1964, section 1, paragraph 3; quoted by Nagel, p. 57).[36]

It is this irrelevance of actual results to the good will's sparkling "like a jewel" that is challenged by Nagel.[37]

Nagel illustrates the relevance of the actual results of one's actions to moral assessment in two types of cases: (a) cases of negligence, (b) cases of decisions under uncertainty. I shall deal with them in turn.

Consider two similar cases, in which one is negligent in not putting out a fire one lights. In one case the fire is fortunately put out by a rainfall, and thus nothing regrettable happens, whereas in the other a nearby house is set on fire and a child is burned to death. It is obvious that the outcome in both these cases is be-yond one's control, in the sense that it was not within one's con-trol to make it the case that a rainfall occurred or did not occur, or that a child was or was not in the house nearby. In this sense, the outcome was a matter of (good or bad) luck.[38] Hence, because, *ex hypothesi*, the two agents were equally negligent, it may seem that both are guilty and responsible to the same degree. But de-spite these facts, we *do* judge the cases differently. We blame the second negligent one far more seriously than the first and view such behavior as much worse from a moral point of view. This is the way one assesses one's own actions too. While the lucky negligent one would feel at most some slight sense of regret, the unfortunate negligent one will reproach himself or herself strongly for the terrible result of such actions.

The relevance of lucky results to the assessment of one's actions is a basic assumption in legal systems. For instance, there is a great difference between the penalty for attempted murder and that for actual murder, though it is often a matter of pure luck whether the attempt succeeds or not.[39] The same with negligence. A driver who drives like a lunatic but does no harm will suffer a much smaller penalty than if somebody had been killed as a result of such driving. Though legal reasoning is sometimes different from moral reasoning, it seems that here the same assumption is presupposed; namely, that one is responsible and blameworthy for the *actual* results of one's actions.

Hence, moral evaluation of actions seems to involve two independent factors. First, in line with Kant, the degree of one's good or ill will. The stronger the will, the more one is held accountable for its results. While some trivial negligence is only a pale expression of ill will, a deliberate murder is a full expression of it and therefore is much more worthy of blame and penalty. Second, contrary to Kant, and here is where luck comes in, the outcome of one's actions. The worse the outcome, the worse the moral evaluation of the agent.[40] Because the outcome of one's actions is a matter of luck, this is a clear case of moral luck.

Another sort of case where moral assessment depends on the outcome is the case of a decision made under uncertainty. In this kind of situation, people decide to act in a certain way on the assumption, or in the hope, that their deeds will have a certain outcome. This outcome is essential for their justification yet it cannot be foreseen with certainty. Hence in making these decisions one is taking a moral risk, and only history will show whether one was justified in taking it.[41]

Conspicuous examples of such decisions are some momentous political choices, well illustrated by Nagel.[42] If one decides to start a revolution against a tyrannical regime, one is taking a terrible moral risk. If one succeeds, one will be a moral hero and savior; if, unfortunately, one fails, one will be responsible for the deaths of many innocent people.[43]

The natural objection to this sort of case is that we should distinguish the making of a reasonable decision, which is under one's control, and its unforeseeable results, which are indeed beyond one's control. That is, if one takes a decision in the light of the best information available to one at the time of decision making, one should not be held responsible for the outcome if it turns out to be different from what one could foresee. If the outcome is bad, this is obviously regrettable, but still one is not blameworthy for it.

Nagel is well aware of this objection (pp. 62–3). Surely, he admits, one's decision could be assessed from the point of view of what one could know at the time of the decision, but not *only* from that point of view. This, argues Nagel, is evident from the fact that one can say *in advance* how the moral verdict will depend on the results. At the time of the decision one can make an hypothetical judgment to the effect that if things turn out in a certain way, one will be praiseworthy, and if they turn out in a different way, one is blameworthy. Such a judgment is possible even when one's decision is absolutely reasonable. Therefore, reasonableness in decision making is not sufficient to guarantee moral justification. We must always await the actual results.

Cases of a decision under uncertainty are different from cases of negligence in an important respect. In the former, the agent might have behaved absolutely reasonably and even so be held responsible for the outcome of the decision. In the latter cases, the agent is morally blameworthy independent of the outcome (just because of negligence), with the outcome determining the degree of blameworthiness and, of course, what that agent is responsible *for*. Nonetheless, both these sorts of cases have an important feature in common; in both of them the agent is judged by the *actual* results of the actions and not just by the agent's good or bad will. Another common feature is the fact that in all of these cases the agent contributes in some way to the results, either by negligence or by a deliberate (lucky or unlucky) decision. According to Nagel, this feature is essential to *moral* luck, as I explained earlier.

The account given by Nagel of the relevance of actual results for moral assessment, as well as that given by Williams, seems to suit our moral intuitions and our moral feelings very well. Indeed, we do seem to regard results as playing a crucial role in moral justification. This, of course, does not prove that these intuitions are appropriate and rational. However any denial of this rationality would have to be supported by weighty reasons. Thus, the best way for the critic of moral luck to take would be to try to show that, on the one hand, contingent results do *not* determine moral worth, and yet, on the other, our common intuitions and feelings are not entirely irrational. This method will be relevant to the assessment of circumstantial luck too.

Let us focus our attention on cases of negligence, particularly on the example of the lorry driver who, as a result of his careless driving, kills a child who happens to jump into the road. Is this driver indeed morally worse than another driver who was negligent in the same way, but was lucky and did not hurt anybody?

Most critics believe that, when we think about it, the answer to this question seems to be negative. That is, on reflection, the moral difference between the two drivers seems to disappear or, at least, to weaken significantly. Therefore the fact that one of the drivers caused a death where the other did not, "says nothing morally interesting about them" (Thomson, p. 204).[44] The justification for this equal judgment lies in our conception of morality as concerned with action guiding and fairness (cf. Jensen, p. 135). A morality that bases a moral verdict on factors beyond human control would be unfair and unjust, its equivalent in legal systems being punishing the innocent. Such a morality would also go against its concern with action guiding, because action can be guided only by requiring one to do what one *can* do.[45]

Nevertheless this does not imply that the guilt feelings of the killer-driver, as opposed to the lucky driver, are irrational— quite the contrary. Because the death of a human being is a bad and a saddening thing, it is quite reasonable that one should feel terrible if one contributes to such a result, even if it is not one's fault. This sense of diminished worth is distinguishable, as many writers rightly observe, from moral fault in the sense of deserving punishment.[46] Hence, though the killer-driver is no more blameworthy than the lucky one, his different feelings are not irrational.

This line of argument is familiar from the recent debate on moral dilemmas. One of the central arguments put forward for the reality of such situations is the 'argument from sentiment,' which argues as follows: since the agent faced with a moral dilemma feels guilt and remorse in any course of action that is chosen, and, moreover, these feelings seem rational and appropriate, then the agent is indeed guilty, and moral dilemmas are situations where one must do wrong. To this argument, opponents of moral dilemmas reply that the agent's guilt feelings can be fully accounted for without supposing that one is *really* guilty.[47]

The same applies to resultant luck. Though the killer-driver is no more blameworthy than the lucky one who does not kill, his (and our) different feelings are understandable and rational. There is a valid distinction between justifying *judgments* of moral worth and blame and justifying the rationality of certain *feelings* concerning these and other moral matters.[48]

Assuming that the moral discredit of our two drivers is indeed equal, does this imply that they are also equally to *blame*? The answer to this question depends on different notions of blame. Judith Thomson distinguishes two such notions (pp. 200–202): (1) a person P is to blame for an unwelcome event, where P caused it by some wrongful act or omission for which P had no adequate excuse;[49] and (2) a person P is to greater or lesser blame for doing something, which is unwelcome, where P's doing it is stronger or weaker reason to think P is a bad person. Now because the killer-driver caused an unwelcome state of affairs (a child's death) by wrongful behavior (his negligent driving), he is no doubt to blame—first notion of "blame"—for it, whereas the second driver is not. However, Thomson argues, the killer-driver is not to blame—*second* notion of "blame"—more than the other driver; the fact that one driver was lucky not to kill somebody, whereas the other was less fortunate is no reason to think the former less bad a person than the latter.

Though this line of argument assumes that, ultimately, moral worth does not depend on factors beyond one's control, still it might admit that luck does play a part in our moral assessment of these cases. Such a different interpretation of moral luck is suggested by Norvin Richards. According to Richards, the driver who kills is morally unfortunate because by killing he made it clear to us that he is a negligent driver and that he deserves to be treated accordingly. Though he deserved this treatment all along, he was lucky that we did not discover it until now. Some negligent drivers are even luckier; they never kill anybody or cause any harm, so no one knows that they really ought to be treated as lunatics or as potential killers. Hence, luck does not affect one's *deserts* but only our *knowledge* of them.[50] Moral bad luck is not luck in one's moral status being hurt, but (bad) luck in one's character becoming transparent to others.

However, it is doubtful to what extent this reinterpretation really reflects our actual apportionment of desert and blame. Jonathan Adler rightly observes in his criticism of Richards, that "legally, emotionally, and socially, the blame we attribute to the reckless driver who runs over the child is far worse than that which we attribute to the driver who doesn't have an accident but whose record indicates equal, if not greater, recklessness" (Adler 1987, p. 248). This shows that our attribution of blame does not "reflect our epistemic shortcomings," as Richards (p. 169) believes, but, rather, our belief in the importance of actual results to moral assessment. This belief might, of course, be mistaken, as Richards, Rescher, Thomson, and others assume, but it cannot be reinterpreted and preserved in a different form.

V

Circumstantial luck is luck in the kind of problems and situations one faces. The example Nagel offers for such luck is the following: "Ordinary citizens of Nazi Germany had an opportunity to behave heroically by opposing the regime, and most of them are culpable for having failed that test. But it is a test to which the citizens of other countries were not subjected, with the result that even if they, or some of them, would have behaved as badly as the Germans in like circumstances, they simply did not and therefore are not similarly culpable." Hence, Nagel concludes: "We judge people for what they actually do or fail to do, not just for what they would have done if circumstances had been different" (p. 66).

If Nagel is right, this is indeed a clear case of moral luck.[51] Some people were morally very lucky not to be German citizens in the 1930s. Others, less fortunate, were such citizens and had to face a momentous moral test, a test that most of them failed, with the result that they collaborated in terrible crimes. It is true that they could have just as equally passed the test. The point is that others were fortunately free from the test altogether.[52]

It is important to notice the difference between circumstantial luck and resultant luck. In a sense, the first is logically prior to the latter. It is first a matter of luck that one happens to live in such circumstances in which one has to decide whether to do a certain action or not, and it is second a matter of luck whether one's decision has good or bad results. So one might be morally lucky in one sense and unlucky in another; one might be unlucky to have to face a difficult moral test, one may fail the test, and yet be lucky that the results of one's behavior turn out, in the end, to be morally desirable.

Assuming that the actual Nazis were free not to collaborate, they are surely responsible to some extent for what they did. Are potential Nazis responsible too? After all, *ex hypothesi*, only luck prevented them from being Nazi murderers.

Richards (pp. 175–77) and Zimmerman (pp. 226–29), as well as Rescher (pp. 154–55), take this challenge and answer the question in the positive. According to Richards, because one's deserts are determined mainly by one's character and because the noncollaborator's character is, *ex hypothesi*, no worse than that of the actual collaborator, therefore, the would-be collaborator deserves blame too. Richards goes even further and argues that the noncollaborator might deserve *more* blame, because his or her bad traits of character have a smaller chance to change: "[A] trait whose enacting is not spectacularly painful for others stands a greater chance to persist." Hence, quite surprisingly, the noncollaborator "is likely to live an entire life in which he takes the pleasures of authority too seriously and the pain of certain others too lightly. This will be a stunted life, as well as a damaging one" (p. 177).

Zimmerman ascribes blame to the noncollaborator not only for his corrupt character but also for what he would have done had he been in the same situation as the collaborator (see principle 6 on p. 225). This naturally raises the question, what is this person to blame *for*? Surely not for collaboration, nor for a *decision* to collaborate, which he, of course, never made. Zimmerman admits he is not sure of the answer to this question (p. 228). One possibility he mentions is that the noncollaborator is to blame but not to blame *for* anything. This does not seem very promising, and Zimmerman tries another answer; that is "he is to blame for being such that he would have made the decision to collaborate had he been in a situation that he believed to be s (where s is the situation that the collaborator believed himself to be in" (ibid.).

This explanation is based on a counterfactual, the truth of which is not easy to determine. Nevertheless, Zimmerman believes this determination is not impossible: "one can imagine setting up controlled laboratory conditions in order to test the noncollaborator's propensity to collaborate" (p. 229). However as these laboratory conditions are not often set up, we cannot usually make judgments with any reasonable certainty. Again this reflects our epistemic shortcomings, as Richards puts it (p. 169), not the real deserts of the agents being judged.

Note how far Zimmerman is prepared to go in his attempt to make morality immune to luck. Every person is held responsible not only for what he or she *does* but also, it appears, for what he or she *would* have done, had circumstances been different. The difficulty in this approach is that too many people are held responsible and blameworthy for too many things, with the result that blame seems to lose much of its meaning and effectiveness. Furthermore, this seems to imply an "unacceptable mitigation of our present apportionment of desert" (Adler 1987, p. 249). If thousands of people would have chosen to be Nazis had they lived in Germany in the 1930s and they are blameworthy for this fact, what is so special about the *actual* Nazi? And why should we think he or she deserves to be punished, indeed very severely punished, whereas the would-be Nazi does not? If our special condemnation of the actual Nazi is to be kept, it seems that some degree of circumstantial luck is unavoidable.

Once again, the critic of moral luck would answer that our special condemnation of the actual Nazi reflects nothing more than our limited and inadequate knowledge. In the eyes of God, the actual and the would-be murderers bear the same blame, and He would have them thrown into the same circle of hell (Thomson, p. 207). What proponents of moral luck need is an example of circumstances where moral luck cannot be dismissed as an expression of our epistemic shortcomings, for it expresses something in the very nature of the situation. This seems to be the case in moral dilemmas.

Moral dilemmas, says Nagel (p. 70, n. 9), are unusual examples of circumstantial moral luck. These are situations where one is faced, through no fault of one's own, with a choice between two evils, in such a way that one cannot avoid doing wrong.[53] These situations are different in an important respect from the situation of the Nazi. While the Nazi could have chosen not to collaborate and not to do wrong, this is not the case in moral dilemmas. In these situations the agent has to do wrong and there is no way of escape. Because one's being trapped in these circumstances is a matter of (bad) luck and because one is forced by these circumstances to behave wrongly, this is a clear case of luck influencing morality. This case is stronger than the standard case of circumstantial (bad) luck, in which one faces a very difficult moral test. It is stronger because in the standard case one *can* pass the test and act morally in spite of the difficulties one faces, whereas in moral dilemmas, according to the preceding thesis, such a victory is impossible and moral wrongdoing is unavoidable.[54]

This strong example of moral luck can be refuted only by offering a different account of moral dilemmas, an account that has been defended recently by a number of philosophers.[55] Briefly, these philosophers deny the possibility of one being in a situation where one must do wrong; that is, the possibility of what are called *genuine* moral dilemmas. They believe that if one chooses the best course of action available to one, one is acting perfectly well from a moral point of view and is not to be blamed for anything. If this account is correct, as I myself believe it to be,[56] moral dilemmas are, after all, not a case of moral luck in the sense just explained. An agent who does the best he or she can in these situations is assessed positively from a moral point of view and nothing in that person's moral worth is lost.

Therefore, moral dilemmas cannot serve as an example of circumstances where one is so morally unfortunate that one has no escape from wrongdoing. Still, even on the account of moral dilemmas just suggested, it must be admitted that moral dilemmas are cases of "standard" circumstantial luck. In such situations one has strong reasons to do two incompatible actions. Granted that only one of them is the right thing to do, the agent has still a strong temptation (a *moral* temptation) to do the other. Assuming that the morally right thing for Agammemnon to do was to kill Iphigenia,[57] he, nonetheless, had a very strong reason not to do so. Thus, one could surely say that Agammemnon faced a very cruel and momentous test. He had bad circumstantial luck.[58]

VI

Critics of moral luck argue in different ways that the problem of moral luck really arises only because we do not reflect enough on the matters under consideration. If we were more reflective and, in effect, more rational, we would ascribe the same responsibility and blame to the driver who kills as to the lucky one who does not, to the actual Nazi as to the potential one. Why, then, should we not be more rational and just abandon our mistaken intuitions?

Williams's answer to this question is that in the less usual cases (such as Gauguin's) the thoughts and experiences that presuppose moral luck are "coherent, and intelligible, and that there is no ground for condemning them as irrational" (p. 37). In the more usual cases, such as the lorry driver's, Williams suggests, "that unless we were to be merely confused or unreflective, life without these experiences would involve a much vaster reconstruction of our sentiments and our view of ourselves than may be supposed" (ibid.). Detaching ourselves from the unintentional aspects of our actions would make it impossible for us to retain our identity and character as agents (p. 44), and viewing morality as supreme and ubiquitous would end in one having no life of one's own, "except for some small area, hygienically allotted, of meaningless privacy" (p. 53).

A powerful defense of Williams is offered by Margaret Walker in her chapter. Walker argues that proponents of moral luck presuppose a picture of what she calls *impure agency,* whereas critics of moral luck presuppose a picture of 'pure agency.' Impure agency is situated within the causal order in ways such as to be variably conditioned by and conditioning parts of that order, without being able to draw a unitary boundary to its exercise at either end. Impure agents' responsibilities are wider than those determined by their domain of control; they are often accountable for results that were neither foreseen nor foreseeable. Pure agency is free from causality that is external to the agent's will (itself understood as a causal power). Pure agents are responsible only for what is within their control, for what has its origin in the agent's free will.

Now Walker's thesis is that a world of pure agents (i.e., a world with no moral luck), would be a bad place to live in; a world where people routinely and with justification would walk away from the harmful, but unforeseeable, results of their actions and where society could justifiably ignore the suffering caused by its hurtful political decisions, provided these were based on the best available information and made bona fide. Fortunately, Walker believes, most of us hold a different picture and live, so to speak, in a different world, one of impure agency. Hence, we can rely on each other in ongoing projects, and we need not fear that our friends will let us down when we need them, even if our need is not something that was within their control; and we can expect parents to take responsibility for their sick children even where they are not accountable—in pure agency terms—for their sickness. Walker points out three interrelated virtues of impure agency: integrity, grace, and lucidity. Each of these virtues, explained at length by Walker, contributes "to our living well in concert with others a distinctively human life" (p. 241). Thus, according to Walker, a world-view that admits moral luck is morally preferable to one that seeks to escape such luck and, so to speak, "purify" agency.

As for Nagel, he believes that in spite of the allure and the reasonableness of Kant's conclusion with regard to moral luck, it remains "intuitively unacceptable." Furthermore, "[w]e may be persuaded that these moral judgments are irrational, but they reappear involuntarily as soon as the argument is over. *This is the pattern throughout the subject*" (p. 65, italics added).

One could, of course, object to this approach and argue that the fact that a certain view is intuitive and "reappears involuntarily as soon as the argument is over" is no reason for holding it but only for correcting our irrational intuitions. This brings us to a well-known and fundamental methodological problem in morality (and in philosophy in general); that is, the question of which source of knowledge is more reliable—moral intuitions or moral arguments? Moral experience or moral theory? We obviously cannot go into this problem here. However Nagel's view on it is very clear and directly relevant to the question we are discussing. In his preface to *Mortal Questions* (1979), of which "Moral Luck" is a part, he explicitly states his philosophical taste: "I believe one should trust problems over solutions, intuition over arguments and pluralistic discord over systematic harmony. . . . If arguments or systematic theoretical considerations lead to results that seem intuitively not to make sense, or if a neat solution to a problem does not remove the conviction that the problem is still there . . . then something is wrong with the argument and more work needs to be done" (Nagel 1979, pp. x–xi).

Thus, according to Nagel, the denial of moral luck would be a typical example of philosophical argument *not* being convincing, and our not being justified in rejecting our basic intuitions.

Is this indeed the case? Can philosophy not offer any convincing arguments for the immunity of morality to luck? Must acceptance of this immunity imply unreasonable results concerning one's personal identity and integrity? I leave these questions for the reader of the following chapters to decide.

Notes

I wish to thank David Heyd, Charlotte Katzoff, and David Widerker
for kindly reading and commenting on earlier drafts of this introduction.
I am also grateful to Martha Nussbaum for her aid in choosing extracts
from her *Fragility of Goodness*, to Nicholas Rescher for his readiness to
revise his original paper on luck to make it more fitting to the locus of
this anthology, and to Bernard Williams who contributed a special postscript to his 1976 paper, thus clarifying and developing his own ideas, on
the one hand, and helping to give this book a more united and integrated
structure, on the other.

1. On the wide ranging effect of luck on our lives and our inability
to control it, see Rescher, pp. 141–45. This effect raises an interesting
question in social philosophy; namely, whether society should take steps
to change the balance of fortune that luck itself has created. This latter
question is discussed at length by Epstein (1988).

2. Both the papers were delivered originally at a symposium of the
Aristotelian Society and appeared in its *Proceedings*, Vol. 50 (1976), Nagel's paper being a reply to that of Williams. Each was reprinted with revisions in Williams (1981), ch. 2, and Nagel (1979), ch. 3. All quotations
are from these latter versions. It is worth mentioning that the revisions
Williams made in the earlier version of "Moral Luck" are more extensive
than those he made in any of the other papers collected in Williams
(1981). Furthermore, he frankly admits that even after these revisions,
he has not entirely succeeded in expressing the main idea of "Moral
Luck," and in deciding to title his book with this term, his aim has been
"not to draw particular attention to that essay, but rather to suggest
something which may indeed have contributed to its imperfections—
that concerns echoed in that title are picked up in different forms in several parts of the book" (Preface to Williams 1981, p. ix).

3. The difference between these two types of moral judgment and
its relevance to moral luck is the central point in Judith Andre's paper.
Cf. Nagel, p. 58; and Williams, Postscript, pp. 251–52.

4. Williams, p. 55, n. 11. Italics added. An interesting topic that
will not be discussed here is the relation between moral luck and
epistemic luck, which is not only formally parallel, but also substantially
connected to moral luck. Just as morality is considered by many philosophers as necessarily immune to luck, so too is knowledge; "knowledge is
essentially a matter of being right non-luckily" (Grant 1980, p. 170). On
knowledge and luck, see Grant 1980; Ravitch 1976; Foley 1984. On the
relation between the role played by luck in morality and that played by
luck in epistemology, see Nagel, p. 60; Williams, p. 40; and more important Williams's Postscript, pp. 252–53; and Statman 1991.

5. The limitation of the good life to the sphere of internal goods is at the heart of what John Kekes calls *the Socratic Ideal*, which Kekes views as "one of the great mistakes in moral philosophy" (1990, p. 14).

6. Though not all kinds of luck, as Williams (p. 35) rightly observes. It is a matter of luck that one is a sage or capable of being one.

7. A comprehensive account of the Epicurean ethics, which focuses on its ideal of invulnerability to luck, can be found in Mitsis (1988).

8. I believe that the ancient and modern concepts of immunity to luck are closer than Williams suggests. According to Williams, although the classical doctrines assumed that "one's *whole* life" is (or can be) immune to luck (p. 35, italics added), the modern doctrines assume that only "one basic form of value" (ibid) is immune to luck, and through this value one is "*partially* immune" to luck (p. 36, italics added). However, the classics never denied that one's health or wealth, for instance, may be subject to luck, and so it is with many other aspects of human existence. They just argued that these various aspects have (or should have) no weight in determining one's worth and well-being. In this respect "one's whole life" is indeed immune to luck, 'whole' not in the sense of including all aspects of life, but only the most important and essential ones. This pattern of thought suits the modern concept of moral luck too. Because morality is supremely valuable, the fact that other aspects of human existence are vulnerable to luck does not discredit the human possibility of attaining a life that in its deepest and most important aspects is immune to luck.

9. See also Kenny (1987).

10. For a different view with regard to facing our vulnerability to the contingencies of life, see Kekes (1990). Kekes acknowledges his debt to Nussbaum but nonetheless disagrees with her on some central points.

11. A similar choice exists in the moral realm too. If, ultimately, there is only one kind of moral value to which all other kinds can be reduced, then moral dilemmas, which are considered cases of bad moral luck (see Section V later), are impossible. But if moral values are plural and incommensurable, such a reduction is impossible, and moral dilemmas are sometimes inescapable. In other words, the richer the realm of values, the more vulnerable the moral agent is to bad luck. Therefore it is not surprising that both Williams (1981, ch. 5) and Nagel (1979, ch. 9) emphasized the plurality and incommensurability of values. See also notes 19 and 54.

12. The interpretation of Kant's ethics by some writers on moral luck creates the impression that, according to Kant, morality is absolutely free from luck and that the moral status of human beings depends

entirely on them. That this is an exaggeration can be seen, for instance, in the important role assigned by Kant to moral education to the extent that "man can only become man by education. He is merely [!] what education makes of him" (Kant 1960, p. 6). Because getting a good education is a matter of luck, Kant, too, would have to admit some influence of luck to morality. For a more tolerant interpretation of Kant, see also Jensen, p. 138.

13. Williams (1985, p. 195) remarks that the conception of human value being immune to luck is in some ways like a religious conception, though unlike any real religion and, in particular, unlike orthodox Christianity, which made human salvation depend on God's grace. However, if Protestantism did indeed have some real influence on Kant, as some commentators believe (see Norman 1984, pp. 94–97), especially in its priority of 'faith' over 'works', to be expressed by Kant in the priority of the good will over one's fortunate actions, then our conception of morality being immune to luck might have some historical roots in religion after all.

14. Williams, p. 36. Cf. MacIntyre (1968), p. 190.

15. See Williams (1981), pp. ix–x, and especially Williams (1985). A good criticism of Williams's objection to moral theories can be found in Scheffler (1987). The rejection of modern ethics, usually accompanied by an endorsement of Greek ethics, can be found in the writings of some other philosophers in the 1980s, too, notably MacIntyre (1981) and Taylor (1985). For discussions of the "Anti-Theory" stream in contemporary ethics, see Clarke (1987) and Louden (1990), and the anthology edited by Clarke and Simpson (1989).

16. This point was also explored by Joel Feinberg (1970), without using this technical term.

17. This naturally raises the question, what rational self-justification has got to do with *moral* justification and moral luck. Williams is aware of this problem and he announces from the outset that he will say very little until the end of the article about the moral. We shall come back to this point later.

18. Williams emphasizes that he is not limited in construing this example by any historical facts about the real Gauguin (Chapter 3, p. 37, Chapter 14, p. 255). As for the motives and behavior of the real Gauguin and their possible philosophical implications, see Levi's paper included in this book.

19. For Gauguin to be justified, the value of his paintings (or his worth as a great painter) must be assumed to override his obligations to his family. Yet this overridingness seems inconsistent with Williams's

(and Nagel's) view on the incommensurability of values, a view that implies that one cannot compare rationally the worths of two different values. On this difficulty, cf. MacIntyre (1983), p. 124.

20. Admittedly, the distinction between the failure of Gauguin and that of the project becomes less clear when we examine possibilities weaker than that of the traffic accident. Suppose Gauguin had fallen in love with one of the beautiful girls of Tahiti, and forgotten all about his painting—is that an intrinsic failure or an extrinsic one? Or, suppose he had missed his children so much that he could not concentrate properly in his work—should we say that *he* had failed, in not managing to devote himself totally to his work, or that the *project* failed, for missing one's children is an "external" factor?

21. For discussions about the concept of agent-regret and its relation to other close concepts, such as guilt and remorse, see Rorty (1980); Baron (1988).

22. The importance of preserving one's personal identity and integrity is a central theme in Williams's thought, in his criticism of both utilitarianism and Kantianism. See Williams (1973), pp. 93–118, especially the famous story about Jim and the Indians on pp. 98–99. For discussions on this story and its philosophical implications, see Hollis (1973); Harris (1974). For a different view of Kant and moral integrity, see Jensen (1989).

23. See Williams (1978), especially p. 99. I shall say more on the relation of moral dilemmas to moral luck in Section V.

24. Levi (pp. 112–13) argues that Gauguin's case is different in this respect from the famous dilemma of Sartre's student, who had to decide whether to stay with his mother or to try and join the Free Forces (Sartre [1948], pp. 35–37), because in the first case the nature of the dilemma could not be known until the project succeeded or failed. This, I believe, is a mistake. In Sartre's case too the nature of the dilemma was unclear, as there was no certainty as to the student's success in reaching the Free Forces and bringing any help to them. And here too his failure could be of an external nature (waiting too long in Spain) or of an internal nature (being useless). The analogy between these two cases can be further developed but I shall not pursue it any further here.

25. Cf. Rescher, p. 159; Hollis and Howe (1987), p. 127.

26. Cf. Slote (1983), pp. 77–93, who takes Gauguin's case as a genuine example of what he calls *admirable immorality*; that is, a case where some trait of character is admirable, though it runs counter to morality. This admirable character, in the case of Gauguin, was his single-minded devotion to his artistic objectives. For a critical discussion

of Slote's thesis, see Flanagan (1986), who shows, among other things, how difficult it is to establish an intrinsic connection between some particular trait of character, e.g., Gauguin's devotion to painting, and any immoral act such as deserting one's family.

27. This is a shift from an earlier view of Williams (1978), in which this distinction still played some role. On this change and its meaning, see Nussbaum (1986), pp. 427–428, n. 10.

28. Cf. Coyne [Walker] (1975), p. 319.

29. See p. 8 earlier.

30. The fact that Williams is more skeptical about our moral conceptions was noticed by Williams himself, p. 55, n. 11. This difference between Williams and Nagel is expressed clearly in each of their later systematic books (Williams [1985] vis-à-vis Nagel [1986a]).

31. The term *constitutive luck* is used by Williams too (pp. 35–6), though in a wider sense. Williams includes under this title not only the luck that affects one's personality, but also that which influences one's motives and intentions. Hereafter I shall be using the term in Nagel's sense. The vulnerability of one's motives and intentions to luck would be classified by Nagel as a different sort of luck, to which I have suggested the term *causal luck*.

32. Following Zimmerman (p. 219). Zimmerman distinguishes this kind of luck from what he calls *situational luck*, under which he includes all Nagel's other sorts of luck.

33. Williams, p. 36; Nagel, p. 66.

34. Jansen and Sverdlik focus their attention on resultant luck; Richards, Thomson, Walker, and Zimmerman on resultant and circumstantial luck; and Andre on resultant and constitutive luck.

35. This kind of consideration is highly relevant in discussions over what are known as *wrongful life* claims. See, for instance, Heyd (1986), especially pp. 577–582.

36. See also Kant (1979), pp. 59–60.

37. Although I shall discuss mainly causal results of actions, I interpret resultant luck in a broader sense, to include many and different ways by which an action might turn out to be right or wrong. Consider, for instance, Rescher's case (p. 152) of the lucky villain who burgles the house of his grandfather, while unbeknownst to him the grandfather has meanwhile died and made him his heir. In this fantastic case, it is true that the burglar's action *turned out* not to be wrong, though not because

of any lucky *results* of it. The same goes for the case put forward by Slote 1983, pp. 56–57.

38. Of course, in a different sense, the outcome was not a matter of luck; behaving negligently belongs to that class of things that, no doubt, are within one's control. However, the crucial point is that the negligent behavior (not putting out a fire), though a necessary condition, was not sufficient to generate the outcome of the child's death. This outcome resulted from other factors too, over which the agent had definitely no control.

39. For a critical review of some suggestions to justify the different attitude toward successful attempts and unsuccessful ones, see Lewis (1989), pp. 53–57. Lewis himself suggests another solution, indeed a very sophisticated one, though he admits that his is not very convincing either, and "probably there is no adequate justification for punishing attempts more severely when they succeed" (ibid. p. 58).

40. An interesting problem within this view would be that of determining the relative weight of each of these factors in assessing the moral value of a pair of actions. Certainly if one of the factors is kept constant and the other varies, the moral value will be determined solely by this second factor. But what about cases where both the factors vary? Which is worse—killing as a result of a trivial negligence, or the unfortunate failure of an attempted murder?

41. Some philosophers believe that resultant luck exists in the domain of virtues too. Let us take the virtue of courage. According to a long-standing philosophical tradition, one can be said to have acted courageously only if one acted toward some good end despite the danger of the means. However, whether one's end turns out to be good is a matter of luck, hence, concludes Walton (1990, p. 238), "there is a certain element of moral luck in carrying out an act later found to be courageous."

42. On political action and moral luck, see Breiner (1989).

43. "An electrifying example" of such moral luck, according to Hollis and Howe (1987) is the job of some social workers who have to decide whether a child, at possible risk from its parents, should be removed from home or left there. A wrong decision is sometimes fatal to the child involved; each year some children, left at home, are abused or killed. Hence, though social work is a morally right and praiseworthy job, it carries with it serious moral risks.

44. Cf. Andre, p. 125; Jensen, p. 135; Richards, p. 171; Zimmerman, p. 227. See also Frankfurt (1988), pp. 55–56, who argues—against

Don Locke—that because the driver did not hit the child freely (= the hitting was a matter of luck), he is not morally responsible for the hitting, only for driving recklessly, which *was* done freely.

45. I believe these two roles of morality are the basis of the famous slogan 'ought implies can'. As opposed to its traditional interpretation, this slogan does not express a logical implication or presupposition, but a second-order normative principle, restricting moral theories in choosing their norms and principles. Cf. Tranoy (1972); Rawls (1972), pp. 236–237.

46. Andre, pp. 127–28; Richards, p. 179; Thomson, pp. 205–6.

47. See Conee 1982, pp. 90–91; McConnell 1978, p. 277.

48. I believe this distinction can be applied to the case of Gauguin too. Even if Gauguin succeeded in Tahiti and, consequently, could justify his decision rationally to himself, surely some kind of regret or sorrow is appropriate on his part for his poor children having to grow up without a father.

49. This notion has a different formulation too but it does not concern us here.

50. Cf. also Zimmerman, p. 227; Rescher, p. 156.

51. Lewis (1989, p. 56) believes that such cases are "[t]he most intelligible cases of moral luck."

52. The first to notice this kind of luck was probably Brandt (1958), p. 30, n. 31, as Zimmerman (p. 230, n. 2) remarks.

53. The subject of moral dilemmas has received considerable attention in the last decade. See the anthology of Gowans (1987), and also Sinnott-Armstrong 1988.

54. In view of the close connection between the notion of moral luck and that of genuine moral dilemmas, one can understand why both Williams and Nagel, as well as Nussbaum, who all confirm the existence of the former, also make a considerable effort to confirm the existence of the latter. See Williams (1978); Nagel (1979), ch. 9; Nussbaum (1986), pp. 47–50. Because the existence of genuine moral dilemmas is often regarded as depending on the incommensurability of values, all these philosophers accept this last idea too. See note 19 earlier.

55. See McConnell (1978); Conee (1982), (1989); Hare (1981); and others.

56. See Statman (forthcoming).

57. Had he not, everybody, including Iphigenia, would have died; see Nussbaum (1986), p. 34, who believes that the killing of Iphigenia was the most rational thing to do.

58. Although I have rejected the strong interpretation of moral dilemmas as a case of (circumstantial) moral luck, I believe that it might be applicable to *some* dilemmas. Certain actions, such as killing, torturing, etc., tend to hurt one's moral sensitivity and innocence, even when *justified*. In this modest respect, some moral dilemmas are strong cases of bad circumstantial luck, cases in which one's moral status is hurt, even if one has overcome all difficulties and temptations and has done the right thing. These are cases where the agent cannot avoid having "dirty hands." Hollis and Howe's account on moral risks in social work (see note 43) implies that social work is a job that sometimes involves something like this. Though it is a morally desirable and important job, it involves a constant hazard to the worker's integrity and innocence (Hollis and Howe 1987, pp. 127, 132).

References

Adler, J. 1987. "Luckless Desert in Different Desert." *Mind* 96: 247–249.

Baron, M. 1988. "Remorse and Agent-Regret." *Midwest Studies in Philosophy* 13: 259–281.

Brandt, R. B. 1958. "Blameworthiness and Moral Obligation." In A. I. Melden, ed., *Essays in Moral Philosophy*, pp. 3–39. Seattle: University of Washington Press.

Breiner, P. 1989. "Democratic Autonomy, Political Ethics, and Moral Luck." *Political Theory* 17: 550–574.

Clarke, S. 1987. "Anti-Theory in Ethics." *American Philosophical Quarterly* 24: 237–244.

——— and Simpson, E., eds. 1989. *Anti-Theory in Ethics and Moral Conservatism*. Albany: SUNY Press.

Conee, E. 1982. "Against Moral Dilemma." *Philosophical Review* 91: 87–97.

———. 1989. "Why Moral Dilemmas are Impossible." *American Philosophical Quarterly* 26: 133–141.

Coyne [Walker], M. U. 1985. "Moral Luck?" *Journal of Value Inquiry* 19: 319–325.

Epstein, R. 1988. "Luck." *Social Philosophy and Policy* 6: 17–38.

32   *Daniel Statman*

Feinberg, J. 1970. "Problematic Responsibility in Law and Morals." In *Doing and Deserving*, pp. 25–37. Princeton N.J.: Princeton University Press.

Flanagan, O. 1986. "Admirable Immorality and Admirable Imperfection." *Journal of Philosophy* 83: 41–60.

Foley, R. 1984. "Epistemic Luck and the Purely Epistemic." *American Philosophical Quarterly* 21: 87–97.

Frankfurt, H. 1988. *The Importance of What We Care About.* Cambridge: Cambridge University Press.

Gowans, C., ed. 1987. *Moral Dilemmas.* Oxford: Oxford University Press.

Grant, B. 1980. "Knowledge, Luck and Charity." *Mind* 89: 161–181.

Hare, R. M. 1981. *Moral Thinking.* Oxford: Oxford University Press.

Harris, J. 1974. "Williams on Negative Responsibility and Integrity." *Philosophical Quarterly* 24: 265–273.

Heyd, D. 1986. "Are 'Wrongful Life' Claims Philosophically Valid?" *Israel Law Review* 21: 574–590.

Hollis, M. 1973. "Jim and the Indians." *Analysis* 43: 36–39.

Hollis, M. and Howe, D. 1987. "Moral Risks in Social Work." *Journal of Applied Philosophy* 4: 123–133.

Jensen, H. 1989. "Kant and Moral Integrity." *Philosophical Studies* 57: 193–205.

Kant, I. 1960. *Education,* trans. A. Churton, Ann Arbor: University of Michigan Press.

——— . 1964. *Groundwork of the Metaphysics of Morals,* trans. H. J. Paton. New York: Harper and Row.

——— . 1979. *Lectures on Ethics,* trans. L. Infield. London: Methuen.

Kekes, J. 1990. *Facing Evil.* Princeton, N.J.: Princeton University Press.

Kenny, A. 1987. "Aristotle on Moral Luck." In J. Dancy, ed., *Human Agency,* pp. 105–119. , Calif.: Stanford University Press.

Lewis, D. 1989. "The Punishment That Leaves Something to Chance." *Philosophy and Public Affairs* 18: 53–67.

Louden, R. B. 1990. "Virtue Ethics and Anti-Theory." *Philosophia* [Israel] 20: 93–114.

MacIntyre, A. 1968. *A Short History of Ethics.* London: Macmillan.

———. 1981. *After Virtue*. London: Duckworth.

———. 1983. "The Magic of the Pronoun 'My'—Review of 'Moral Luck' by Williams." *Ethics* 94: 113–125.

McConnell, T. C. 1978. "Moral Dilemmas and Consistency in Ethics." *Canadian Journal of Philosophy* 7: 269–287.

Mitsis, P. 1988. *Epicurus' Ethical Theory: The Pleasures of Invulnerability*. Ithaca, N.Y.: Cornell University Press.

Nagel, T. 1979. *Mortal Questions*. Cambridge: Cambridge University Press.

———. 1986a. *The View from Nowhere*. New York: Oxford University Press.

———. 1986b. "A Review of 'Ethics and the Limits of Philosophy'." *Journal of Philosophy* 83: 351–360.

Norman, R. 1984. *The Moral Philosophers*. Oxford: Oxford University Press.

Nussbaum, M. 1986. *The Fragility of Goodness—Luck and Ethics in Greek Tragedy and Philosophy*. Cambridge: Cambridge University Press.

Ravitch, H. 1976. "Knowledge and the Principle of Luck." *Philosophical Studies* 30: 347–349.

Rawls, J. 1972. *A Theory of Justice*. Oxford: Oxford University Press.

Rorty, A. 1980. "Agent-Regret." In A. O. Rorty, ed., *Explaining Emotions*, pp. 489–506. Berkeley: University of California Press.

Sartre, J. P. 1948. *Existentialism and Humanism*, trans. by P. Mairet. London: Methuen.

Scheffler, S. 1987. "Morality Through Thick and Thin—A Critical Notice of 'Ethics and the Limits of Philosophy'." *The Philosophical Review* 65: 411–434.

Sinnott-Armstrong, W. 1988. *Moral Dilemmas*. Oxford: Blackwell.

Slote, M. 1983. *Goods and Virtues*. Oxford: Clarendon Press.

Statman, D. (forthcoming). *Moral Dilemmas*. Value Inquiry Book Series (Editor, Robert Ginsberg). Amsterdam: Rodopi.

———. 1991. "Moral and Epistemic Luck." *Ratio* (new series) 4: 146–156.

Taylor, R. 1985. *Ethics, Faith and Reason*. Englewood Cliffs, N.J.: Prentice-Hall.

Tranoy, K. E. 1972. " 'Ought' Implies 'Can'—A Bridge from Fact to Norm?" *Ratio* 14: 116–130.

Walton, D. 1990. "Courage, Relativism and Practical Reasoning." *Philosophia* [Israel] 20: 227–240.

Williams, B. 1973. "A Critique of Utilitarianiam." In B. Williams and J. Smart, eds., *Utilitarianism—For and Against*, pp. 77–150. Cambridge: Cambridge University Press.

————. 1978. "Ethical Consistency." In J. Raz, ed., *Practical Reasoning*, pp. 91–109. Oxford: Oxford University Press.

————. 1981. *Moral Luck*. Cambridge: Cambridge University Press.

————. 1985. *Ethics and the Limits of Philosophy*. London: Fontana Press.

2

Moral Luck*

Bernard Williams

There has been a strain of philosophical thought which identifies the end of life as happiness, happiness as reflective tranquillity, and tranquillity as the product of self-sufficiency— what is not in the domain of the self is not in its control, and so is subject to luck and the contingent enemies of tranquillity. The most extreme versions of this outlook in the Western tradition are certain doctrines of classical antiquity, though it is a notable fact about them that while the good man, the sage, was immune to the impact of incident luck, it was a matter of what may be called constitutive luck that one was a sage, or capable of becoming one: for the many and vulgar this was not (on the prevailing view) an available course.

The idea that one's whole life can in some such way be rendered immune to luck has perhaps rarely prevailed since (it did not prevail, for instance, in mainstream Christianity), but its place has been taken by the still powerfully influential idea that there is one basic form of value, moral value, which is immune to luck and—in the crucial term of the idea's most rigorous exponent—'unconditioned'. Both the disposition to correct moral judgment, and the objects of such judgment, are on this view free from external contingency, for both are, in their related ways, the product of the unconditioned will. Anything which is the product of happy or unhappy contingency is no proper object of moral assessment, and no proper determinant of it, either.[1] Just as, in the realm of character, it is motive that counts, not style, or powers, or endowment, so in action it is not changes actually effected in the world, but intention. With these considerations there is sup-

---

*From *Moral Luck* (Cambridge: Cambridge University Press, 1981), ch. 2.

posed to disappear even that constitutive luck from which the ancient sages were happy to benefit. The capacity for moral agency
is supposedly present to any rational agent whatsoever, to anyone
for whom the question can even present itself. The successful
moral life, removed from considerations of birth, lucky upbringing, or indeed of the incomprehensible Grace of a non-Pelagian
God, is presented as a career open not merely to the talents, but
to a talent which all rational beings necessarily possess in the
same degree. Such a conception has an ultimate form of justice at
its heart, and that is its allure. Kantianism is only superficially
repulsive—despite appearances, it offers an inducement, solace
to a sense of the world's unfairness.

It can offer that solace, however, only if something more is
granted. Even if moral value were radically unconditioned by
luck, that would not be very significant if moral value were merely
one kind of value among others. Rather, moral value has to possess some special, indeed supreme, kind of dignity or importance. The thought that there is a kind of value which is, unlike
others, accessible to all rational agents, offers little encouragement if that kind of value is merely a last resort, the doss-house of
the spirit. Rather, it must have a claim on one's most fundamental concerns as a rational agent, and in one's recognition of that
one is supposed to grasp, not only morality's immunity to luck,
but one's own partial immunity to luck through morality.

Any conception of 'moral luck', on this view, is radically incoherent. The phrase indeed sounds strange. This is because the
Kantian conception embodies, in a very pure form, something
which is basic to our ideas of morality. Yet the aim of making morality immune to luck is bound to be disappointed. The form of
this point which is most familiar, from discussion of freewill, is
that the dispositions of morality, however far back they are placed
in the direction of motive and intention, are as 'conditioned' as
anything else. However, the bitter truth (I take it to be both) that
morality is subject, after all, to constitutive luck is not what I am
going to discuss. The Kantian conception links, and affects, a
range of notions: morality, rationality, justification, and ultimate
or supreme value. The linkage between those notions, under Kantian conception, has a number of consequences for the agent's reflective assessment of his own actions—for instance, that, at the
ultimate and most important level, it cannot be a matter of luck
whether he was justified in doing what he did.

It is this area that I want to consider. I shall in fact say very
little until the end about the moral, concentrating rather on ideas

of rational justification. This is the right place to start, I believe, since almost everyone has some commitment to ideas of this kind about rationality and justification, while they may be disposed to think, so far as morality is concerned, that all that is in question is the pure Kantian conception, and that conception merely represents an obsessional exaggeration. But it is not merely that, nor is the Kantian attempt to escape luck an arbitrary enterprise. The attempt is so intimate to our notion of morality, in fact, that its failure may rather make us consider whether we should not give up that notion altogether.

I shall use the notion of 'luck' generously, undefinedly, but, I think, comprehensibly. It will be clear that when I say of something that it is a matter of luck, this is not meant to carry any implication that it is uncaused. My procedure in general will be to invite reflection about how to think and feel about some rather less usual situations, in the light of an appeal to how we—many people—tend to think and feel about other more usual situations, not in terms of substantive moral opinions or 'intuitions' but in terms of the experience of those kinds of situation. There is no suggestion that it is impossible for human beings to lack these feelings and experiences. In the case of the less usual there is only the claim that the thoughts and experiences I consider are possible, coherent, and intelligible, and that there is no ground for condemning them as irrational. In the case of the more usual, there are suggestions, with the outline of a reason for them, that unless we were to be merely confused or unreflective, life without these experiences would involve a much vaster reconstruction of our sentiments and our view of ourselves than may be supposed—supposed, in particular, by those philosophers who discuss these matters as though our experience of our own agency and the sense of our regrets not only could be tidied up to accord with a very simple image of rationality, but already had been.

Let us take first an outline example of the creative artist who turns away from definite and pressing human claims on him in order to live a life in which, as he supposes, he can pursue his art. Without feeling that we are limited by any historical facts, let us call him *Gauguin*. Gauguin might have been a man who was not at all interested in the claims on him, and simply preferred to live another life, and from that life, and perhaps from that preference, his best paintings came. That sort of case, in which the claims of others simply have no hold on the agent, is not what concerns me here, though it serves to remind us of something related to the present concerns, that while we are sometimes guided by the notion that it would be the best of worlds in which morality were universally respected and all men were of a disposition to affirm it, we have in fact deep and persistent reasons to be grateful that that is not the world we have.

Let us take, rather, a Gauguin who is concerned about these claims and what is involved in their being neglected (we may suppose this to be grim), and that he nevertheless, in the face of that, opts for the other life. This other life he might perhaps not see very determinately under the category of realising his gifts as a painter, but, to make things simpler, let us add that he does see it determinately in that light—it is as a life which will enable him really to be a painter that he opts for it. It will then be clearer what will count for him as eventual success in his project—at least, some possible outcomes will be clear examples of success (which does not have to be the same thing as recognition), however many others may be unclear.

Whether he will succeed cannot, in the nature of the case, be foreseen. We are not dealing here with the removal of an external obstacle to something which, once that is removed, will fairly predictably go through. Gauguin, in our story, is putting a great deal on a possibility which has not unequivocally declared itself. I want to explore and uphold the claim that in such a situation the only thing that will justify his choice will be success itself. If he fails—and we shall come shortly to what, more precisely, failure may be—then he did the wrong thing, not just in the sense in which that platitudinously follows, but in the sense that having done the wrong thing in those circumstances he has no basis for the thought that he was justified in acting as he did. If he succeeds, he does have a basis for that thought.

As I have already indicated, I will leave to the end the question of how such notions of justification fit in with distinctively moral ideas. One should be warned already, however, that, even if Gauguin can be ultimately justified, that need not provide him with any way of justifying himself to others, or at least to all others. Thus he may have no way of bringing it about that those who suffer from his decision will have no justified ground of reproach. Even if he succeeds, he will not acquire a right that they accept what he has to say: if he fails, he will not even have anything to say.

The justification, if there is to be one, will be essentially retrospective. Gauguin could not do something which is thought to be essential to rationality and to the notion of justification itself, which is that one should be in a position to apply the justifying considerations at the time of the choice and in advance of knowing whether one was right (in the sense of its coming out right). How this can be in general will form a major part of the discussion. I do not want, at this stage of the argument, to lay much weight on the notion of morality, but it may help to throw some light on the matter of prior justification if we bring in briefly the narrower question whether there could be a prior justification for Gauguin's choice in terms of moral rules.

A moral theorist, recognizing that some value attached to the success of Gauguin's project and hence possibly to his choice, might try to accommodate that choice within a framework of moral rules, by forming a subsidiary rule which could, before the outcome, justify that choice. What could that rule be? It could not be that one is morally justified in deciding to neglect other claims if one is a great creative artist: apart from doubts about its content, the saving clause begs the question which at the relevant time one is in no position to answer. On the other hand, ' . . . if one is convinced that one is a great creative artist' will serve to make obstinacy and fatuous self-delusion conditions of justification, while ' . . . if one is reasonably convinced that one is a great creative artist' is, if anything, worse. What is reasonable conviction supposed to be in such a case? Should Gauguin consult professors of art? The absurdity of such riders surely expresses an absurdity in the whole enterprise of trying to find a place for such cases within the rules.

Utilitarian formulations are not going to contribute any more to understanding these situations than do formulations in terms of rules. They can offer the thought 'it is better (worse) that he did it', where the force of that is, approximately, 'it is better (worse) that it happened', but this in itself does not help towards a characterization of the agent's decision or its possible justification, and Utilitarianism has no special materials of its own to help in that. It has its own well-known problems, too, in spelling out the content of the 'better'—on standard doctrine, Gauguin's decision would seem to have been a better thing, the more popular a painter he eventually became. But there is something more interesting than that kind of difficulty. The Utilitarian perspective, not uniquely but clearly, will miss a very important dimension of such cases, the question of what 'failure' may relevantly be. From the perspective of consequences, the goods or benefits for the sake of which Gauguin's choice was made either

materialize in some degree, or do not materialize. But it matters considerably to the thoughts we are considering, in what
way the project fails to come off, if it fails. If Gauguin sustains
some injury on the way to Tahiti which prevents his ever painting again, that certainly means that his decision (supposing it
now to be irreversible) was for nothing, and indeed there is
nothing in the outcome to set against the other people's loss. But
that train of events does not provoke the thought in question,
that after all he was wrong and unjustified. He does not, and
never will, know whether he was wrong. What would prove him
wrong in his project would not just be that it failed, but that
he failed.

This distinction shows that while Gauguin's justification is
in some ways a matter of luck, it is not equally a matter of all
kinds of luck. It matters how intrinsic the cause of failure is to the
project itself. The occurrence of an injury is, relative to these undertakings at least, luck of the most external and incident kind.
Irreducibly, luck of this kind affects whether he will be justified or
not, since if it strikes, he will not be justified. But it is too external for it to unjustify him, something which only his failure as a
painter can do; yet still that is, at another level, luck, the luck of
being able to be as he hoped he might be. It might be wondered
whether that is *luck* at all, or, if so, whether it may not be luck of
that constitutive kind which affects everything and which we
have already left on one side. But it is more than that. It is not
merely luck that he is such a man, but luck relative to the deliberations that went into his decision, that he turns out to be such
a man: he might (epistemically) not have been. That is what sets
the problem.

In some cases, though perhaps not in Gauguin's, success in
such decisions might be thought not to be a matter of epistemic
luck relative to the decision. There might be grounds for saying
that the person who was prepared to take the decision, and was
in fact right, actually knew that he would succeed, however sub-
jectively uncertain he may have been. But even if this is right for
some cases, it does not help with the problems of retrospective
justification. For the concept of knowledge here is itself applied
retrospectively, and while there is nothing wrong with that, it
does not enable the agent at the time of his decision to make any
distinctions he could not already make. As one might say, even if
it did turn out in such a case that the agent did know, it was still
luck, relative to the considerations available to him at the time

and at the level at which he made his decision, that he should turn out to have known.

Some luck, in a decision of Gauguin's kind, is extrinsic to his project, some intrinsic; both are necessary for success, and hence for actual justification, but only the latter relates to unjustification. If we now broaden the range of cases slightly, we shall be able to see more clearly the notion of intrinsic luck. In Gauguin's case the nature of the project is such that two distinctions do, roughly, coincide. One is a distinction between luck intrinsic to the project, and luck extrinsic to it; the other is a distinction between what is, and what is not, determined by him and by what he is. The intrinsic luck in Gauguin's case concentrates itself on virtually the one question of whether he is a genuinely gifted painter who can succeed in doing genuinely valuable work. Not all the conditions of the projects' coming off lie in him, obviously, since others' actions and refrainings provide many necessary conditions of its coming off—and that is an important locus of extrinsic luck. But the conditions of its coming off which are relevant to unjustification, the locus of intrinsic luck, largely lie in him—which is not to say, of course, that they depend on his will, though some may. This rough coincidence of two distinctions is a feature of this case. But in others, the locus on intrinsic luck (intrinsic, that is to say, to the project) may lie partly outside the agent, and this is an important, and indeed the more typical, case.

Consider an equally schematized account of another example, that of Anna Karenina. Anna remains conscious in her life with Vronsky of the cost exacted from others, above all from her son. She might have lived with that consciousness, we may suppose, if things had gone better, and relative to her state of understanding when she left Karenin, they could have gone better. As it turns out, the social situation and her own state of mind are such that the relationship with Vronsky has to carry too much weight, and the more obvious that becomes, the more it has to carry; and that I take that to be a truth not only about society but about her and Vronsky, a truth which, however inevitable Tolstoy ultimately makes it seem, could, relative to her earlier thoughts, have been otherwise. It is, in the present terms, a matter of intrinsic luck, and a failure in the heart of her project. But its locus is not by any means entirely in her, for it also lies in him.

It would have been an intrinsic failure, also, if Vronsky had actually committed suicide. It would not have been that, but rather an extrinsic misfortune, if Vronsky had been accidentally killed. Though her project would have been at an end, it would not have failed as it does fail. This difference illustrates precisely the thoughts we are concerned with. If Anna had then committed suicide, her thought might have been something like: 'there is nothing more for me'. But I take it that as things are, her thought in killing herself is not just that, but relates inescapably also to the past and to what she has done. What she did, she now finds insupportable, because she could have been justified only by the life she hoped for, and those hopes were not just negated, but refuted, by what happened.

It is such thoughts that I want to place in a structure which will make their sense plainer. The discussion is not in the first place directed to what we or others might say or think of these agents (though it has implications for that), but on what they can be expected coherently to think about themselves. A notion we shall be bound to use in describing their state of mind is *regret*, and there are certain things that need, first, to be said about this notion.

The constitutive thought of regret in general is something like 'how much better if it had been otherwise', and the feeling can in principle apply to anything of which one can form some conception of how it might have been otherwise, together with consciousness of how things would have been better. In this general sense of regret, what are regretted are states of affairs, and they can be regretted, in principle, by anyone who knows of them. But there is a particularly important species of regret, which I shall call 'agent-regret', which a person can feel only towards his own past actions (or, at most, actions in which he regards himself as a participant). In this case, the supposed possible difference is that one might have acted otherwise, and the focus of the regret is on that possibility, the thought being formed in part by first-personal conceptions of how one might have acted otherwise. 'Agent-regret' is not distinguished from regret in general solely or simply in virtue of its subject-matter. There can be cases of regret directed to one's own past actions which are not cases of agent-regret, because the past action is regarded purely externally, as one might regard anyone else's action. Agent-regret requires not merely a first-personal subject-matter, nor yet merely a particular kind of psychological content, but also a particular kind of expression.

The sentiment of agent-regret is by no means restricted to *voluntary* agency. It can extend far beyond what one intentionally did to almost anything for which one was causally responsible in virtue of something one intentionally did. Yet even at deeply accidental or non-voluntary levels of agency, sentiments of agent-regret are different from regret in general, such as might be felt by a spectator, and are acknowledged in our practice as being different. The lorry driver who, through no fault of his, runs over a child, will feel differently from any spectator, even a spectator next to him in the cab, except perhaps to the extent that the spectator takes on the thought that he himself might have prevented it, an agent's thought. Doubtless, and rightly, people will try, in comforting him, to move the driver from this state of feeling, move him indeed from where he is to something more like the place of a spectator, but it is important that this is seen as something that should need to be done, and indeed some doubt would be felt about a driver who too blandly or readily moved to that position. We feel sorry for the driver, but that sentiment co-exists with, indeed presupposes, that there is something special about his relation to this happening, something which cannot merely be eliminated by the consideration that it was not his fault. It may be still more so in cases where agency is fuller than in such an accident, though still involuntary through ignorance.

The differences between agent-regret and regret felt by a spectator comes out not just in thoughts and images that enter into the sentiment, but in differences of expression. The lorry-driver may act in some way which he hopes will constitute or at least symbolize some kind of recompense or restitution, and this will be an expression of his agent-regret. But the willingness to give compensation, even the recognition that one should give it, does not always express agent-regret, and the preparedness to compensate can present itself at very different levels of significance in these connexions. We may recognize the need to pay compensation for damage we involuntarily cause, and yet this recognition be of an external kind, accompanied only by regret of a general kind, or by no regret at all. It may merely be that it would be unfair for the sufferer to bear the cost if there is an alternative, and there is an alternative to be found in the agent whose intentional activities produced the damage as a side-effect.

In these cases, the relevant consciousness of having done the harmful thing is basically that of its having happened as a

consequence of one's acts, together with the thought that the cost
of its happening can in the circumstances fairly be allocated to
one's account. A test of whether that is an agent's state of mind in
acknowledging that he should compensate is offered by the question whether from this point of view insurance cover would do at
least as well. Imagine the premiums already paid (by someone
else, we might add, if that helps to clarify the test): then if knowledge that the victim received insurance payments would settle
any unease the agent feels, then it is for him an external case.
It is an obvious and welcome consequence of this test that
whether an agent can acceptably regard a given case externally
is a function not only of his relations to it, but of what sort of
case it is—besides the question of whether he should compensate rather than the insurance company, there is the question
whether it is the sort of loss that can be compensated at all by
insurance. If it is not, an agent conscious that he was uninten-
tionally responsible for it might still feel that he should do something, not necessarily because he could actually compensate
where insurance money could not, but because (if he is lucky)
his actions might have some reparative significance other than
compensation.

    In other cases, again, there is no room for any appropriate
action at all. Then only the desire to make reparation remains,
with the painful consciousness that nothing can be done about
it; some other action, perhaps less directed to the victims, may
come to express this. What degree of such feeling is appropriate,
and what attempts at reparative action or substitutes for it, are
questions for particular cases, and that there is room in the area
for irrational and self-punitive excess, no one is likely to deny. But
equally it would be a kind of insanity never to experience sentiments of this kind towards anyone, and it would be an insane
concept of rationality which insisted that a rational person never
would. To insist on such a conception of rationality, moreover,
would, apart from other kinds of absurdity, suggest a large false-
hood: that we might, if we conducted ourselves clear-headedly
enough, entirely detach ourselves from the unintentional aspects
of our actions, relegating their costs to, so to speak, the insurance fund, and yet still retain our identity and character as
agents. One's history as an agent is a web in which anything that
is the product of the will is surrounded and held up and partly
formed by things that are not, in such a way that reflection can go
only in one of two directions: either in the direction of saying that

responsible agency is a fairly superficial concept, which has a limited use in harmonizing what happens, or else that it is not a superficial concept, but that it cannot ultimately be purified—if one attaches importance to the sense of what one is in terms of what one has done and what in the world one is responsible for, one must accept much that makes its claim on that sense solely in virtue of its being actual.[2]

The examples of Gauguin and Anna Karenina are, of course, cases of voluntary agency, but they share something with the involuntary cases just mentioned, for the 'luck' of the agents relates to those elements which are essential to the outcome but lie outside their control, and what we are discussing is in this way a very drastic example of determination by the actual, the determination of the agents' judgments on their decisions by what, beyond their will, actually occurs. Besides that, the discussion of agent-regret about the involuntary also helps us to get away from a dichotomy which is often relied on in these matters, expressed in such terms as *regret* and *remorse*, where 'regret' is identified in effect as the regret of the spectator, while 'remorse' is what we have called 'agent-regret', but under the restriction that it applies only to the voluntary. The fact that we have agent-regret about the involuntary, and would not readily recognize a life without it (though we may think we might), shows already that there is something wrong with this dichotomy: such regret is neither mere spectator's regret, nor (by this definition) remorse.

There is a difference between agent-regret as we have so far discussed it, and the agents' feelings in the present cases. As we elicited it from the non-voluntary examples, agent-regret involved a wish on the agent's part that he had not done it. He deeply wishes that he had made changes which, had he known it, was in his power and which would have altered the outcome. But Gauguin or Anna Karenina, as we have represented them, wish they had acted otherwise only if they are unsuccessful. (At least, that wish attends their unsuccess under the simplifying assumption that their subsequent thoughts and feelings are still essentially formed by the projects we have ascribed to them. This is an oversimplification, since evidently they might form new projects in the course of unsuccess itself; though Anna did not. I shall sustain the assumption in what follows). Whatever feelings these agents had after their decision, but before the declaration of their success or failure, lacked the fully-developed wish to have acted otherwise—that wish comes only when failure is declared.

Regret necessarily involves a wish that things had been otherwise, for instance that one had not had to act as one did. But it
does not necessarily involve the wish, all things taken together,
that one had acted otherwise. An example of this, largely independent of the present issues, is offered by the cases of conflict between two courses of action each of which is morally required,
where either course of action, even if it is judged to be for the
best, leaves regrets—which are, in our present terms, agent-
regrets about something voluntarily done.[3] We should not entirely assimilate agent-regret and the wish, all things taken
together, to have acted otherwise. We must now look at some connexions of these to each other, and to certain ideas of justification. This will add the last element to our attempt to characterize
our cases.

It will be helpful to contrast our cases with more straightforward cases of practical deliberation and the types of retrospective
reflexion appropriate to them. We may take first the simplest
cases of pure egoistic deliberation, where not only is the agent's
attention confined to egoistic projects, but moral critics would
agree that it is legitimately so confined. Here, in one sense the
agent does not have to justify his deliberative process, since there
is no one he is answerable to, but it is usually supposed that
there is some sense in which even such an agent's deliberative
processes can be justified or unjustified—the sense, that is, in
which his decision can be reasonable or unreasonable relative to
his situation, whatever its actual outcome. Considerations bearing on this include at least the consistency of his thoughts, the
rational assessment of probabilities, and the optimal ordering of
actions in time.[4]

While the language of justification is used in this connexion,
it is less clear than is usually assumed what its content is, and, in
particular, what the point is of an agent's being retrospectively
concerned with the rationality of his decision, and not just with
its success. How are we to understand the retrospective thought
of one who comes to see a mismatch between his deliberations
and the outcome? If he deliberates badly, and as a result of this
his projects go wrong, it is easy to see *in that case* how his regret
at the outcome appropriately attaches itself to his deliberations.
But if he deliberates well, and things go wrong; particularly if, as
sometimes happens, they would have gone better if he had deliberated worse; what is the consciousness that he was 'justified'
supposed to do for the disposition of his undoubted regret about

how things actually turned out? His thought that he was justified seems to carry with it something like this: while he is sorry
that things turned out as they did, and, in a sense corresponding
to that, he wishes he had acted otherwise, at the same time he
does not wish he had acted otherwise, for he stands by the processes of rational deliberation which led to what he did. Similarly
with the converse phenomenon, where having made and too late
discovered some mistake of deliberation, the agent is by luck successful, and indeed would have been less successful if he had
done anything else. Here his gladness that he acted as he did (his
lack of a wish to have acted otherwise) operates at a level at which
it is compatible with such feelings as self-reproach or retrospective alarm at having acted as he did.

These observations are truisms, but it remains obscure
what their real content is. Little is effected by talk of self-reproach
or regret at all, still less of co-existent regret and contentment,
unless some expression of such sentiments can be identified.
Certainly it is not to be identified in this case with any disposition
to compensate other persons, for none is affected. Connected
with that, criticism by other persons would be on a different basis
from criticism offered where they had a grievance, as in a case
where an agent risks goods of which he is a trustee, through error, oversight, or (interestingly) merely through the choice of a
high-risk strategy to which he would be perfectly entitled if he
were acting solely in his own interests. The trustee is not entitled
to gamble with the infants' money even if any profits will certainly
go to the infants, and success itself will not remove, or start to
remove, that objection. That sort of criticism is of course not appropriate in the purely egoistic case, and in fact there is no reason to think that criticism by others is more than a consequential
consideration in the egoistic case, derived from others' recommendation of the virtues of rational prudence, which need to be
explained first.

Granted that there is no issue of compensation to others in
the purely egoistic case, the form of expression of regret seems
necessarily to be, as Richards has said,[5] the agent's resolutions
for his future deliberations. His regrets about his deliberations
express themselves as resolves to think better next time; satisfaction with the deliberation, however disappointing the particular outcome, expresses itself in this, that he finds nothing
to be *learned* from the case, and is sure that he will have no
better chance of success (at a given level of pay-off) next time by

changing his procedures. If this is right, then the notions of regret or lack of regret at the past level of deliberative excellence
makes sense only in the context of a policy or disposition of rational deliberation applied to an on-going class of cases.

This is a modest enough conception—it is important to see
how modest it is. It implies a class of cases sufficiently similar for
deliberative practices to be translated from one to another of
them; it does not imply that these cases are all conjointly the subject of deliberative reasoning. I may make a reasoned choice between alternatives of a certain kind today, and, having seen how
it turns out, resolve to deal rather differently with the next choice
of that kind, but I need not either engage in or resolve to engage
in any deliberative reasoning which weighs the options of more
than one such occasion together.[6]

Insofar as the outcomes of different such situations affect
one another, there is indeed pressure to say that rational deliberation should in principle consider them together. But if one knew
enough, virtually any choice would be seen to affect all later ones,
so it has seemed to some that the ideal limit of this process is
something which is far more ambitious than the modest notion
of an ongoing disposition to rational deliberation. This is the
model of rational deliberation as directed to a *life-plan*, in Rawls'
sense, which treats all times of one's life as of equal concern to
one.[7] The theorists of this picture agree that as a matter of fact
ignorance and other factors do usually make it rational to dis-
count over remoteness in time, but these are subsequent considerations brought to a model which is that of one's life as a
rectangle, so to speak, presented all at once and to be optimally
filled in. This model is presented not only as embodying the ideal
fulfilment of a rational urge to harmonize all one's projects. It is
also supposed to provide a special grounding for the idea that a
more fundamental form of regret is directed to deliberative error
than to mere mistake. The regret takes the form of self-reproach,
and the idea is that we protect ourselves against reproaches from
our future self if we act with deliberative rationality: 'nothing can
protect us from the ambiguities and limitations of our knowledge,
or guarantee that we find the best alternative open to us. Acting
with deliberative rationality can only ensure that our conduct is
above reproach, and that we are responsible to ourselves as one
person over time.'[8] These strains come together in Rawls' advo-
cacy of 'the guiding principle that a rational individual is always
to act so that he need never blame himself no matter how things
finally transpire'.[9]

Rawls seems to regard this injunction as, in a sense, formal, and as not determining how risky or conservative a strategy the agent should adopt, but it is worth remarking that if any grounding for self-reproach about deliberative error is to be found in the notion of the recriminations of one's later self, the injunction will in fact have to be taken in a more materially cautious sense. The grounding relies on an analogy with the responsibility to other persons: I am a trustee for my own future. If this has any force at all, it is hard to see why it does not extend to my being required, like any other trustee, to adopt a cautious strategy with the entrusted goods—which are, in this case, almost everything I have.

However that may be, the model that gives rise to the injunction is false. Apart from other difficulties,[10] it implicitly ignores the obvious fact that what one does and the sort of life one leads condition one's later desires and judgments. The standpoint of that retrospective judge who will be my later self will be the product of my earlier choices. So there is no set of preferences both fixed and relevant, relative to which the various fillings of my life-space can be compared. If the fillings are to be evaluated by reference to what I variously, in them, want, the relevant preferences are not fixed, while if they are to be evaluated by what I now (for instance) want, this will give a fixed set of preferences, but one that is not necessarily relevant. The recourse from this within the life-space model is to assume (as Utilitarianism does) that there is some currency of satisfactions, in terms of which it is possible to compare quite neutrally the value of one set of preferences together with their fulfillments, as against a quite different set of preferences together with their fulfilments. But there is no reason to suppose that there is any such currency, nor that the idea of practical rationality should implicitly presuppose it.

If there is no such currency, then we can only to a limited extent abstract from the projects and preferences we actually have, and cannot in principle gain a standpoint from which the alternative fillings of our life-rectangle could be compared without prejudice. The perspective of deliberative choice on one's life is constitutively *from here*. Correspondingly the perspective of assessment with greater knowledge is necessarily *from there*, and not only can I not guarantee how factually it will then be, but I cannot ultimately guarantee from what standpoint of assessment my major and most fundamental regrets will be.

For many decisions which are part of the agent's ongoing activity (the 'normal science', so to speak, of the moral life) we can see why it is that the presence or absence of regrets is more basically conditioned by the retrospective view of the deliberative processes, than by the particular outcomes. Oneself and one's viewpoint are more basically identified with the dispositions of rational deliberation, applicable to an ongoing series of decisions, than they are with the particular projects which succeed or fail on those occasions. But there are certain other decisions, as in the cases we are considering, which are not like this. There is indeed some room for the presence and subsequent assessment of deliberative rationality. The agents in our cases might well not be taken as seriously as they would otherwise if they did not, to the limited extent that the situation permits, take such rational thought as they can about the realities of their situation. But this is not the aspect under which they will primarily look back on it, nor is it as a contribution to a series of deliberative situations that it will have its importance for them. Though they will learn from it, it will not be in that way. In these cases, the project in the interests of which the decision is made is one with which the agent is identified in such a way that if it succeeds, his standpoint of assessment will be from a life that then derives an important part of its significance for him from that very fact; if he fails, it can, necessarily, have no such significance in his life. If he succeeds, it cannot be that while welcoming the outcome he more basically regrets the decision. If he fails, his standpoint will be of one for whom the ground project of the decision has proved worthless, and this (under the simplifying assumption that other adequate projects are not generated in the process) must leave him with the most basic regrets. So if he fails, his most basic regrets will attach to his decision, and if he succeeds, they cannot. That is the sense in which his decision can be justified, for him, by success.

On this account, it is clear that the decisions we are concerned with are not merely very risky ones, or even very risky ones with a substantial outcome. The outcome has to be substantial in a special way—in a way which importantly conditions the agent's sense of what is significant in his life, and hence his standpoint of retrospective assessment. It follows from this that they are, indeed, risky, and in a way which helps to explain the importance for such projects of the difference between extrinsic and intrinsic failure. With an intrinsic failure, the project which generated the decision is revealed as an empty thing, incapable of grounding the agent's life. With extrinsic failure, it is not so revealed, and while he must acknowledge that it has failed, nevertheless it has not been discredited, and may, perhaps in the form of some new aspiration, contribute to making sense of what is left. In his retrospective thought, and its allocation of basic regret, he cannot in the fullest sense identify with his decision, and so does not find himself justified; but he is not totally alienated from it either, cannot just see it as a disastrous error, and so does not find himself unjustified.

What is the relation of all this, finally, to morality? Does it have any very direct relation? Thomas Nagel,[11] who agrees that morality is deeply and disquietingly subject to luck, denies that an example such as Gauguin's shows that to be so—rather, it shows that Gauguin's most basic retrospective feelings do not have to be moral.

One reason that Nagel gives for this understanding of the matter is that (as I suggested earlier) Gauguin may not be able to justify himself to others, in the sense that they will have no justified grievance. However, this consideration just in itself will not carry great weight unless one makes a strong assumption about the nature of ethical consistency, to the effect that, if someone had acted justifiably from a moral point of view, then no-one can justifiably complain, from that point of view, of his so acting. But this as a general requirement is unrealistically strong, as can be seen from political cases,[12] for instance, in which we can have reason to approve of the outcome, and of the agent's choice to produce that outcome, and of his being an agent who is able to make that choice, while conscious that there has been a 'moral cost'. It is not reasonable, in such a case, to expect those particular people who have been cheated, used or injured to approve of the agent's action, nor should they be subjected to the patronising thought that, while their complaints are not justified in terms of the whole picture, they are too closely involved to be able to see that truth. Their complaints are, indeed, justified, and they may quite properly refuse to accept the agent's justification which the rest of us may properly accept. The idea that there has been a moral cost itself implies that something bad has been done, and, very often, that someone has been wronged, and if the people who have been wronged do not accept the justification, then no-one can demand that they should. It is for them to decide how far they are prepared to adopt the perspective within which the justification counts. This is just one of the ways—the distancing of time is another—in which, if the moral sentiments are to be part of life as it is actually experienced, they cannot be modelled on a view of the world in which every happening and every person is at the same distance.

Our cases are admittedly different from the case of the politician. There, the justifying conditions relate to issues of what we want effected, what system of government we want, what persons we want to work within that system, and those wants may themselves be shaped by what are, in an everyday sense, moral considerations. With the agents in our examples, it is not the same, and there is, moreover, a difference between the examples themselves. If Gauguin's project succeeds, it can yield a good for the world as Anna's success could not. The moral spectator has to consider the fact that he has reason to be glad that Gauguin succeeded, and hence that he tried—or if a particular spectator finds that he has no disposition to be grateful for Gauguin's paintings, or for paintings, then there will be some other case.

It may be said that this merely represents our gratitude that morality does not always prevail—that moral values have been treated as one value among others, not as unquestionably supreme. I think that that misdescribes our relation to *this* Gauguin, at least, but it is important also to bear in mind the grounds, the scope and the significance of that gratitude, which I mentioned earlier, for the limitations of morality. If the moral were really supreme, it would have to be ubiquitous: like Spinoza's substance, if it were to be genuinely unconditioned, there would have to be nothing to condition it.

That is a demand which, only too familiarly, can extend itself among the feelings. The ultimate justice which the Kantian outlook so compellingly demands requires morality, as immune to luck, to be supreme, and while that does not formally require that there be no other sentiments or attachments, in fact it can, like the Robespierrean government to which Heine compared the Kantian system in general, steadily grow to require a wider conformity of the sentiments. Justice requires not merely that *something I am* should be beyond luck, but that *what I most fundamentally am* should be so, and, in the light of that, admiration or liking or even enjoyment of the happy manifestations of luck can seem to be treachery to moral worth. That guilty leveling of the sentiments can occur even if one recognizes, as Kant recognized, that there are some things that one is responsible for, and others for which one is not. The final destruction occurs when the Kantian sense of justice is joined to a Utilitarian conception of negative responsibility, and one is left, at any level of importance, only with purely moral motivations and no limit to their application. There is, at the end of that, no life of one's own, except perhaps for some small area, hygienically allotted, of meaningless privacy.

Because that is a genuine pathology of the moral life, the limitation of the moral is itself something morally important. But to regard Gauguin's decision simply as a welcome incursion of the amoral is anyway too limited. It will be adequate only if he is the amoral Gauguin we put aside at the beginning. If he is not, then he is himself open to regrets for what he has done to others, and, if he fails, then those regrets are not only all that he has, but, as I have tried to explain, he no longer even has the perspective within which something else could have been laid against them. That can make a difference to the moral spectator. While he may admire the amoral Gauguin's achievements, and indeed admire him, this other Gauguin is someone who shares the same world of moral concerns. The risk these agents run is a risk within morality, a risk which amoral versions of these agents would not run at all.

The fact that these agents' justifications, if they acquired them, would not properly silence all complaints, does not itself lead to the conclusion that they are not moral justifications. However, perhaps we should, all the same, accept that conclusion. Their moral luck, we should then say, does not lie in acquiring a moral justification. It lies rather in the relation of their life, and of their justification or lack of it, to morality. That relation has to be seen in the first instance in their perspective, one in which, if they fail, there is simply regret. But their life is recognizably part of moral life, and it has a significance for us as well.

There is now, however, a pressing question—how much is being done by the concept of the moral, and how much *by this stage of the argument* does it matter what happens to it? In reminding ourselves of the significance of luck to the moral life— whether it is constitutive luck, or that which affects the relations of one's decisions to morality, or that which affects merely what one will turn out to have done—we essentially use the concept, because we are working out in reflection from central applications of the concept to question what may be a basic motive for using it all:[13] the motive of establishing a dimension of decision and assessment which can hope to transcend luck. Once that motive is understood and questioned, it has to be asked once more what the concept is for, and, by the same token, how many other features of it can be taken for granted.

Scepticism about the freedom of morality from luck cannot leave the concept of morality where it was, any more than it can remain undisturbed by skepticism about the very closely related image we have of there being a moral order, within which our actions have a significance which may not be accorded to them by mere social recognition. These forms of skepticism will leave us with *a* concept of morality, but one less important, certainly, than ours is usually taken to be; and that will not be ours, since one thing that is particularly important about ours is how important it is taken to be.

Notes

1. Kant's own account of this centrally involves the role of the Categorical Imperative. On that issue, I agree with what I take to be the substance of Philippa Foot's position ("Morality as a System of Hypothetical Imperatives," *Phil. Rev.* 1972; and her reply to Frankena, *Philosophy* 1975), but not at all with her way of putting it. In so far as there is a clear distinction between categorical and hypothetical imperatives, and in so far as morality consists of imperatives, it consists of categorical imperatives. The point is that the fact that an imperative is in this sense, categorical provides no reason at all for obeying it. Nor need Kant think it does: the authority of the Categorical Imperative is supposed (mysteriously enough) to derive not just from its being (in this sense) categorical, but from its being categorical and self-addressed by the agent as a rational being.

2. That acceptance is central to tragedy, something which itself presses the question of how we want to think about these things. When Oedipus says 'I did not do it' (Sophocles *Oedipus at Colonus* 539) he speaks as one whose exile and blindness proclaim that he did do it, and to persons who treat him as quite special because he did. Could we have, and do we want, a concept of agency by which what Oedipus said would be simply true, and by which he would be seeing things rightly if for him it was straight off as though he had no part in it? (These questions have little to do with how the law should be: punishment and public amends are a different matter.)

3. For some discussion of this see "Ethical Consistency," in *Problems of the Self* (Cambridge 1973), pp. 166–86.

4. A useful outline of such considerations is in D. A. J. Richards, *A Theory of Reasons for Action* (Oxford 1971), ch. 3.

5. Op. cit., pp. 70–1, and cf. ch. 13 [*Moral Luck* (Cambridge: Cambridge University Press, 1981)]

6. The notion of treating cases together, as opposed to treating them separately but in the light of experience, applies not only to deliberation which yields in advance a conjunctive resolution of a number of cases, but also to deliberation which yields hypothetical conclusions to the effect that a later case will receive a certain treatment if an earlier case turns out in a certain way: as in a staking system.

7. John Rawls, *A Theory of Justice* (Oxford, 1972), esp. ch. VII; Thomas Nagel, *The Possibility of Altruism* (Oxford, 1970).

8. Rawls, pp. 422–3.

9. P. 422.

10. It ignores also the very basic fact that the size of the rectangle is up to me; see Chapter 1 [*Moral Luck*].

11. In his contribution to the symposium for which this paper was originally written: *Proc. Arist. Soc.* Supp. Vol. L (1976), reprinted with revisions in his *Mortal Questions* (Cambridge, 1979) [see chapter 3]. I have benefited from Nagel's paper and from discussion with him. I entirely agree with him that the involvement of morality with luck is not something that can simply be accepted without calling our moral conceptions into question. That was part of my original point; I have tried to state it more directly in the present version of this paper. A difference between Nagel and myself is that I am more skeptical about our moral conceptions than he is.

12. See Chapter 4 [*Moral Luck*].

13. As Nagel points out, the situation resembles to some degree that with skepticism about knowledge. The same idea indeed seems to be involved in both cases: the knower is one whose belief is non-accidentally true (for discussion, see my *Descartes, the Project of Pure Enquiry* (Harmondsworth, 1978), pp. 37 seq). However, the path taken by skepticism from these similar starting points, and its eventual effectiveness, seem to be very different in the two cases.

3

Moral Luck*

Thomas Nagel

Kant believed that good or bad luck should influence neither our moral judgment of a person and his actions, nor his moral assessment of himself.

> The good will is not good because of what it effects or accomplishes or because of its adequacy to achieve some proposed end; it is good only because of its willing, i.e., it is good of itself. And, regarded for itself, it is to be esteemed incomparably higher than anything which could be brought about by it in favor of any inclination or even of the sum total of all inclinations. Even if it should happen that, by a particularly unfortunate fate or by the niggardly provision of a stepmotherly nature, this will should be wholly lacking in power to accomplish its purpose, and if even the greatest effort should not avail it to achieve anything of its end, and if there remained only the good will (not as a mere wish but as the summoning of all the means in our power), it would sparkle like a jewel in its own right, as something that had its full worth in itself. Usefulness or fruitlessness can neither diminish nor augment this worth.[1]

He would presumably have said the same about a bad will: whether it accomplishes its evil purposes is morally irrelevant. And a course of action that would be condemned if it had a bad outcome cannot be vindicated if by luck it turns out well. There cannot be moral risk. This view seems to be wrong, but it arises

---

*From *Mortal Questions* (New York: Cambridge University Press, 1979), ch. 3.

in response to a fundamental problem about moral responsibility to which we possess no satisfactory solution.

The problem develops out of the ordinary conditions of moral judgment. Prior to reflection it is intuitively plausible that people cannot be morally assessed for what is not their fault, or for what is due to factors beyond their control. Such judgment is different from the evaluation of something as a good or bad thing, or state of affairs. The latter may be present in addition to moral judgment, but when we blame someone for his actions we are not merely saying it is bad that they happened, or bad that he exists: we are judging *him*, saying he is bad, which is different from his being a bad thing. This kind of judgment takes only a certain kind of object. Without being able to explain exactly why, we feel that the appropriateness of moral assessment is easily undermined by the discovery that the act or attribute, no matter how good or bad, is not under the person's control. While other evaluations remain, this one seems to lose its footing. So a clear absence of control, produced by involuntary movement, physical force, or ignorance of the circumstances, excuses what is done from moral judgment. But what we do depends in many more ways than these on what is not under our control—what is not produced by a good or a bad will, in Kant's phrase. And external influences in this broader range are not usually thought to excuse what is done from moral judgment, positive or negative.

Let me give a few examples, beginning with the type of case Kant has in mind. Whether we succeed or fail in what we try to do nearly always depends to some extent on factors beyond our control. This is true of murder, altruism, revolution, the sacrifice of certain interests for the sake of others—almost any morally important act. What has been done, and what is morally judged, is partly determined by external factors. However jewel-like the good will may be in its own right, there is a morally significant difference between rescuing someone from a burning building and dropping him from a twelfth-storey window while trying to rescue him. Similarly, there is a morally significant difference between reckless driving and manslaughter. But whether a reckless driver hits a pedestrian depends on the presence of the pedestrian at the point where he recklessly passes a red light. What we do is also limited by the opportunities and choices with which we are faced, and these are largely determined by factors beyond our control. Someone who was an officer in a concentration camp might have led a quiet and harmless life if the Nazis had never come to power in Germany. And someone who led a quiet and harmless life in Argentina might have become an officer in a concentration camp if he had not left Germany for business reasons in 1930.

I shall say more later about these and other examples. I introduce them here to illustrate a general point. Where a significant aspect of what someone does depends on factors beyond his control, yet we continue to treat him in that respect as an object of moral judgment, it can be called moral luck. Such luck can be good or bad. And the problem posed by this phenomenon, which led Kant to deny its possibility, is that the broad range of external influences here identified seems on close examination to undermine moral assessment as surely as does the narrower range of familiar excusing conditions. If the condition of control is consistently applied, it threatens to erode most of the moral assessments we find it natural to make. The things for which people are morally judged are determined in more ways than we at first realize by what is beyond their control. And when the seemingly natural requirement of fault or responsibility is applied in light of these facts, it leaves few pre-reflective moral judgments intact. Ultimately, nothing or almost nothing about what a person does seems to be under his control.

Why not conclude, then, that the condition of control is false—that it is an initially plausible hypothesis refuted by clear counter-examples? One could in that case look instead for a more refined condition which picked out the *kinds* of lack of control that really undermine certain moral judgments, without yielding the unacceptable conclusion derived from the broader condition, that most or all ordinary moral judgments are illegitimate.

What rules out this escape is that we are dealing not with a theoretical conjecture but with a philosophical problem. The condition of control does not suggest itself merely as a generalization from certain clear cases. It seems *correct* in the further cases to which it is extended beyond the original set. When we undermine moral assessment by considering new ways in which control is absent, we are not just discovering what *would* follow given the general hypothesis, but are actually being persuaded that in itself the absence of control is relevant in these cases too. The erosion of moral judgment emerges not as the absurd consequence of an over-simple theory, but as a natural consequence of the ordinary idea of moral assessment, when it is applied in view of a more complete and precise account of the facts. It would therefore be a mistake to argue from the unacceptability of the conclusions to the need for a different account of the conditions of moral responsibility. The view that moral luck is paradoxical is not a *mistake*, ethical or logical, but a perception of one of the ways in which the intuitively acceptable conditions of moral judgment threaten to undermine it all.

It resembles the situation in another area of philosophy, the theory of knowledge. There too conditions which seem perfectly natural, and which grow out of the ordinary procedures for challenging and defending claims to knowledge, threaten to undermine all such claims if consistently applied. Most skeptical arguments have this quality: they do not depend on the imposition of arbitrarily stringent standards of knowledge, arrived at by misunderstanding, but appear to grow inevitably from the consistent application of ordinary standards.[2] There is a substantive parallel as well, for epistemological skepticism arises from consideration of the respects in which our beliefs and their relation to reality depend on factors beyond our control. External and internal causes produce our beliefs. We may subject these processes to scrutiny in an effort to avoid error, but our conclusions at this next level also result, in part, from influences which we do not control directly. The same will be true no matter how far we carry the investigation. Our beliefs are always, ultimately, due to factors outside our control, and the impossibility of encompassing those factors without being at the mercy of others leads us to doubt whether we know anything. It looks as though, if any of our beliefs are true, it is pure biological luck rather than knowledge.

Moral luck is like this because while there are various respects in which the natural objects of moral assessment are out of our control or influenced by what is out of our control, we cannot reflect on these facts without losing our grip on the judgments.

There are roughly four ways in which the natural objects of moral assessment are disturbingly subject to luck. One is the phenomenon of constitutive luck—the kind of person you are, where this is not just a question of what you deliberately do, but of your inclinations, capacities, and temperament. Another category is luck in one's circumstances—the kind of problems and situations one faces. The other two have to do with the causes and effects of action: luck in how one is determined by antecedent circumstances, and luck in the way one's actions and projects turn out. All of them present a common problem. They are all opposed by the idea that one cannot be more culpable or estimable for anything than one is for that fraction of it which is under one's control. It seems irrational to take or dispense credit or blame for matters over which a person has no control, or for their influence on results over which he has partial control. Such things may create the conditions for action, but action can be judged only to the extent that it goes beyond these conditions and does not just result from them.

Let us first consider luck, good and bad, in the way things turn out. Kant, in the above-quoted passage, has one example of this in mind, but the category covers a wide range. It includes the truck driver who accidentally runs over a child, the artist who abandons his wife and five children to devote himself to painting,[3] and other cases in which the possibilities of success and failure are even greater. The driver, if he is entirely without fault, will feel terrible about his role in the event, but will not have to reproach himself. Therefore this example of agent-regret[4] is not yet a case of *moral* bad luck. However, if the driver was guilty of even a minor degree of negligence—failing to have his brakes checked recently, for example—then if that negligence contributes to the death of the child, he will not merely feel terrible. He will blame himself for the death. And what makes this an example of moral luck is that he would have to blame himself only slightly for the negligence itself if no situation arose which required him to brake suddenly and violently to avoid hitting a child. Yet the *negligence* is the same in both cases, and the driver has no control over whether a child will run into his path.

The same is true at higher levels of negligence. If someone has had too much to drink and his car swerves on to the sidewalk, he can count himself morally lucky if there are no pedestrians in its path. If there were, he would be to blame for their deaths, and would probably be prosecuted for manslaughter. But if he hurts no one, although his recklessness is exactly the same, he is guilty of a far less serious legal offence and will certainly reproach himself and be reproached by others much less severely. To take another legal example, the penalty for attempted murder is less than that for successful murder—however similar the intentions and motives of the assailant may be in the two cases. His degree of culpability can depend, it would seem, on whether the victim happened to be wearing a bullet-proof vest, or whether a bird flew into the path of the bullet—matters beyond his control.

Finally, there are cases of decision under uncertainty—common in public and in private life. Anna Karenina goes off with Vronsky, Gauguin leaves his family, Chamberlain signs the

Munich agreement, the Decembrists persuade the troops under their command to revolt against the czar, the American colonies declare their independence from Britain, you introduce two people in an attempt at match-making. It is tempting in all such cases to feel that some decision must be possible, in the light of what is known at the time, which will make reproach unsuitable no matter how things turn out. But this is not true; when someone acts in such ways he takes his life, or his moral position, into his hands, because how things turn out determines what he has done. It is possible *also* to access the decision from the point of view of what could be known at the time, but this is not the end of the story. If the Decembrists had succeeded in overthrowing Nicholas I in 1825 and establishing a constitutional regime, they would be heroes. As it is, not only did they fail and pay for it, but they bore some responsibility for the terrible punishments meted out to the troops who had been persuaded to follow them. If the American Revolution had been a bloody failure resulting in greater repression, then Jefferson, Franklin and Washington would still have made a noble attempt, and might not even have regretted it on their way to the scaffold, but they would also have had to blame themselves for what they had helped to bring on their compatriots. (Perhaps peaceful efforts at reform would eventually have succeeded.) If Hitler had not overrun Europe and exterminated millions, but instead had died of a heart attack after occupying the Sudetenland, Chamberlain's action at Munich would still have utterly betrayed the Czechs, but it would not be the great moral disaster that has made his name a household word.[5]

In many cases of difficult choice the outcome cannot be foreseen with certainty. One kind of assessment of the choice is possible in advance, but another kind must await the outcome, because the outcome determines what has been done. The same degree of culpability or estimability in intention, motive, or concern is compatible with a wide range of judgments, positive or negative, depending on what happened beyond the point of decision. The *mens rea* which could have existed in the absence of any consequences does not exhaust the grounds of moral judgment. Actual results influence culpability or esteem in a large class of unquestionably ethical cases ranging from negligence through political choice.

That these are genuine moral judgments rather than expressions of temporary attitude is evident from the fact that one can say *in advance* how the moral verdict will depend on the results. If one negligently leaves the bath running with the baby in it, one will realize, as one bounds up the stairs toward the bathroom, that if the baby has drowned one has done something awful, whereas if it has not one has merely been careless. Someone who launches a violent revolution against an authoritarian regime knows that if he fails he will be responsible for much suffering that is in vain, but if he succeeds he will be justified by the outcome. I do not mean that *any* action can be retroactively justified by history. Certain things are so bad in themselves, or so risky, that no results can make them all right. Nevertheless, when moral judgment does depend on the outcome, it is objective and timeless and not dependent on a change of standpoint produced by success or failure. The judgment after the fact follows from an hypothetical judgment that can be made beforehand, and it can be made as easily by someone else as by the agent.

From the point of view which makes responsibility dependent on control, all this seems absurd. How is it possible to be more or less culpable depending on whether a child gets into the path of one's car, or a bird into the path of one's bullet? Perhaps it is true that what is done depends on more than the agent's state of mind or intention. The problem then is, why is it not irrational to base moral assessment on what people do, in this broad sense? It amounts to holding them responsible for the contributions of fate as well as for their own—provided they have made some contribution to begin with. If we look at cases of negligence or attempt, the pattern seems to be that overall culpability corresponds to the product of mental or intentional fault and the seriousness of the outcome. Cases of decision under uncertainty are less easily explained in this way, for it seems that the overall judgment can even shift from positive to negative depending on the outcome. But here too it seems rational to subtract the effects of occurrences subsequent to the choice, that were merely possible at the time, and concentrate moral assessment on the actual decision in light of the probabilities. If the object of moral judgment is the *person*, then to hold him accountable for what he has done in the broader sense is akin to strict liability, which may have its legal uses but seems irrational as a moral position.

The result of such a line of thought is to pare down each act to its morally essential core, an inner act of pure will assessed by motive and intention. Adam Smith advocates such a position in

The Theory of Moral Sentiments, but notes that it runs contrary to our actual judgments.

> But how well soever we may seem to be persuaded of the truth of this equitable maxim, when we consider it after this manner, in abstract, yet when we come to particular cases, the actual consequences which happen to proceed from any action, have a very great effect upon our sentiments concerning its merit or demerit, and almost always either enhance or diminish our sense of both. Scarce, in any one instance, perhaps, will our sentiments be found, after examination, to be entirely regulated by this rule, which we all acknowledge ought entirely to regulate them.[6]

Joel Feinberg points out further that restricting the domain of moral responsibility to the inner world will not immunize it to luck. Factors beyond the agent's control, like a coughing fit, can interfere with his decisions as surely as they can with the path of a bullet from his gun.[7] Nevertheless the tendency to cut down the scope of moral assessment is pervasive, and does not limit itself to the influence of effects. It attempts to isolate the will from the other direction, so to speak, by separating out constitutive luck. Let us consider that next.

Kant was particularly insistent on the moral irrelevance of qualities of temperament and personality that are not under the control of the will. Such qualities as sympathy or coldness might provide the background against which obedience to moral requirements is more or less difficult, but they could not be objects of moral assessment themselves, and might well interfere with confident assessment of its proper object—the determination of the will by the motive of duty. This rules out moral judgment of many of the virtues and vices, which are states of character that influence choice but are certainly not exhausted by dispositions to act deliberately in certain ways. A person may be greedy, envious, cowardly, cold, ungenerous, unkind, vain, or conceited, but *behave* perfectly by a monumental effort of will. To possess these vices is to be unable to help having certain feelings under certain circumstances, and to have strong spontaneous impulses to act badly. Even if one controls the impulses, one still has the vice. An envious person hates the greater success of others. He can be morally condemned as envious even if he congratulates them cordially and does nothing to denigrate or spoil their success. Conceit, likewise, need not be displayed. It is fully present in someone who cannot help dwelling with secret satisfaction on the superiority of his own achievements, talents, beauty, intelligence, or virtue. To some extent such a quality may be the product of earlier choices; to some extent it may be amenable to change by current actions. But it is largely a matter of constitutive bad fortune. Yet people are morally condemned for such qualities, and esteemed for others equally beyond control of the will: they are assessed for what they are *like*.

To Kant this seems incoherent because virtue is enjoined on everyone and therefore must in principle be possible for everyone. It may be easier for some than for others, but it must be possible to achieve it by making the right choices, against whatever temperamental background.[8] One may want to have a generous spirit, or regret not having one, but it makes no sense to condemn oneself or anyone else for a quality which is not within the control of the will. Condemnation implies that you should not be like that, not that it is unfortunate that you are.

Nevertheless, Kant's conclusion remains intuitively unacceptable. We may be persuaded that these moral judgments are irrational, but they reappear involuntarily as soon as the argument is over. This is the pattern throughout the subject.

The third category to consider is luck in one's circumstances, and I shall mention it briefly. The things we are called upon to do, the moral tests we face, are importantly determined by factors beyond our control. It may be true of someone that in a dangerous situation he would behave in a cowardly or heroic fashion, but if the situation never arises, he will never have the chance to distinguish or disgrace himself in this way, and his moral record will be different.[9]

A conspicuous example of this is political. Ordinary citizens of Nazi Germany had an opportunity to behave heroically by opposing the regime. They also had an opportunity to behave badly, and most of them are culpable for having failed this test. But it is a test to which the citizens of other countries were not subjected, with the result that even if they, or some of them, would have behaved as badly as the Germans in like circumstances, they simply did not and therefore are not similarly culpable. Here again one is morally at the mercy of fate, and it may seem irrational upon reflection, but our ordinary moral attitudes

66   *Thomas Nagel*

would be unrecognizable without it. We judge people for what
they actually do or fail to do, not just for what they would have
done if circumstances had been different.[10]

This form of moral determination by the actual is also paradoxical, but we can begin to see how deep in the concept of responsibility the paradox is embedded. A person can be morally
responsible only for what he does; but what he does results from
a great deal that he does not do; therefore he is not morally responsible for what he is and is not responsible for. (This is not a
contradiction, but it is a paradox.)

It should be obvious that there is a connection between
these problems about responsibility and control and an even
more familiar problem, that of freedom of the will. That is the last
type of moral luck I want to take up, though I can do no more
within the scope of this essay than indicate its connection with
the other types.

If one cannot be responsible for consequences of one's acts
due to factors beyond one's control, or for antecedents of one's
acts that are properties of temperament not subject to one's will,
or for the circumstances that pose one's moral choices, then how
can one be responsible even for the stripped-down acts of the will
itself, if *they* are the product of antecedent circumstances outside
of the will's control?

The area of genuine agency, and therefore of legitimate moral
judgment, seems to shrink under this scrutiny to an extension-
less point. Everything seems to result from the combined influence of factors, antecedent and posterior to action, that are not
within the agent's control. Since he cannot be responsible for
them, he cannot be responsible for their results—though it may
remain possible to take up the aesthetic or other evaluative ana-
logues of the moral attitudes that are thus displaced.

It is also possible, of course, to brazen it out and refuse to
accept the results, which indeed seem unacceptable as soon as we
stop thinking about the arguments. Admittedly, if certain sur-
rounding circumstances had been different, then no unfortunate
consequences would have followed from a wicked intention, and
no seriously culpable act would have been performed; but since
the circumstances were *not* different, and the agent *in fact* succeeded in perpetrating a particularly cruel murder, *that* is what
he did, and that is what he is responsible for. Similarly, we may
admit that if certain antecedent circumstances had been different, the agent would never have developed into the sort of person

who would do such a thing; but since he *did* develop (as the inevitable result of those antecedent circumstances) into the sort of swine he is, and into the person who committed such a murder, *that* is what he is blameable for. In both cases one is responsible for what one actually does—even if what one actually does depends in important ways on what is not within one's control. This compatibilist account of our moral judgments would leave room for the ordinary conditions of responsibility—the absence of coercion, ignorance, or involuntary movement—as part of the determination of what someone has done—but it is understood not to exclude the influence of a great deal that he has not done.[11]

The only thing wrong with this solution is its failure to explain how skeptical problems arise. For they arise not from the imposition of an arbitrary external requirement, but from the nature of moral judgment itself. Something in the ordinary idea of what someone does must explain how it can seem necessary to subtract from it anything that merely happens—even though the ultimate consequence of such subtraction is that nothing remains. And something in the ordinary idea of knowledge must explain why it seems to be undermined by any influences on belief not within the control of the subject—so that knowledge seems impossible without an impossible foundation in autonomous reason. But let us leave epistemology aside and concentrate on action, character, and moral assessment.

The problem arises, I believe, because the self which acts and is the object of moral judgment is threatened with dissolution by the absorption of its acts and impulses into the class of events. Moral judgment of a person is judgment not of what happens to him, but of him. It does not say merely that a certain event or state of affairs is fortunate or unfortunate or even terrible. It is not an evaluation of a state of the world, or of an individual as part of the world. We are not thinking just that it would be better if he were different, or did not exist, or had not done some of the things he has done. We are judging *him*, rather than his existence or characteristics. The effect of concentrating on the influence of what is not under his control is to make this responsible self seem to disappear, swallowed up by the order of mere events.

What, however, do we have in mind that a person must *be* to be the object of these moral attitudes? While the concept of agency is easily undermined, it is very difficult to give it a positive characterization. That is familiar from the literature on Free Will.

I believe that in a sense the problem has no solution, because something in the idea of agency is incompatible with actions being events, or people being things. But as the external
determinants of what someone has done are gradually exposed,
in their effect on consequences, character, and choice itself, it becomes gradually clear that actions are events and people things.
Eventually nothing remains which can be ascribed to the responsible self, and we are left with nothing but a portion of the larger
sequence of events, which can be deplored or celebrated, but not
blamed or praised.

Though I cannot define the idea of the active self that is thus
undermined, it is possible to say something about its sources.
There is a close connexion between our feelings about ourselves
and our feelings about others. Guilt and indignation, shame and
contempt, pride and admiration are internal and external sides of
the same moral attitudes. We are unable to view ourselves simply
as portions of the world, and from inside we have a rough idea of
the boundary between what is us and what is not, what we do
and what happens to us, what is our personality and what is an
accidental handicap. We apply the same essentially internal conception of the self to others. About ourselves we feel pride, shame,
guilt, remorse—and agent-regret. We do not regard our actions
and our characters merely as fortunate or unfortunate episodes—
though they may also be that. We cannot *simply* take an external
evaluative view of ourselves—of what we most essentially are and
what we do. And this remains true even when we have seen that
we are not responsible for our own existence, or our nature, or the
choices we have to make, or the circumstances that give our acts
the consequences they have. Those acts remain ours and we remain ourselves, despite the persuasiveness of the reasons that
seem to argue us out of existence.

It is this internal view that we extend to others in moral
judgment—when we judge *them* rather than their desirability or
utility. We extend to others the refusal to limit ourselves to external evaluation, and we accord to them selves like our own. But in
both cases this comes up against the brutal inclusion of humans
and everything about them in a world from which they cannot be
separated and of which they are nothing but contents. The external view forces itself on us at the same time that we resist it. One
way this occurs is through the gradual erosion of what we do by
the subtraction of what happens. [12]

The inclusion of consequences in the conception of what we have done is an acknowledgment that we are parts of the world, but the paradoxical character of moral luck which emerges from this acknowledgment shows that we are unable to operate with such a view, for it leaves us with no one to be. The same thing is revealed in the appearance that determinism obliterates responsibility. Once we see an aspect of what we or someone else does as something that happens, we lose our grip on the idea that it has been done and that we can judge the doer and not just the happening. This explains why the absence of determinism is no more hospitable to the concept of agency than is its presence—a point that has been noticed often. Either way the act is viewed externally, as part of the course of events.

The problem of moral luck cannot be understood without an account of the internal conception of agency and its special connection with the moral attitudes as opposed to other types of value. I do not have such an account. The degree to which the problem has a solution can be determined only by seeing whether in some degree the incompatibility between this conception and the various ways in which we do not control what we do is only apparent. I have nothing to offer on that topic either. But it is not enough to say merely that our basic moral attitudes toward ourselves and others are determined by what is actual; for they are also threatened by the sources of that actuality, and by the external view of action which forces itself on us when we see how everything we do belongs to a world that we have not created.

Notes

1. *Foundations of the Metaphysics of Morals*, first section, third paragraph.

2. See Thompson Clarke, "The Legacy of Skepticism," *Journal of Philosophy*, LXIX, no. 20 (November 9, 1972), 754–69.

3. Such a case, modelled on the life of Gauguin, is discussed by Bernard Williams in 'Moral Luck' *Proceedings of the Aristotelian Society*, supplementary vol. L (1976), 115–35 (to which the original version of this essay was a reply). He points out that though success or failure cannot be predicted in advance, Gauguin's most basic retrospective feelings about the decision will be determined by the development of his talent. My disagreement with Williams is that his account fails to explain why

such retrospective attitudes can be called moral. If success does not permit Gauguin to justify himself to others, but still determines his most
basic feelings, that shows only that his most basic feelings need not be
moral. It does not show that morality is subject to luck. If the retrospective judgment were moral, it would imply the truth of a hypothetical
judgment made in advance, of the form 'If I leave my family and become
a great painter, I will be justified by success; if I don't become a great
painter, the act will be unforgivable.'

4. Williams' term (ibid.).

5. For a fascinating but morally repellent discussion of the topic
of justification by history, see Maurice Merleau-Ponty, *Humanisme et
Terreur* (Paris: Gallimard, 1947), translated as *Humanism and Terror*
(Boston: Beacon Press, 1969).

6. Pt II, sect. 3, Introduction, para. 5.

7. "Problematic Responsibility in Law and Morals," in Joel Feinberg, *Doing and Deserving* (Princeton: Princeton University Press,
1970).

8. "If nature has put little sympathy in the heart of a man, and if
he, though an honest man, is by temperament cold and indifferent to the
sufferings of others, perhaps because he is provided with special gifts of
patience and fortitude and expects or even requires that others should
have the same—and such a man would certainly not be the meanest
product of nature—would not he find in himself a source from which to
give himself a far higher worth than he could have got by having a good-
natured temperament?" (*Foundations of the Metaphysics of Morals*,
first section, eleventh paragraph).

9. Cf. Thomas Gray, "Elegy Written in a Country Churchyard":

Some mute inglorious Milton here may rest,
Some Cromwell, guiltless of his country's blood.

An unusual example of circumstantial moral luck is provided by the
kind of moral dilemma with which someone can be faced through no
fault of his own, but which leaves him with nothing to do which is not
wrong. See chapter 5; and Bernard Williams, "Ethical Consistency," *Proceedings of the Aristotelian Society*, supplementary vol. XXXIX (1965),
reprinted in *Problems of the Self* (Cambridge: Cambridge University
Press, 1973), pp. 166–86.

10. Circumstantial luck can extend to aspects of the situation other
than individual behavior. For example, during the Vietnam War even U.S.
citizens who had opposed their country's actions vigorously from the
start often felt compromised by its crimes. Here they were not even re-

sponsible; there was probably nothing they could do to stop what was happening, so the feeling of being implicated may seem unintelligible. But it is nearly impossible to view the crimes of one's own country in the same way that one views the crimes of another country, no matter how equal one's lack of power to stop them in the two cases. One *is* a citizen of one of them, and has a connexion with its actions (even if only through taxes that cannot be withheld)—that one does not have with the other's. This makes it possible to be ashamed of one's country, and to feel a victim of moral bad luck that one was an American in the 1960s.

11. The corresponding position in epistemology would be that knowledge consists of true beliefs formed in certain ways, and that it does not require all aspects of the process to be under the knower's control, actually or potentially. Both the correctness of these beliefs and the process by which they are arrived at would therefore be importantly subject to luck. The Nobel Prize is not awarded to people who turn out to be wrong, no matter how brilliant their reasoning.

12. See P. F. Strawson's discussion of the conflict between the objective attitude and personal reactive attitudes in "Freedom and Resentment," *Proceedings of the British Academy,* 1962, reprinted in *Studies in the Philosophy of Thought and Action,* ed. P. F. Strawson (London: Oxford University Press, 1968), and in P. F. Strawson, *Freedom and Resentment and Other Essays* (London: Methuen, 1974).

4

Luck and Ethics*

Martha C. Nussbaum

I

'But human excellence grows like a vine tree, fed by the green dew, raised up, among wise men and just, to the liquid sky.'[1] So Pindar displays a problem that lies at the heart of Greek thought about the good life for a human being. He is a poet who has dedicated his career to writing lyric odes in praise of human excellence. This career presupposes, on the part of both poet and audience, the belief that the excellence of a good person is something of that person's own, for whose possession and exercise that person can appropriately be held accountable.[2] He has just been praying to die as he had lived, as one 'who praised what deserves praise and sowed blame for wrong-doers'. His 'but', which might equally well be translated 'and', both continues and qualifies that prayer. The excellence of the good person, he writes, is like a young plant: something growing in the world, slender, fragile, in constant need of food from without.[3] A vine tree must be of good stock if it is to grow well. And even if it has a good heritage, it needs fostering weather (gentle dew and rain, the absence of sudden frosts and harsh winds), as well as the care of concerned and intelligent keepers, for its continued health and full perfection. So, the poet suggests, do we. We need to be born with adequate capacities, to live in fostering natural and social circumstances, to stay clear of abrupt catastrophe, to develop confirming associations with other human beings. The poem's next lines are, "We have all kinds of needs for those we love: most

---

*From *The Fragility of Goodness: Luck and Ethics in Greek Tragedy and Philosophy* (Cambridge: Cambridge University Press, 1986), pp. 1–8, 322–340.

of all in hardships, but joy, too, strains to track down eyes that it can trust." Our openness to fortune and our sense of value, here again, both render us dependent on what is outside of us: our openness to fortune, because we encounter hardships and can come to need something that only another can provide; our sense of value, because even when we do not need the *help* of friends and loved ones, love and friendship still matter to us for their own sake. Even the poet's joy is incomplete without the tenuous luck of seeing it confirmed by eyes on whose understanding, good will, and truthfulness he can rely. His joy is like a hunter, straining on the track of an elusive quarry.[4] Much of the poem has been about envy, the way lies can make the world rotten. The one trusted friend invoked by the poet is dead, beyond the reach even of his poetic words. And all these needs for all these things that we do not humanly control are pertinent, clearly, not only to feelings of contentment or happiness. What the external nourishes, and even helps to constitute, is excellence or human worth itself.

The vine-tree image, standing near the poem's end, between the wish to die a praiser of goodness and the invocation of the dead friend, confronts us with a deep dilemma in the poet's situation, which is also ours. It displays the thorough intermingling of what is ours and what belongs to the world, of ambition and vulnerability, of making and being made, that are present in this and in any human life. In so doing, it asks a question about the beliefs that sustain human ethical practices. How can Pindar be a praise poet, if human goodness is nourished, and even constituted, by external happenings? How can we be givers and receivers of praise, if our worth is just a plant in need of watering? The audience is invited to inspect its own self-conception. To what extent *can* we distinguish between what is up to the world and what is up to us, when assessing a human life? To what extent *must* we insist on finding these distinctions, if we are to go on praising as we praise? And how can we improve this situation, making progress by placing the most important things, things such as personal achievement, politics, and love, under our control?

The problem is made more complex by a further implication of the poetic image. It suggests that part of the peculiar beauty of *human* excellence just *is* its vulnerability. The tenderness of a plant is not the dazzling hardness of a gem. There seem to be two, and perhaps two incompatible, kinds of value here. Nor, perhaps, is the beauty of a true human love the same as that of the love of two immortal gods, only shorter. The liquid sky that covers these people and circumscribes their possibilities also lends to their environment a quick, gleaming splendor that would not, we suspect, be the climate of heaven. (A later poet will speak of the moist, 'dewy' freshness of the young Ganymede drying himself after a bath—as a beauty and a sexuality *gone* from him from the moment that the god, out of love, gave him immortality, dooming his own passion.)[5] Human excellence is seen, in Pindar's poem and pervasively in the Greek poetic tradition, as something whose very nature it is to be in need, a growing thing in the world that could not be made invulnerable and keep its own peculiar fineness. (The hero Odysseus chose the mortal love of an aging woman over Calypso's unchanging splendor.)[6] The contingencies that make praise problematic are also, in some as yet unclear way, constitutive of that which is there for praising.

If this picture of the passive vine tree begins to strike us as incompatible with some aspiration we have for ourselves as human agents (and so it is likely to have struck this poem's audience), there is the consolation that, so far, Pindar has apparently left something out. However much human beings resemble lower forms of life, we are unlike, we want to insist, in one crucial respect. We have reason. We are able to deliberate and choose, to make a plan in which ends are ranked, to decide actively what is to have value and how much. All this must count for something. If it is true that a lot about us is messy, needy, uncontrolled, rooted in the dirt and standing helplessly in the rain, it is also true that there is something about us that is pure and purely active, something that we could think of as 'divine, immortal, intelligible, unitary, indissoluble, ever self-consistent and invariable'.[7] It seems possible that this rational element in us can rule and guide the rest, thereby saving the whole person from living at the mercy of luck.

This splendid and equivocal hope is a central preoccupation of ancient Greek thought about the human good. A raw sense of the passivity of human beings and their humanity in that world of nature, and a response of both horror and anger at the passivity, lived side by side with and nourished the belief that reason's activity could make safe, and thereby save, our human lives—indeed, must save them, if they were to be humanly worth living. This need for a livable life preoccupied most of the early Greek thinkers, including some whom tradition calls philosophers and some who usually receive other titles (for example poet, dramatist, historian). Indeed, it was this need above all that seems to have motivated the founders of a human and ethical philosophy to press their search for a new art that would make progress beyond ordinary beliefs and practices; and the Greek philosophical tradition always remained centrally dedicated to the realization of a good human life, even, frequently, in its pursuit of metaphysical and scientific inquiries.

But on the other side of this pursuit of self-sufficiency, complicating and constraining the effort to banish contingency from human life, was always a vivid sense of the special beauty of the contingent and the mutable, that love for the riskiness and openness of empirical humanity which finds its expression in recurrent stories about gods who fall in love with mortals. The question of life-saving thus becomes a delicate and complicated one for any thinker of depth. It becomes, in effect, the question of the human good: how can it be reliably good and still be beautifully human? It was evident to all the thinkers with whom we shall be concerned that the good life for a human being must to some extent, and in some ways, be self-sufficient, immune to the incursions of luck. How far a life can and how far it should be made self-sufficient, what role reason plays in the search for self-sufficiency, what the appropriate kind of self-sufficiency is for a rational human life—these questions elicited and became a part of the general question: who do we think we are, and where (under what sky) do we want to live?

This book will be an examination of the aspiration to rational self-sufficiency in Greek ethical thought: the aspiration to make the goodness of a good human life safe from luck through the controlling power of reason. I shall use the word 'luck' in a not strictly defined but, I hope, perfectly intelligible way, closely related to the way in which the Greeks themselves spoke of *tuchē*.[8] I do not mean to imply that the events in question are random or uncaused. What happens to a person by luck will be just what does not happen through his or her own agency, what just *happens* to him, as opposed to what he does or makes.[9] In general, to eliminate luck from human life will be to put that life, or the most important things in it, under the control of the agent (or of those elements in him with which he identifies himself), removing the element of reliance upon the external and undependable that was captured in the plant image. And my general question will be, how much luck do these Greek thinkers believe we can humanly live with? How much *should* we live with, in order to live the life that is best and most valuable for a human being?

This question was, as I have said, central for the Greeks. I have already suggested that I believe it to be important for us as well. But in some periods of history it would have been thought not to be a genuine question at all. The enormous influence of Kantian ethics[10] on our intellectual culture has led to a long-standing neglect of these issues in work on Greek ethics. When they are treated, it is often suggested that the way the Greeks pose the problems of agency and contingency is primitive or mis-guided. For the Kantian believes that there is one domain of value, the domain of moral value, that is altogether immune to the assaults of luck. No matter what happens in the world, the moral value of the good will remains unaffected. Furthermore, the Kantian believes that there is a sharp distinction to be drawn between this and every other type of value, *and* that moral value is of overwhelmingly greater importance than anything else. If these beliefs are all true, then an inquiry such as ours can only serve to uncover false beliefs about the important and true beliefs about the trivial. It can show that Greek thinkers held the false and primitive view that moral value is vulnerable to luck; and it can show that they had the true but relatively unimportant belief that other sorts of value are vulnerable. It will surely reveal, in the process, the primitive character of an ethical thought that does not even attempt to make a sharp distinction between moral value and other types of value. When the truth of these Kantian beliefs, and the importance of the Kantian distinction between moral and non-moral value,[11] are taken as the starting-point for inquiry into Greek views of these matters,[12] the Greeks do not, then, fare well. There appears to be something peculiar about the way they agonize about contingency, lamenting an insoluble prac-tical conflict and the regret it brings in its wake, pondering the risks of love and friendship, weighing the value of passion against its destructive excesses. It is as if they were in difficulties because they had not discovered what Kant discovered, did not know what we Kantians all know.

But if we do not approach these texts armed with a point of view from which their questions cannot even be seen, it proves difficult to avoid feeling, ourselves, the force of these questions.[13] I begin this book from a position that I believe to be common: the position of one who finds the problems of Pindar's ode anything but peculiar and who has the greatest difficulty understanding how they might ever cease to be problems. That I am an agent, but also a plant; that much that I did not make goes towards making me whatever I shall be praised or blamed for being; that I must constantly choose among competing and apparently incommensurable goods and that circumstances may force me to a position in which I cannot help being false to something or doing some wrong; that an event that simply happens to me may, without my consent, alter my life; that it is equally problematic to entrust one's good to friends, lovers, or country and to try to have a good life without them—all these I take to be not just the material of tragedy, but everyday facts of lived practical reason.

On the other hand, it seems equally impossible, or equally inhuman, to avoid feeling the force of the Platonic conception of a self-sufficient and purely rational being, cleansed of the 'barnacles' and the 'seaweed' of passion, the 'many stony and wild things that have been encrusted all over it',[14] freed from contingent limitations on its power. Plato shows us how Glaucon, an ordinary gentleman, discovers in himself, through conversation with Socrates, an intense love for the pure and stable activity of mathematical reasoning, a love that requires the denigration of much that he had previously valued. Even so, as we read and are gripped by these works, we are likely to recollect an aspiration to purity and to freedom from luck that is also a deep part of humanness and stands in a complex tension with other empirical perceptions. And if to feel this tension is not an idiosyncratic or rare experience, but a fact in the natural history of human beings, then good human practical reasoning about the self-sufficiency of the good life seems to require an inquiry that explores both pictures, feeling the power of each.

We shall be investigating the role played by luck in the area of human excellence[15] and the activities associated with it, leaving aside the countless ways in which luck affects mere contentment or good feeling.[16] Central to our inquiry will be three questions. The first concerns the role in the human good life of activities and relationships that are, in their nature, especially vulnerable to reversal. How much should a rational plan of life allow for elements such as friendship, love, political activity, attachments to property or possessions, all of which, being themselves vulnerable, make the person who stakes his or her good to them similarly open to chance? These 'external goods' can enter into the excellent life not only as necessary instrumental means to good living but also, if we value them enough, as ends in themselves; their contingent absence, then, may deprive the agent not only of resources but of intrinsic value itself and living well itself.

Is all of this reason not to ascribe such value to them or to include them as components in a rational plan?

Closely connected with the question about the individual constituents of the good life is our second question, which concerns the relationship among these components. Do they coexist harmoniously, or are they capable, in circumstances not of the agent's own making, of generating conflicting requirements that can themselves impair the goodness of the agent's life? If an agent ascribes intrinsic value to, and cares about, more than one activity, there is always a risk that some circumstances will arise in which incompatible courses of action are both required; deficiency therefore becomes a natural necessity. The richer my scheme of value,[17] the more I open myself to such a possibility; and yet a life designed to ward off this possibility may prove to be impoverished. This problem is connected with the first in several ways. For a life centered around activities that are always in the agent's power to pursue regardless of circumstances will give few opportunities for conflict; and strategies of reason adopted to minimize conflict will significantly (as we shall see) diminish the fragility of certain important values, taken singly.

We have spoken so far of what we might call 'external contingency'[18]—of luck coming to the agent from the world outside of him, and from his own value system insofar as it links him to the outside. This will be the primary focus of our concern. But we must also raise a third problem, concerning the relationship between self-sufficiency and the more ungovernable parts of the human being's internal makeup. We will be led by our other two problems to ask, in particular, about the ethical value of the so-called "irrational parts of the soul": appetites, feelings, emotions. For our bodily and sensuous nature, our passions, our sexuality, all serve as powerful links to the world of risk and mutability. The activities associated with the bodily desires not only exemplify mutability and instability in their own internal structure; they also lead us and bind us to the world of perishable objects and, in this way, to the risk of loss and the danger of conflict. The agent who ascribes value to activities connected with the appetites and emotions will *eo ipso* be depending on the external, upon resources and other persons, for his possibilities of ongoing good activity. Furthermore, these 'irrational' attachments import, more than many others, a risk of practical conflict and so of contingent failure in virtue. And even when passional activities are not deemed in themselves valuable, the passions can still figure as sources of disruption, disturbing the agent's rational planning as if from without and producing distortion of judgment, inconstancy or weakness in action. To nourish them at all is thus to expose oneself to a risk of disorder or 'madness'.[19] We need to ask, then, whether a restructuring of the human being, a transformation or suppression of certain familiar parts of ourselves, could lead to greater rational control and self-sufficiency, and whether this would be the appropriate form of self-sufficiency for a rational human life.

To ask any of these three questions is, of course, also to ask about a conception of human reason. If it is reason, and reason's art, philosophy, that are supposed to save or transform our lives, then, as beings with an interest in living well, we must ask what this part of ourselves is, how it works to order a life, how it is related to feeling, emotion, perception. The Greeks characteristically, and appropriately, link these ethical questions very closely to questions about the procedures, capabilities, and limits of reason. For it is their instinct that some projects for self-sufficient living are questionable because they ask us to go beyond the cognitive limits of the human being; and, on the other hand, that many attempts to venture, in metaphysical or scientific reasoning, beyond our human limits are inspired by questionable ethical motives, motives having to do with closedness, safety, and power. Human cognitive limits circumscribe and limit ethical knowledge and discourse; and an important topic *within* ethical discourse must be the determination of an appropriate human attitude towards those limits. For both of these reasons our ethical inquiry will find it necessary to speak about first principles, truth, and the requirements of discourse.

[We are making a transition to Nussbaum's discussion of Aristotle in Chapter 11. Ed.]

II

'Nevertheless, it is evident that *eudaimonia*[20] stands in need of good things from outside, as we have said: for it is impossible or difficult to do fine things without resources' (*EN* 1099a31–3). We must now examine Aristotle's articulation and defense of this claim, as he argues against his opponents.

The opponents of luck assert that the good human life is completely invulnerable to *tuchē*. That which we ourselves control is in every case sufficient to secure it. Aristotle clearly sympathizes with their general motivation and wishes to preserve many of the same beliefs. He and the opponents are on common ground when they insist that the good life should be available by effort to the person who has not been ethically 'maimed' (1099b18–19, cf. 1096b34), and when they demand a life that is "one's own and hard to take away" (1095b25–6), 'stable and in no way easily subject to change' (1100b2–3). But complete invulnerability is purchased, Aristotle will argue, at too high a price: by imagining (as does the Platonist) a life bereft of certain important values; or by doing violence (as does the good-condition theorist) to our beliefs about activity and its worth.[21]

. . . We turn now to the good-condition opponent and to Aristotle's elaboration, against this opponent, of a view about the value and the vulnerability of excellent activity.

The good-condition theorist argues that *eudaimonia* is invulnerable because it consists simply in having a good ethical state or condition[22] and because this condition is itself stable even under the direst circumstances. To oppose such an opponent Aristotle can, then, adopt more than one strategy. He can argue that states of character *are* vulnerable to external influences. Or he can argue that good states are not by themselves sufficient for good living. If he takes the second course he must, in addition, argue that the further element that must be added to good states is itself not invulnerable. Aristotle's argument, as we shall see, is a complex combination of these two lines of attack. We shall start by following him as he pursues the second line, establishing, first, that *eudaimonia* requires actual activity for its completion, and, second, that good human activity can be disrupted or decisively impeded by various forms of luck. There is, then, a gap between being good and living well. The investigation of this gap will eventually lead Aristotle to the first line as well—since it will turn out that some forms of interfering luck eventually affect the virtuous condition itself.

We agree, Aristotle says, that our end is *eudaimonia*; but we agree on just about nothing concerning it, except the name (1095a17ff.). One further agreement, however, emerges near the beginning of the *Nicomachean Ethics:* it concerns the connection of *eudaimonia* with activity. "Both the many and the refined . . . believe that living well and acting well are the same as *eudaimonia*" (1095a19–20). Later he repeats, *"Eudaimonia* has been said to be good living and good acting." In the *Eudemian*

Ethics he brings forward a "belief held by all of us", the belief that "acting well and living well are the same thing as *eudaimonein:* both are forms of use and activity" (1219a40–b2). So we can see from the start that the opponent who makes the good life consist in a non-active state or condition, removing it altogether from its realization in activity, is going against beliefs of ours that are so broadly shared as any ever brought forward by Aristotle in the ethical works. This seems to put his thesis in trouble from the start.

But Aristotle must also show the depth and importance of these beliefs; for to show that they are *widely* held is not all that the method of appearances requires. Therefore, instead of contenting himself with this general point, he examines the consequences of the good-condition thesis for concrete types of cases, showing that thesis has intuitively unacceptable results. We can take, first, the most extreme and therefore clearest case and move towards cases which offer greater potential for controversy.

The starkest and clearest test case for the good-condition view would be one in which there was a good virtuous condition but *no* activity of any kind issuing from this condition. We get such a case if we imagine a person with a well-formed character who, upon becoming an adult (for to imagine this person virtuous we must, in Aristotle's view, imagine him or her as active during the process of formation), goes to sleep and sleeps all through his adult life, doing nothing at all. We could make the case contemporary and plausible by considering a case of irreversible coma—though to match Aristotle's it would have to be one in which the internal structure of goodness was in no way permanently removed or impaired: excellence of character must remain constant. Now our question is, can such a person be said to be living a good life? Can he appropriately be praised and congratulated? According to the good-condition theorist, he can: for the excellent state is the sole appropriate object of these ethical attitudes. Aristotle objects (in both the *Nicomachean Ethics* and the *Eudemian Ethics* [henceforth 'EN' and 'EE', respectively]) that this just is not in harmony with our practices and our beliefs. We simply do not think that a state or condition that never *does* anything is sufficient for living well. It seems incomplete, frustrated, cut off from its fulfillment. Indeed, we tend to think that having such a condition makes little real difference, if one is never active from it: to sleep through life is like being a vegetable and not a human at all (*EE* 1216a3–5, cf. *EN* 1176a34–5). Just as we do not think a fetus, who lives a purely vegetative existence, without awareness, lives a full human life (*EE* 1216a6–8), so we are not going to be willing to praise and congratulate the life of this hopelessly inactive adult. The *EN* concludes, 'Nobody would say that a person living in such a way was living well, unless he were defending a theoretical position at all costs" (1096a1–2). The case shows us, the parallel passage in *EN* x concludes, that *eudaimonia* cannot be simply a *hexis*, a condition or state (1176a33–5).

Later on in *EN* I Aristotle returns to the same point, insisting that, although 'it is possible for a state to be present and accomplish nothing good, as is true for the sleeper and in some cases of waking people as well', nonetheless, such a person will not receive the ethical attitudes of praise and congratulation that we associate with the judgment that someone is living a good human life (1098b33–99a2). He uses an athletic analogy: in a race we applaud, as runners, only those who actually compete, not the ones who might be thought to be in general the strongest and most fit. Just as we will not say of a well-conditioned non-runner that he or she runs well, so we will not praise the virtuous sleeper for living virtuously (1099a3–7). It is important to see that Aristotle does not claim here that the good life is a kind of competition, or that only success is praised. His point is that the endowment and condition are not sufficient for praise: the person has to *do* something, show how he or she can be active. Just as our assessments of people as runners depend upon there being some actual running (though of course they depend, too, on our belief that this good running was caused by their good condition, not by some external force), so too our ethical assessments are based on actual effort and activity, as well as upon the presence of a stable character that is the cause of the activity. Character alone is not sufficient. Furthermore, the opponent's very account of the case may be incoherent: for we do not know what it means to say of someone in irreversible coma that a virtuous condition is retained. At the very least, there is an insuperable epistemological difficulty; but it may be more than that—it may be a logical difficulty as well, given the strong conceptual connection of *hexis* with a pattern of activity. Aristotle points to this problem when he says that 'the good and the bad are not at all distinct in sleep . . . for sleep is the idleness of that element of the soul in virtue of which it is said to be fine or base' (1102b5–8). It is not clear, then, that it is even appropriate to say of this totally non-active person that he or she has a virtuous character.[23]

We can summarize the general point against the good-condition theorist this way. The good condition of a virtuous character, like good athletic conditioning, is a kind of preparation for the activity; it finds its natural fulfillment and flourishing in activity. To deprive the person of that natural expression of the condition *is* to make a difference in the quality of the person's life. It is to make the condition fruitless or pointless, cut off. Just as a runner who gets into good condition and is then prevented from running would be pitied more than praised, so we pity the virtuous person in situations of impediment. Activity, *energeia*, is the coming-forth of that good condition from its state of concealment or mere potentiality; it is its flourishing or blooming. Without that the good condition is seriously incomplete. Like an actor who is always waiting in the wings and never gets a chance to appear on the stage, it is not doing its job, and, in consequence, is only in a shadowy way itself.[24]

The opponent might grant that *total* cessation of awareness and activity was a diminution or cessation of good living, and yet still try to salvage some of his position by making a distinction between external, worldly activity and a full internal health, or health of condition, that includes thought and awareness. He might say, then, that so long as cognitive functioning and ethical awareness go on in the good person, it does not matter at all that his or her body is altogether prevented from carrying out such projects as the moral imagination forms.[25] So long as he is able to form virtuous intentions and to think good thoughts, so long he is living well—even if he is in prison, enslaved, or tortured. Aristotle needs to argue in reply that the functioning available to a person in such circumstances is not sufficient for acting well and living well. This he does in a passage in *EN* VII: "No activity *(energeia)* is complete if it is impeded; but *eudaimonia* is something complete. So the *eudaimōn* persons needs the goods of the body and external goods and goods of luck, in addition, so that his activities should not be impeded. Those who claim that the person who is being tortured on the wheel, or the person who has encountered great reversals of fortune, is *eudaimōn*, so long as he is good, are not saying anything—whether that is their intention or not" (1153b16–21).[26]

Once again, the opponent has specified what *eudaimonia* is in a way that makes it by definition immune to external changes of circumstance: external reversals impede action, not the virtuous state, and the virtuous state (including, presumably, some sort of waking inner life) is sufficient for living well. Once again,

Aristotle insists that doing does matter. Being excellent in character is not yet acting according to excellence. But action according to excellence requires certain external conditions: of the body, of social context, of resources. The person on the wheel cannot act justly, generously, moderately; he cannot help his friends or participate in politics. How, then, can he be said to live well? The opponent's case here is more intuitively gripping than the sleeper example was, because we have allowed the person to wake up, restoring at least that awareness of internal goodness that might seem to be a necessary part of goodness of character, goodness totally impeded and cut off is not enough to justify our most serious praise and congratulation.

Aristotle suggests a further point as well. Insofar as the opponent's case is initially plausible, it is so because we imagine the tortured person as leading some sort of complex inner life. We might imagine him, for example, as imagining, forming intentions, having appropriate feelings and responses, even reflecting philosophically or proving truths of mathematics. If we pack all of this into 'being good' as opposed to 'acting', then being good looks closer to what might satisfy us than it did in the sleeper's case, where 'being good' was something completely inert and inactive. But now we notice that 'being good' looks like a kind of being active—and, like any being active, it looks itself vulnerable to impediment. Aristotle's talk of impeded activity makes us ask whether the inner activity of the tortured person cannot itself be impeded by pain and deprivation. Thoughts, emotions and reactions, speculative and scientific thinking, are not impervious to circumstance; they can, like projects in the external world, fail to reach completion or perfection. Torture can harm them.[27] In short: the distinction 'inner/outer' is not the same as the distinction 'state/activity'. If the opponent makes the latter the salient distinction, ascribing all value to the state, this will perhaps give him something really immune to luck; but it will make the human being into little more than a vegetable. If he makes the salient distinction the former one, ascribing all value to inner activities, then he will have something richer and more interesting—but something that is, after all, just because it is active, open to chance and upset.

III

Now, however, Aristotle must describe in more detail the ways in which good activity is vulnerable to circumstances; and he must, in particular, ask to what degree calamities that are temporary or partial should be thought to diminish *eudaimonia*. For while the consideration of extreme cases may suffice to refute the views of the most extreme type of good-condition opponent, they do not go far towards grappling with problems that most of us are likely to face in the course of our lives. The more common practical problems are also, frequently, more subtle and more controversial.

Before we approach Aristotle's treatment of 'tragic' reversal and the case of Priam, we need to point out that there are four rather different ways in which uncontrolled circumstances may, in these cases, interfere with excellent activity. They may (1) deprive it of some instrumental means or resource. This resource, in turn, may be either (a) absolutely necessary for excellent activity, so that its absence altogether blocks the activity; or (b) its absence may simply constrain or impede the performance of the activity. (2) Circumstances may block activity by depriving it, not merely of an external instrument, but of the very object or recipient of the activity. (The death of a friend blocks friendship in this more intimate way.) Here again, the activity may be either (a) completely blocked, if the loss is permanent and complete; or (b) impeded, if the loss is temporary and/or partial. We shall concentrate on (Ia) and (Ib) here, reserving the loss of an object for the next chapter. But Aristotle does not explicitly draw these distinctions, and his examples are drawn from all groups.

'It is impossible or not easy to do fine things without resources', Aristotle said in the passage with which we began this chapter, as he opened his discussion of the power of luck. He goes on to enumerate various types of necessary 'resources': "For many things are done through *philoi** and wealth and political capability, as through tools. And deprivation of some things defiles blessedness *(to makarion)*: for example good birth, good children,

---

*In this chapter and the next, *philos* and *philia* (usually rendered "friend" and "friendship") will usually remain untranslated; the issues are discussed in Ch. 12. Briefly: *philia* is extensionally wider than friendship—it takes in family relations, the relation between husband and wife, and erotic relationships, as well as what we would call 'friendship'. It is also, frequently, affectively stronger: it is a requirement of *philia* that the partners should be linked by affectionate feeling; and, as we see, *philia* includes the very strongest and most intimate of our affective ties. We can say that two people are 'just friends'; no such thing could be said with *philia*.

good looks. For nobody will entirely live well (be *eudaimonikos)* if he is entirely disgusting to look at, or basely born, or both solitary and childless; still less, perhaps, if he has terribly bad children or *philoi,* or has good ones who die" (1099a33–b6). Some of these are deprivations of instrumental means towards activity; some (the cases of friends and children) involve the loss both of instrumental means towards further activities (for friends are also 'tools') and of an object for one kind of excellent activity itself. In some cases, we can imagine that the absence of the instrumental means or object will altogether block excellent activity. Lifelong enslavement, severe chronic illness, extreme poverty, the death of all one's loved ones—any of these could make one or more of the excellences impossible to exercise. (Even extreme physical ugliness, as Aristotle elsewhere explicitly says,[28] can altogether block the formation of deep friendships.) In other cases, we imagine that good activity, while not altogether blocked, will be significantly impeded or cut back. The person disadvantaged in social position may lack opportunities for good political activity that are available to the well-placed; the death of a child can cramp the quality or spirit of many types of activity; sickness can do the same. These are not rare disasters, nor does Aristotle here seem to view them that way. They are regular parts of the course of many human lives. Aristotle's list makes us begin to notice the extent to which an average life is hedged round by dangers of impediment. Unconstrained activity begins to look like the rare or lucky item.

Having made these general observations about the power of circumstance to disrupt good activity, Aristotle is ready to test our intuitions against a particular case: "For many reversals and all sorts of luck come about in the course of a life; and it is possible for the person who was most especially going well to encounter great calamities in old age, as in the stories told about Priam in the Trojan war. But when a person has such misfortunes and ends in a wretched condition, nobody says that he is living well *(oudeis eudaimonizei)"* (1100a5–10). The story of Priam is a good test case for Aristotle's ethical theory here. For it begins with a person who had, presumably, developed and maintained a stably virtuous character through life, had acted well and according to excellence—but who was then deprived by war of family, children, friends, power, resources, freedom. In his final pitiable state Priam's capacity to act well is very much diminished; for he cannot, given the constraints upon him, exercise many of the

human excellences for which he was previously known. We deeply
pity Priam, feeling that he has lost something of great importance
in losing his sphere of activity, something that is deeper than
mere contented feeling. On the other hand, even an ethical theorist who rejects the extremes of the good-condition view may wish
to maintain here that calamity does not impair the quality of Priam's life, since he has displayed good character in action consistently through the course of a long life. Aristotle's challenge is to
sketch a response that will do justice to these competing
intuitions.

His strategy here, as elsewhere, is two-pronged. Against the
opponent of luck he will insist on luck's real importance, explor-
ing our belief that it is possible to be dislodged from living well. At
the same time, he shows us that, given a conception of good living that values stable excellences of character and activity according to these, such drastic upsets will be rare. Making excellences
and their activities—rather than, say, honor or success—the primary bearers of value (or, better, acknowledging that we really believe that they *are* the primary bearers of value, for Aristotle
argues that those who say something else will change if they
think harder about the full range of their beliefs) helps us to avoid
seeing ourselves as, and being, mere victims of luck.

Aristotle's remarks about Priam and related cases go against
a well-established tradition in moral philosophy, both ancient
and modern, according to which moral goodness, that which is
an appropriate object of ethical praise and blame, cannot be
harmed or affected by external circumstances. For Plato, the good
person could not be harmed by the world: his life is no less good
and praiseworthy because of adverse circumstances.[29] For the
good-condition theorist, the same is evidently true, though for
slightly different reasons. For Kant, whose influence upon modern Aristotle commentators and their audiences cannot, here
again, be overestimated, *happiness* can be augmented or diminished by fortune; but that which is truly deserving of ethical
praise and blame, true moral worth, cannot be.[30] This Kantian
view has so influenced the tradition of subsequent ethical theory
that it has come to seem to many a hallmark of truly moral thinking. It is not surprising, then, that interpreters under the influence of one or more of these traditions and anxious to make
Aristotle look morally respectable have read the Priam passage
oddly, so that it no longer says what would be most shocking,
namely that ethical praiseworthiness of life, not just happy feeling, can be augmented or diminished by chance reversals. The in-

terpretative view that acquits Aristotle of this immoral doctrine is
as follows. Aristotle is, in these passages, drawing a distinction
between two of his central ethical notions: between *eudaimonia*
and *makariotēs*, living well and being blessed or happy. The
former consists in activity according to excellence; the latter in
this, plus the blessings of fortune. According to this story, which
has been put forward by Kant-influenced commentators such as
Sir David Ross and H. H. Joachim,[31] the gifts and reversals of fortune can never diminish *eudaimonia*, i.e., that for which Priam
can be praised and blamed; but because they can diminish his
enjoyment of his good activity, they do diminish contentment and
good feeling. This reading bases itself upon a sentence in the
Priam passage that says, 'If things are so, the *eudaimōn* person
will never become wretched; nor, however, will he be *makarios*, if
he encounters the luck of Priam' (1101a6–7). We shall later inves-
tigate this sentence in its context and ask whether it is really
making the distinction desired by the interpreter.

It is a famous distinction; and its closeness to the Kantian
distinction between moral worth and happiness makes us suspicious of it right away as a reading of Aristotle, especially given the
anti-Kantian force of Aristotle's remarks about the person on the
wheel. Nor does it give us confidence to find that Aristotle's first
remark about Priam's case is, 'As for someone who has luck like
that and dies in a wretched condition, nobody says that he is living well (nobody *eudaimonizei* him)' (1100a9–10). Priam is from
the beginning denied not just contentment, but *eudaimonia* itself. But perhaps this is an unreflective belief of the many that
Aristotle is going to criticize. So we need to look further to see
whether the text as a whole supports the interpreters' distinction.

In fact it does not. Aristotle makes no significant distinction,
in these passages, between *eudaimonia* and *makariotēs*; and he
clearly claims that both can be damaged or disrupted by certain
kinds of luck, though not by all the kinds that some of his contemporaries supposed.

The textual evidence can be succinctly set out: first, passages claiming that *eudaimonia* is vulnerable to catastrophe;
second, passages indicating that Aristotle here treats '*eudaimon*' and '*makarion*' as interchangeable; those then allow us to
draw upon his remarks about the *makarion* for our picture of
eudaimonia.

(1) As we have already seen, the passage about the person
on the wheel from *EN* VII = *EE* VI clearly asserts that external
circumstances are required for *eudaimonia*; the same was

obviously true of the passage from *Magna Moralia* II.8 that we quoted at the beginning of this chapter. *Eudemian Ethics* VIII.2 argues at length that 'practical wisdom is not the only thing that makes acting well according to excellence *(eupragian kat' areten*, the definiens of *eudaimonia)*, but we say that the fortunate, too, do well *(eu prattein)*, implying that good fortune is a cause of good activity just as knowledge is" (1246b37—42a2). The friendship books will argue that *philoi*, as 'external goods', are necessary for full *eudaimonia* (cf. esp. 1169b2ff.). But we do not need to look so far afield. For the very disputed passages in *EN* 1 tell the same story. Nobody calls Priam *eudaimon* (1100a7—8). Because it is difficult or impossible to *do fine things (ta kala prattein)* without resources, it is obvious that *eudaimonia* stands in need of the external goods (1099a29—31). And at the conclusion of the Priam passage, Aristotle summarizes, 'What, then, prevents us from saying that a person is *eudaimon* if and only if that person is active according to complete excellence and is sufficiently equipped with the external goods not for some chance period of time, but for a complete life?' (1101a14—15). Here the presence of "sufficient" external goods is introduced, in a passage as formally definitional as any in the *EN*, as a separate necessary condition for *eudaimonia* itself.

(2) If we now attend to passages in which *'makarion'* and *'eudaimon'* occur together, we find that these passages confirm and do not disrupt this general picture. For the words are, in fact, treated as interchangeable. This is generally true in the ethical works. To take just a single salient example outside of our present context: in *EN* IX.9, Aristotle reports a debate about the value of *philia*:

> There is a debate as to whether the *eudaimon* needs *philoi* or not. For they say that *makarioi* and self-sufficient people have no need of *philoi*, since they have all good things already . . . But it seems peculiar to give all good things to the *eudaimon* and to leave out *philoi*, which seem to be the greatest of the external goods . . . And surely it is peculiar to make the *makarios* a solitary: for nobody would choose to have all the good things in the world all by himself. For the human being is a political creature and naturally disposed to living-with. And this is true of the *eudaimon* as well . . . Therefore the *eudaimon* needs *philoi*. (1169b3—10, 16—19,

22; for a detailed discussion of the argument of the passage, see Ch. 12)

Nobody could reasonably doubt that the two words are used here with no salient distinction, more or less as stylistic variants. Both in the paraphrase of the opponent's position and in Aristotle's own remarks, this is so. Nor could anyone doubt that the external good of *philia* is held here to be necessary for *eudaimonia*, not just for *makariotēs*.

The same is in fact true of our present context, as we can see if we reexamine its opening passage, part of which we have quoted previously:

> Nonetheless, *eudaimonia* evidently needs the external goods as well, as we said. For many things are done through *philoi* and wealth and political capability, as through tools. And deprivation of some things defiles the condition of being *makarion;* for example good birth, good children, good looks. For nobody will entirely be *eudaimonikos* if he is entirely disgusting to look at, or basely born, or both solitary and childless; still less, perhaps, if he has terribly bad children or *philoi*, or has good ones who die. As we said, then, it seems to require this sort of fortunate climate in addition. This is why some have identified *eudaimonia* with good fortune, and others with excellence. (1099a33–b8)

This passage shows very clearly that Aristotle draws no distinction of an important kind between *makariotēs* and *eudaimonia*, and that he is fully prepared to assert that *eudaimonia* itself is disrupted by absence of certain external goods. The entire passage concerns the need of *eudaimonia* for external goods. (The subject of the first quoted sentence is not explicit in the Greek, but must be supplied from the previous sentence, whose last word is '*eudaimonia*'; there is no other candidate subject.) The general point is now further explained (NB 'for') by a passage that speaks of the defilement of the *makarion*; this, in turn, is further explained (another 'for') by a passage that once again speaks in terms of *eudaimonia*. The 'it' in the final conclusion plainly refers to *eudaimonia*: it is this which requires a fortunate climate, as the final sentence of our citation makes clear. The absence of certain necessary conditions for good living impairs good living

itself, presumably by impeding the doing of fine actions in which
good living consists. So far, *'makarion'* and *'eudaimon'* do not
come apart.

Now we must look closely at the context of the passage that
forms the basis for the opposing interpretation, the passage in
which Aristotle delivers his verdict about the case of Priam. He
asks how secure our judgments of *eudaimonia* are during the
course of a person's life, given the vulnerability of human good living to reversals in fortune. He then once again reasserts his position that human good living does 'need in addition' (*prosdeitai*,
1100b8) the external goods of luck. But, he goes on, this does not
make *eudaimonia* entirely at the mercy of luck, or the *eudaimōn*
'a chameleon and resting on a rotten basis' (1100b6–7). For these
goods are not the most important factors in living well: 'the well
or badly does not reside in these' (8).[32] They are not the actual
constituents of good living: 'activities according to excellence, or
their opposites, are what are in charge of[33] *eudaimonia* or its
opposite' (1100b8–10). Such activity, though to some degree
vulnerable, is just about the most stable and enduring thing
in human life, one of the hardest things to lose hold of or forget
or have taken away (1100b12ff.). The person who is living and acting well (Aristotle first calls this person the *makarios*, then
switches in the next sentence to the *eudaimōn*—16, 18) will go on
doing so throughout his or her entire life. 'For he will always or
more than anything else do and consider the things according to
excellence; and he will bear luck most nobly and in every way harmoniously, if he is really good and "four-square without blame" '
(1100b19–22).

So much is fairly clear. Now the complexities begin, as Aristotle begins to ask in what ways this stable good life, based upon
steady character and consisting in activity according to the excellences of character and intellect, *is* vulnerable. Small pieces of either good or bad fortune, he now tells us, will not produce a
'decisive change of life' (*rhopē tēs zōēs*, 22–5). But big and numerous contingencies can, if they happen well, make life more
makarion because the opportunities they afford will be used nobly and well; on the other hand, correspondingly great misfortunes will 'crush and pollute the (condition of being) *makarion*—
for they bring pain and get in the way of many activities'
(1100b23–30). So far, then, only the word *'makarion'* has been
used, in the immediate context, of that which can be augmented
by great good fortune and diminished by great misfortune. But,

in addition to our other evidence, the reasons given here, which all have to do with the way fortune augments or impedes excellent *activity*, show us that the *makarion* cannot be some merely supervenient pleasure or feeling of contentment. Aristotle is maintaining, as elsewhere, that some of the component activities in which good living consists can be increased or blocked by external happenings. We are probably supposed to think of both instrumental and more direct effects of fortune. An inheritance gives, instrumentally, scope for fine and generous action; sudden illness impedes good acting in every area by taking away one's energy. Political reversals and deaths of loved ones more directly remove other sorts of good activity, by removing their objects; conversely, the birth of a child or the acquisition of adult political rights makes a direct contribution to excellent action by providing it with an object.

All of this seems to be about *eudaimonia* itself and its constituents, not some supervenient good. Aristotle shortly makes this explicit: "The *eudaimōn* person is not variable and easily changed. For he will not be easily dislodged from his *eudaimonia*, nor by just any misfortune that happens his way, but only by big and numerous misfortunes; and out of these he will not become *eudaimōn* again in a short time, but, if ever, in a long and complete time, if, in that time, he gets hold of big and fine things" (1101a8–14). (There follows the definitional passage that we have already discussed on p. 330.) Aristotle here very clearly asserts that misfortunes of a severe kind, prolonged over a period of time, impair good living itself. He uses '*eudaimon*' where above he had used '*makarion*', making no distinction. (Several lines later, at 1101a19–20, he paraphrases his concluding definition, now substituting '*makarion*' for '*eudaimon*'.) Such disruptions are rare, he says, since human excellence, once developed, is something stable; but if they are big or deep or frequent enough, catastrophes will 'pollute' good activity, and therefore the good life, so severely that only time and much good luck, if anything, will bring *eudaimonia* back.

Aristotle inserts an important qualification in the intervening section. Since this passage includes the sentence from which we began our criticism of the Kantian interpretation, we should now study its context in full:

If activities are the main thing in life, as we said, nobody who is *makarios* will ever become basely wretched (*athlios*).

For he will never engage in hateful and base actions. We
think that the really good and reasonable person will bear
his luck with dignity and always do the finest thing possible
given the circumstances, just as the good general will make
the most warlike use of the army he has and the good shoemaker will make the best shoe he can out of the hides he is
given—and so on for all craftsmen. If this is right, then the
eudaimōn person would never become basely wretched;
nonetheless, he will still not be *makarios*, if he encounters
the luck of Priam. Nor indeed is he variable and easily
changed, for he will not be easily dislodged from his *eudaimonia* . . . etc. (1100b33–1101a10)

Now that we can examine the entire passage some of whose bits
we have seen separately, we can understand Aristotle's final judgment concerning Priam. He does concede that such extreme bad
luck *could* dislodge a good person from full *eudaimonia*. But he
reminds us that a person of good character and practical wisdom
will often be able to resist this damage, finding a way to act nobly
even in circumstances of adversity. Like a general who does the
best he can with the troops he has, or the shoemaker who makes
the best shoes he can with the available materials, so even the
wise and virtuous person will use life's 'materials' as well as possible, finding for excellence some expression in action. Indeed,
part of the 'art' of Aristotelian practical wisdom, as we saw in
Chapter 10, seems to consist in being keenly responsive to the
limits of one's 'material' and figuring out what is best given the
possibilities, rather than rigidly aiming at some inflexible set of
norms. Aristotelian practical excellence is prepared for the contingencies of the world and is not easily diminished by them. But
none of this will suffice to prevent the loss of *eudaimonia* in a
very extreme case such as Priam's.

Finally, Aristotle feels it important to stress that a person of
good and stable character will not act diametrically against character just because of continued misfortune; the stability of character will stand between him and really *bad* action. But only
bad action makes a person truly *athlios*, if actions are the main
thing in life. If *eudaimonia* were constituted by wealth or power,
a person could go from the top to the very bottom, from the most
praiseworthy condition to the condition most worthy of scorn, as
a result of luck. Activity according to excellence may be squeezed
or blocked; but the person to whom that happens does not,

just on account of this, go to the very bottom of the scale of ethical assessment. Even if we do not wish to grant that the good person on the wheel is living a flourishing and fully praiseworthy life, we can also acknowledge that his life is not evil, despicable, or blameworthy.

In short, an Aristotelian conception of *eudaimonia*, which bases excellent activity on stable goodness of character, makes the good life tolerably stable in the face of the world. But this stability is not limitless. There is a real gap between being good and living well; uncontrolled happening can step into this gap, impeding the good state of character from finding its proper fulfillment in action. . . .

Aristotle adds a further observation. This is, that certain valued excellences, particularly courage, political commitment, and love of friends, will take the good agent, far more often than the defective agent, into situations in which the requirements of character conflict with the preservation of life itself—therefore with the continued possibility of all excellent activity. This is a special type of value conflict. The good Aristotelian agent will see it as a choice in which something of real value is forgone—though not, admittedly, one in which evil action is forced. In his discussion of sacrifices for the sake of friendship or love, Aristotle stresses the fact that the person of excellence will think little of comfort or safety or money compared to the chance to do something noble; but he goes on to say that love of friends or country will sometimes call for a sacrifice more intimately connected to good living: a sacrifice of the opportunity to act well, or even of life itself (1169a18–b2).

The good-condition theorist, and other defenders of the view that the good life cannot be diminished by such chance collisions, might try to say that there is no real loss here—for the person's goodness is intact, and the nobility of his choice guarantees that he will suffer no diminution in *eudaimonia*. Aristotle, as we might expect, does not agree. The loss of activity and of life, he argues elsewhere, is even a greater loss to the excellent person than to the base. The more excellent he is, the richer his life is in value—and, therefore, the more painful the choice to risk losing it:

By so much as the courageous person has all of excellence and the more *eudaimōn* he is, so much more will he be pained at the prospect of death. For such a person, above

others, has a value worthy of living, and he will be aware that
he is being deprived of the greatest goods. That is a painful
thing. But he will nonetheless be courageous, and perhaps
even more so because he chooses what is fine in war over
these other things. In fact we don't have pleasant activity in
the case of all the excellences—except insofar as they reach
their end. (1117b10–16)

Excellence, in this case and others like it, diminishes self-
sufficiency and increases vulnerability: it gives you something of
high value and it enjoins that in certain situations of luck you be
ready to give it up. But that excellence should bring risk and pain
is no surprise, says Aristotle—unless you are in the grip of the
false notion that excellence is necessarily linked with having a
good time. There is pleasure when the noble activity reaches its
end; but if the world should prevent this fulfillment, the good person still chooses to act nobly.

IV

So far, Aristotle's reply to the good-condition theorist has
spoken only of impeded activity. It has not spoken of chance-
caused damage to the good condition or state of character itself.
But Aristotle plainly does believe that our worldly circumstances
affect, for better or for worse, adult good character itself, not just
its expression. It is obvious that the world, in his view, affects decisively the character-formation he convincingly made out. We
can sketch the case by pointing to four pieces of evidence: (1) the
Priam passage itself; (2) evidence concerning *philia* and the political context; (3) the *Rhetoric's* discussion of the relationship between character and time and/or experience of life; (4) the account
of the so-called 'goods of fortune' in both *Rhetoric* and *EN*.

The good person, Aristotle said, could not easily be dislodged
from *eudaimonia*, but only by 'big and numerous misfortunes'.
Once so dislodged, however, 'he will not become *eudaimōn* again
in a short time, but, if ever, in a long and complete time, if, in that
time, he gets hold of big and fine things'. We must now look more
closely into the nature of the damage that dislodges the good person. For misfortunes can 'pollute' good activity in two ways: by
disrupting the expression of good dispositions in action, or by affecting the internal springs of action themselves. The former possibility is prominent in the context; but the latter seems

important, as well, for the explication of this particular passage. A purely external impediment to good action could be set right *immediately* by the restoration of good fortune. A person who has been enslaved in wartime can be set free in a moment. A sick person can as quickly be cured. A childless person can suddenly conceive or beget a child. What does take time and repeated good fortune to heal is the corruption of desire, expectation, and thought that can be inflicted by crushing and prolonged misfortune. Aristotle's repeated use of words suggesting spoilage or pollution,[34] and his assertion that the damages of luck are reversed, if at all, only over a long period of time, suggest that he is thinking also of this deeper, more internal sort of damage. It takes a long time to restore to the slave a free person's sense of dignity and self-esteem, for the chronic invalid to learn again the desires and projects characteristic of the healthy person, for the bereaved person to form new and fruitful attachments.

This possibility is made more concrete in the books concerning *philia*. For there Aristotle both shows love to be a vulnerable good and ascribes to it an important role in the development and maintenance of adult good character. The same can be said of his discussions of the function of a supporting political context. Since we shall discuss these arguments in detail in our next chapter, we can now turn to the little-known and highly interesting material from the *Rhetoric*.[35]

In *Rhetoric* 11.12–14, Aristotle makes a series of observations about the relationship between character and time of life; these show us clearly to what extent the experience of reversal and misfortune can wound character itself. Young people, he tells us, have certain virtues of character of which the elderly are frequently no longer capable. They are of a noble simplicity: they are *euētheis*, open or guileless, rather than *kakoētheis*, guileful or malignant, 'because they have not yet seen much wickedness' (1389a17–18).[36] They are capable of trust because they have not yet been often deceived (1389a18–19). They are courageous because they are capable of high hope, and this makes for confidence (1389a26–7). They are capable of the central Aristotelian virtue of *megalopsuchia*, greatness of soul, 'because they have not yet been humbled by life, but they lack experience of necessities' (1389a31–2). (The *EN*, too, stresses the importance of good luck for this 'crown of the virtues'—1124a20ff.) They lack excessive concern for money because they have little experience of need (1389a14–15). They form friendships easily because they take pleasure in the company of others and do not calculate everything with an eye to advantage (a35–b2). They are easily moved to pity, since they have a good opinion of others and so easily believe that they are suffering unjustly (b8–9). They are fond of laughter, so they have the social excellence of *eutrapelia,* charm or ready wit (b10–11). They have certain tendencies to excess as well, Aristotle tells us, which are the outgrowth of their inexperience and their keenness of passion. But what most interests us, in this remarkable set of observations, is that they are capable of certain good and high things just on account of their lack of certain bad experiences.

We see more clearly what this claim means when we turn to the account of the character of the elderly, whose deficiencies result from just that experience of life that the trusting and hopeful young have not yet had. This little known but very important passage deserves to be quoted at length:

> Because they have lived many years and have been deceived many times and made many mistakes, and because their experience is that most things go badly, they do not insist upon anything with confidence, but always less forcefully than is appropriate. They *think,* but never *know;* they have views on both sides of a question and are always adding in 'perhaps' and 'probably'; they say everything this way, and nothing unequivocally. And they are malignant *(kakoëtheis):* for it is malignant to interpret everything in the worst light. Furthermore, they are excessively suspicious because of their lack of trust *(apistia),* and lacking in trust because of their experience. And they neither love nor hate intensely for these reasons, but, as in the saying of Bias, they love as if they were going to hate tomorrow, and hate as if they were going to love tomorrow. And they are small of soul *(mikropsuchoi)* because they have been humbled by life: for they desire nothing great or excellent, but only what is commensurate with life. And they are ungenerous. For property is one of the necessary things; and in, and through, their experience they know how hard it is to get it and how easy to lose it. And they are cowardly and fear everything beforehand—for they have, in this respect, the opposite character from the young. For they are chilly, and the young are warm; so old age prepares the way for cowardice, since fear, too, is a kind of chilling . . . And they are self-

loving more than is appropriate; for this, too, is a kind of smallness of soul. And they live for advantage and not for the noble, more than is appropriate, because they are self-loving. For the advantageous is good for oneself; the noble is good *simpliciter* . . . And the elderly, too, feel pity, but not for the same reason as the young: for the young feel it through love of humanity, the old through weakness—for they think every suffering is waiting for them, and this inspires pity. For this reason they are given to grieving, and are neither charming nor fond of laughter. (1389b13–1390a24)

These remarkable observations show us clearly to what extent Aristotle is willing to acknowledge that circumstances of life can impede character itself, making even acquired virtues difficult to retain. Especially at risk are those virtues that require openness or guilelessness rather than self-defensiveness, trust in other people and in the world rather than self-protecting suspiciousness. And it seems to be Aristotle's view that quite a few of the virtues require this element. Love and friendship require trust in the loved person; generosity is incompatible with continual suspicion that the world is about to take one's necessary goods away; greatness of soul requires high hope and expectation; even courage requires confidence that some good can come of fine action. (In Chapter 13, I show the importance of this idea for Aristotle's connection with Euripidean tragedy.) The virtues require a stance of openness towards the world and its possibilities: as the *Antigone* also suggested, a yielding and receptive character of soul that is not compatible with an undue emphasis on self-protection. This openness is both itself vulnerable and a source of vulnerability for the person's *eudaimonia:* for the trusting person is more easily betrayed than the self-enclosed person, and it is the experience of betrayal that slowly erodes the foundation of the virtues. Virtue contains in this way (in a world where most people's experience is that 'things go badly') the seeds of its own disaster.

    This is a treatise for orators who will address a mixed group of ordinary people; it therefore aims to say what is so for the average mediocre type, and it does not stress the abilities of the person of superior character.[37] We can assume, with *EN* 1, that such a person would not be corroded by a few bad experiences and that in a wide range of circumstances he or she would be able to act well with the 'materials' at hand, preserving character intact. And yet this passage tells us clearly that character itself can be affected; the mechanisms of its decline are, clearly, present in the good as well as the mediocre life. (Most of the circumstances mentioned are common; some even appear natural and inevitable.) Indeed, we might say that the good are in certain ways more at risk than the bad: for it is the good *euēthēs* person who trusts in uncertain things and therefore risks the pain of disillusionment. We shall see in Euripides' portrait of Hecuba both how difficult it is to sway the character of a really good person *and* how horrible is the spectacle of a decline, once trust is no longer available.

We can now summarize Aristotle's argument against the opponent of luck. First of all, he has argued that the good condition of a virtuous person is not, by itself, sufficient for full goodness of living. Our deepest beliefs about value, when scrutinized, show us that we require more. We require that the good condition find its completion or full expression in activity; and this activity takes the agent to the world, in such a way that he or she becomes vulnerable to reversals. Any conception of good living that we will consider rich enough to be worth going for will contain this element of risk. The vulnerability of the good person is not unlimited. For frequently, even in diminished circumstances, the flexible responsiveness of his practical wisdom will show him a way to act well. But the vulnerability is real: and if deprivation and diminution are severe or prolonged enough, this person can be 'dislodged' from *eudaimonia* itself. Aristotle's final point against the good-condition opponent is that even then virtuous condition is not, itself, something hard and invulnerable. Its yielding and open posture towards the world gives it the fragility, as well as the beauty, of a plant.

Notes

[All chapter references are to *The Fragility of Goodness*, from which these extracts are taken. Ed.]

1. Pindar, *Nemean* VIII.40–2; the following citations are from lines 39 and 42–4. 'Vine tree' results from an emendation by Bury, now widely, though not universally, accepted; the unemended text would read 'as a tree shoots upward'. This issue makes no difference to my argument. On *aretē*, 'excellence', see below, note 15.

2. The conventions of the epinician genre received penetrating study in the now classic work of the late Elroy Bundy (*Studia Pindarica* (Berkeley 1962)), which transformed Pindar criticism by showing the extent to which shared convention, and not idiosyncratic autobiographical fact, shapes the poet's self-presentation and other features of his practice. On these developments in criticism, see H. Lloyd-Jones, "Modern interpretation of Pindar," *Journal of Hellenic Studies* 93 (1973) 109–37; for a penetrating introduction to the poet and the criticism about him, see H. Lloyd-Jones, "Pindar," Lecture on a Master Mind, *Proceeding of the British Academy* (1982), 139–63. Two recent studies of the epinician tradition and Pindar's place in it are M. R. Lefkowitz, *The Victory Ode* (Park Ridge, N.J. 1976) and K. Crotty, *Song and Action* (Baltimore 1982).

3. The plant imagery is deeply traditional: see, for example, the *Homeric Hymn to Demeter* 237–41, *Iliad* XVIII. 54–60, 437–41, of the growth of the hero. Other later occurrences will be discussed in Chs. 3, 4, 6, 7, and 13. For a very interesting discussion of the connection between plant imagery and lamentation, which supports our idea that the plant image expresses a picture of specifically mortal and vulnerable excellence, see G. Nagy, *The Best of the Achaeans* (Baltimore 1979) 181ff. Nagy offers a perceptive account of the development, in the early poetic tradition, of a picture of human excellence that is unavailable in, and contrasted with, the condition of a self-sufficient or needless being. (I have discussed earlier work of Nagy on this subject in my "*Psuchē* in Heraclitus, II," *Phronesis* 17 (1972) 153–70, where I ascribe to Heraclitus a contrast between the self-sufficient excellence of gods and the needy excellence of vulnerable humans.) For other related material concerning traditional conceptions of the 'human situation' in early Greek poetry, see J. Redfield's *Nature and Culture in the Iliad* (Chicago 1975), esp. 60–6, 85–8. Aristotle's more pejorative use of the plant image will be discussed below, Chs. 8 and 11. See also Plato, *Timaeus* 90A, which insists that we are not earthly but heavenly plants. Some relevant Platonic and Aristotelian material is discussed in E. N. Lee, 'Hoist with his own petard,' in Lee, E. N. Lee, A. P. D. Mourelates and R. M. Rorty, eds., *Exegesis and Argument: Studies in Greek Philosophy Presented to Gregory Vlastos, Phronesis Suppl.* I, Assen, 1973. For other use of plant imagery in the poem, see *eblasten* line 12 (the child 'sprouts forth'), *phututheis* line 28 (wealth can be 'planted and tended' with a god's help).

4. This seems to be the implication of the verb *masteuei* here: compare Aes. *Ag.* 1093–4, and the commentary on the passage by E. Fraenkel, *Aeschylus: Agamemnon* (Oxford 1950) *ad loc.* The word seems to mean, in general, 'seek out', 'search after', 'pursue the track of'. In the Aeschylus passage, Clytemnestra is explicitly compared to a hunting dog sniffing out the trail of blood; the subsequent sentence *mateuei d' bōn aneurēsei phonon* is translated by Fraenkel, 'she is on the track of the

murder . . . '; similar versions are offered by others. It is a little difficult, given the relative rarity of the word, to know whether its presence alone implies the idea of hunting or tracking. We can at least infer from the Aeschylus passage that it was felt to be particularly appropriate for the sort of eager, intense searching that a hunting dog performs. The phrase *en ommasi thesthai piston*, which follows the verb, is difficult and multiply ambiguous. Literally, it can be rendered, 'to place for oneself the trustworthy in eyes'. This can, in turn, be taken at least four ways: (1) to repose trust (locate the trustworthy for oneself) in someone's (the friend's) eyes; (2) to place something or someone trustworthy (viz., the friend) before one's eyes; (3) to make visible (place before eyes) a sure or trustworthy item (viz., perhaps, the poem?); (4) to make a trustworthy bond or pledge before people's eyes. In short—we cannot determine whether the eyes in question are those of the person, of the friend, or of the group; and we also do not know whether *to piston* is the friend, the poem, a specific pledge, or the trustworthy in the abstract. I have chosen and translated the reading (I), also favored and well defended by Farnell (*The Works of Pindar* (London 1932)); each of the other versions has had its influential defenders. I am not eager to disambiguate in an arbitrary way a suggestive phrase some of whose ambiguity is doubtless deliberate. But it seems to me that (1) and (2) fit the context in some ways better than (3) and (4). The whole passage before and after is concerned with personal friendship, the bond of trust and reliance linking one friend with another. The overall sense must, in general, be: 'We have all sorts of needs for beloved friends, especially in difficulty (or labor); but we need to be able to rely on them in joyful times too (or to share with them our joy in victory, as with someone whom we trust). This I cannot do in this present case, since Megas is dead and I cannot bring him back. My desire to share this joy with him is empty and vain. But I can at least write this poem . . . ' Either (1) or (2) suits this overall meaning; (1) seems slightly easier because *en ommasi* more easily means 'within' than 'before' the eyes; but there are a few precedents for the latter, so we cannot decide firmly. (The scholiast compares Euripides' *Ion* 732, *es ommat' eunou phōtos emblepein gluku*, 'to look at sweetness in the eyes of a well-disposed person', showing that he understands the passage in sense (1).) (3), which (at least as articulated to me informally by Professor Lloyd-Jones) has these lines already making reference to the poem as a token of friendship, does not seem to me to work well, since we do not then expect the poet to say that his hopes have been frustrated by Megas's death. If the hope *en ommasi thesthai piston* is frustrated, it cannot be the hope to write the poem. The poem is presented not as the fulfillment of this hope—this, I think, is quite important for Pindar's view of the magnitude and ethical importance of the loss of friendship—but as a substitute or consolation, after the termination of friendship and its exchange of trust by death. As for (4), it is not altogether clear to me what pledge its defenders have in mind; nor have I seen convincing parallels for *thesthai piston* in this sense. One final reason for preferring (1) lies in the idea it conveys, that eyes are the seat of trust between one friend and another. This deeply rooted and pervasive Greek idea, which will be further exemplified and discussed in Chs. 3 and 13, is a most appropriate one for Pindar to allude to in this context; it enriches the poem's meaning.

5. Euripides, *Trojan Women* 820ff. Ganymede will reappear, as an example of specifically human and vulnerable excellence, in Plato's *Phaedrus*—cf. Ch. 7.

6. *Odyssey* V. 214–20.

7. Plato, *Phaedrus* 80B.

8. For further discussion of the notion of *tuchē* in pre-Platonic thought, and of the antithesis between *tuchē* and rational *technē*, see Ch. 4 and references.

9. The problem of masculine and feminine pronouns has bothered me all through the writing of this manuscript. To use 'he or she' as the unmarked pronoun in every instance seemed intolerably cumbersome. To opt for 'he' everywhere seemed repugnant to my political sensibilities and also false to the current state of the language, where, increasingly, efforts are being made to give 'she' equal time. It also seems clear to me that in the contexts where 'he' most often would so occur in this book (referring back to 'the philosopher', 'the poet', 'the good agent'), its presence is far from being really unmarked: it does encourage the imagination to picture the character in question as male. Nor is this an irrelevant concern in writing about this material. For the tragedians all have a claim to be taken seriously as thinkers about the privileges and the moral status of women; in each of the plays that we shall discuss, a woman defends her claim to moral and political equality. Plato has a good claim to be called the first feminist philosopher—though his position is more radical still: for it is the denial that the body, therefore gender, is of any ethical significance at all (cf. Ch. 5). He is also the first thinker I know who pointed out that feminism ought to lead to changes in unmarked linguistic gender. At *Republic* 540C, Socrates expresses concern that Glaucon's failure to use both masculine and feminine participles, when referring to the rulers, may give rise to the false impression that they are talking only about males. Aristotle's conspicuous anti-feminism is an issue that we shall discuss. My first idea, as I considered these questions, was to adopt the completely arbitrary 'solution' of using 'he' as unmarked in even-numbered chapters, 'she' in odd. But this proved distracting and harsh to readers of widely varying political beliefs. Nor, clearly, was it a

solution that the natural language could ever adopt. I therefore decided, on reflection, to follow Plato's practice in the above-mentioned passage, by using 'he or she' fairly frequently, in order to remind the reader not to think of men only, but reverting (as Plato does) to the masculine in between, in order to avoid cumbersome sentence rhythms. I have also been sensitive to the context—since there is no use pretending that 'he or she' is appropriate when speaking of an Aristotelian ruler as imagined by Aristotle; whereas there is great use in employing this form for Plato.

10. There are of course several other post-classical views that would significantly affect the appreciation of these questions: for example Stoic and Christian views concerning divine providence and Christian views concerning the relationship between human goodness and divine grace. I focus on the influence of Kant because, as I shall go on to show (especially in Chapters 2, 11, 12, 13, and Interlude 2), Kantian views have profoundly affected the criticism and evaluation of these Greek texts; and it is the pervasive influence of these views in our time that constitutes the greatest obstacle to a proper estimation of the texts' importance. Except in Chapter 2, where I do discuss Kant's views about conflict of obligation, I speak of 'Kantians' and Kant's influence, rather than of Kant's usually more complex and subtle positions.

11. I shall, in fact, try to avoid not only the Kantian moral/non-moral distinction, but all versions of that distinction and of the related distinctions between moral and non-moral practical reasoning, moral and non-moral practical conflict. The Greek texts make no such distinction. They begin from the general question, 'How should we live?' and consider the claim of all human values to be constituent parts of the good life; they do not assume that there is any one group that has even a *prima facie* claim to be supreme. I believe that their approach is faithful to the way that our intuitive practical reasoning does in fact proceed, and that it recaptures aspects of our practical lives that tend to be obscured in works beginning from that distinction, however understood. In Chapter 2 I describe various versions of the distinction and show why they would be inappropriate starting-points for our inquiry. Our discussions of justice, civic obligation, and religious requirement are, however, intended to satisfy the convinced partisan of the distinction that our points about fragility apply even to values that would, on most versions of the distinction, standardly be considered as central moral values.

12. As, for example, in the influential work of A. W. H. Adkins, especially his *Merit and Responsibility* (Oxford, 1960), which begins with the claim (p. 2) that 'We are all Kantians now', and makes use of Kantian assumptions throughout in both exegesis and assessment. I have criticized Adkins's methodology in Nussbaum, "Consequences and Character in Sophocles' *Philoctetes*", *Philosophy and Literature* 1 (1976–7), pp. 25–35. For other valuable criticisms, see Lloyd-Jones, *JZ*; A. A. Long;

"Morals and values in Homer," *Journal of Hellenic Studies* 90 (1970) 121–39; K. J. Dover, "The portrayal of moral evaluation in Greek poetry," *Journal of Hellenic Studies* 103 (1983) 35–48.

13. Two recent articles that, in different ways, challenge Kantian views about luck are B. A. O. Williams, "Moral luck," *Proceedings of the Aristotelian Society, Supplementary Volume* 50 (1956), reprinted in Williams, *Moral Luck* (Cambridge: Cambridge University Press, 1981) 20–39 [see ch. 2. Ed.], and Thomas Nagel, "Moral luck," *Proceedings of the Aristotelian Society, Supplementary Volume* 50 (1976) reprinted in *Mortal Questions* (Cambridge 1979) 24–38 [see ch. 3. Ed.]. Williams's views about Greek ethical thought on these issues are discussed in this chapter, pp. 18–21, and in Ch. 2, p. 29.

14. *Republic* 612A.

15. Excellence *(aretē)* should here be understood broadly, not as presupposing any separation of a special group of moral excellences; we so far include all features of persons in virtue of which they live and act well, i.e. so as to merit praise. We thus include, at the least, both what Aristotle would call 'excellences of character' (a group not equivalent to the 'moral virtues', although this phrase is the most common English translation—cf. Ch. 11) and Aristotle's other major group, the excellences of the intellect.

16. Some texts we shall discuss are rendered obscure on this point by the common translation of Greek *'eudaimonia'* by English 'happiness'. Especially given our Kantian and Utilitarian heritage in moral philosophy, in both parts of which 'happiness' is taken to be the name of a feeling of contentment or pleasure, and a view that makes happiness the supreme good is assumed to be, by definition, a view that gives supreme value to psychological states rather than to activities, this translation is badly misleading. To the Greeks, *eudaimonia* means something like 'living a good life for a human being'; or, as a recent writer, John Cooper, has suggested, 'human flourishing'. Aristotle tells us that it is equivalent, in ordinary discourse, to 'living well and doing well'. Most Greeks would understand *eudaimonia* to be something essentially active, of which praiseworthy activities are not just productive means, but actual constituent parts. It is possible for a Greek thinker to argue that *eudaimonia* is equivalent to a state of pleasure; to this extent activity is not a conceptual part of the notion. But even here we should be aware that many Greek thinkers conceive of pleasure as something active rather than stative (cf. Ch. 5); an equation of *eudaimonia* with pleasure might, then, not mean what we would expect it to mean in a Utilitarian writer. The view that *eudaimonia* is equivalent to a *state* of pleasure is an unconventional and *prima facie* counterintuitive position in the Greek tradition (cf. Ch. 4). A very common position would be Aristotle's,

that *eudaimonia* consists in activity according to excellence(s). In the terms of this view, then, we shall be investigating the ways in which luck affects *eudaimonia* and the excellences that are its basis. Where it is important for clarity of our argument, the Greek word will be left untranslated.

I shall also be leaving aside one part of the question about excellence, namely the luck of birth or constitution—the role of factors the agent does not control in endowing him with the various initial abilities requisite for living humanly well. I shall only assume, as the texts assume, that the answer to this question is not such as to close off all of our other questions.

17. Anyone who is dubious about the use of the English word 'value' where Greek ethical texts are concerned will, I hope, be reassured as we go along, as it becomes clear why this is an appropriate notion to use to render certain Greek ethical terms. There is no one word for which 'value' is always and only the appropriate translation; but it is frequently the best word for certain uses of *'agathon'*, 'good', and especially *'kalon'*, 'fine', 'intrinsically good'. On *kalon*, see further in Ch. 6, p. 178. Other relevant locations are 'that which is worthy *(axion)'*, 'that which is choiceworthy *(haireton)'*, and various verbal locations involving words of estimating, esteeming, choosing.

18. This is terminology used by Williams, *Moral Luck* (Cambridge: Cambridge University Press, 1981). Although I have been using these expressions 'internal' and 'external contingency' for a long time and find them natural, it is likely that I first heard them in a seminar of Williams's at Harvard in 1973.

19. On madness *(mania)* and Plato's view of its role in the good life, see Ch. 7.

20. On *eudaimonia*, which will remain untranslated, see note 16 above.

21. I am making Aristotle's argument sound more systematic than it really is: in fact, the two groups of opponents are considered separately in different books of the *EN*; but there seems no reason not to bring them together in this way.

22. Aristotle's word (presumably the opponent's also) is *hexis*, frequently translated 'disposition'. I use 'state' or 'condition' to indicate that it is supposed to be something with psychological reality, that can be there in the person whether or not any action is going on. To call it a disposition would make the opponent's position seem even more paradoxical than it is; on the other hand, as we shall see, Aristotle believes that the criteria for ascription of a *hexis* are not present in the case of the totally inactive person.

23. It is not entirely clear whether Aristotle is saying (1) that the *hexis* might still be intact, but that we have an insuperable epistemological problem about telling whether it is; (2) that the notion of *hexis* is *logically* connected with activity, in such a way that it does not make sense to ascribe it apart from the presence of activity; (3) that *hexis* and action are *causally* interdependent, in such a way that an inactive person would be likely to lose her *hexis*. He certainly believes both (1) and (3); and (3) is, for him, not incompatible with (2), as we have seen in Ch. 9. But we know that he does not believe that a *hexis* goes away the minute no actual activity is being performed; it is a stable (or relatively stable) condition of the person. So whatever logical connection there is between *hexis* and activity, it cannot be this strong a connection.

24. See the excellent account of these matters in L. A. Kosman, 'Substance, being, and *Energeia*,' *Oxford Studies in Ancient Philosophy* 2 (1984) 121–49.

25. At this point, the good-condition theorist comes very close to the Platonist: for if what this person calls 'being' includes this sort of mental functioning, it will be *energeia*, as Plato's arguments understand it.

26. Although I have used 'his or her' in my own discussion, it seems inappropriate to translate Aristotle this way.

27. Contemplative activity is, of course, less vulnerable to reversal by the external than other activities; but, in Aristotle's view, it too has some external necessary conditions—cf. Ch. 12.

28. See the remarks on old age and *philia* in Ch. 12.

29. *Republic* 388A–B, *Apologia* 41C–D, etc. Here again, we need to point out that Plato differs from the good-condition theorist by requiring actual activity for *eudaimonia*; he will insist, however, that contemplative activity is altogether self-sufficient, requiring no special worldly conditions for its attainment beyond life itself.

30. Cf. for example, *Groundwork of the Metaphysics of Morals* (Berlin 1785), trans. H. J. Paton (New York 1960), Akad. p. 394, cf. Int. 2 n. 13.

31. H. H. Joachim, *The Nicomachean Ethics* (Oxford 1951) *ad loc.*; W. D. Ross, *The Works of Aristotle* (London 1923) 192.

32. For Aristotle's use of *en* ('in') in the sense of 'causally dependent' on, see esp. *Ph.* 210b21–2; also *Metaph.* 1023a8–11, 23–5; *EN* 1109b23; and see my discussion in Nussbaum, *De Motu Animalium* (Princeton 1978) Essay 3, p. 153.

33. The word used is *kurios*.

34. Compare the use of these words by Euripides and Thucydides—cf. Ch. 13; Aristotle may be using a traditional metaphor.

35. For the *Rhetoric*, the only edition to use is that of R. Kassel (Berlin 1976); see my review in *American Journal of Philology* 63 (1981) 346–50.

36. On *to euēthes* and its traditional association with excellence, cf. Ch. 13.

37. It might be objected, too that these sections of the *Rhetoric* deal with *endoxa*, prevalent ordinary beliefs not yet sifted and scrutinized. But Aristotle is telling the orator what young and old people are like in part so that he will know how best to persuade them. The success of his teaching here depends on its being right about the way their characters in fact are, not just about how they are seen.

5

What's Luck Got to Do With It?*

Don S. Levi

Sometimes you get lucky when doing philosophy. You are perplexed by a problem, you work on it and it leads to something interesting or even significant. You can find this development quite surprising especially if, like most philosophers, so many of your investigations have not led anywhere. This is where luck enters into it. Whether or not you were right to take up the problem depends on how things turn out.

Take this paper for example. I became interested in the role of a key example in illustrating the concept of moral luck. I was interested in it because the example dealt with someone quite fascinating—Paul Gauguin—and I was sceptical about any philosopher's moralizing about him. But if I knew why I was interested in the example, I did not know what would come of that interest. And as you read this paper you will wonder whether I got lucky and was able to make something out of the problems I have with the example.

In 1889 Paul Gauguin painted a self-portrait in which he sees himself as an angel, albeit a satanic fallen angel. There is a halo over his head; as an artist he is angelic in his power to excite us. A red and a green apple dangle temptingly by his head, a snake entwines itself between his fingers, and he seems to be leering at us; as an artist he is satanic in his power to tempt us to do things respectable people are not supposed to do.

This self-portrait is not without its ambiguities and ironies. As a painter Gauguin may have the power to stir unconscious desires in us; but he is only a painter and however powerful his work he cannot get us to act on these desires. Ironically,

*From *Philosophical Investigations* 12 (1989):1—13.

in portraying himself as a fallen angel he also seems to be mocking himself.

And there is an ambiguity in how the artist sees himself. He paints himself as a tempter, but he also seems to have succumbed to temptation. By seeing himself as a *fallen* angel he seems to be saying that he is living out the very fantasies that he is stirring in us.

It is this last theme that interests me. It is an expression of what I think of as bohemianism, the idea that to be really creative the artist must live the part: there should be no difference between who he is in his painting and who he is in his life. What this means is perhaps best illustrated in the case of Gauguin. He seems to have thought that in order to depict an instinctual world controlled by mysterious forces he had to be one of the savages whom he thought of as being more conscious of living in such a world. "You were mistaken that day in saying that I was wrong to call myself a savage. I am a savage, and civilized people feel it, for there is nothing in my work which astonishes, perplexes, if it is not this 'savage-in-spite-of myself.' That's why my work is inimitable. The work of the man is the explanation of the man."[1] To abandon himself in his art to savagery he also had to abandon himself to it in his life.

As I see it there are problems with bohemianism. I wonder why the artist cannot explore the dark, satanic side of himself without being satanic. And I question why the artist cannot nurture and support others without compromising her integrity or diminishing her powers as an artist. She may have less time for painting (and bohemian activities) but why should taking care of others mean that when she paints she will be less creative? Few artists can support themselves from the sale of their work (and just imagine how things were before art dealers and tax laws created a market for paintings). And few can turn all their energies to painting after working at other jobs. But bohemianism in its transvaluation of values seems to make creativity the only value; why should she have to abandon her family in order to do her best work? I would suggest that the answer is that she does not have to do so; and even though as the husband of a painter I have something invested in this answer, I hope that there is more to it than wishful thinking.

In his essay "Moral Luck" Bernard Williams seems to be saying that the bohemian artist is justified in his transvaluation of values if he succeeds in 'realising his gifts as a painter.'[2] No doubt

Williams will be surprised to find his argument discussed in the context of bohemianism, but, as I hope to show, that is how it should be understood.

In "Moral Luck" the target is the view that, by contrast with happiness, doing what is (rationally) justified is completely up to the agent and is not dependent on 'external contingencies.' To attack this view Williams introduces the concept of moral luck and illustrates it with the case of "the creative artist [Gauguin] who turns away from definite and pressing human claims in order to live a life in which, as he supposes, he can pursue his art."[3] Gauguin cannot know at the time of his decision how justified he might be in taking this step. Of course he might get sick and die before he has a chance to succeed, but that would not mean that Gauguin was wrong to have decided as he did. What Williams has in mind is an external contingency that is intrinsic to the project itself, the contingency of whether or not Gauguin succeeds in realising his gifts as an artist. Where Gauguin turns away from pressing human claims in order to pursue his art and the project turns out to be a failure then, as luck would have it, the original choice was not justified.

Williams is attacking the conception of morality that ignores the importance of a project like Gauguin's (or Anna Karenina's in abandoning her husband for the sake of love) that gives meaning to the life of the person with the project. As Williams sees it, Gauguin is leaving his family to carry out a *ground project* that Williams defines as 'providing the motive force which propels him into the future, and gives him a reason for living.'[4]

The ground project propels him into the future but when he arrives there and looks back on his decision how he thinks about it then will depend on an external contingency.

That contingency is whether the project was a success or failure; after he has succeeded or failed 'his standpoint of assessment will be from a life which then derives an important part of its significance for him from that very fact.'[5] This is what luck has to do with it: his endorsement of what he did will depend, at least in part, on whether or not his project was successful, something that is not completely in his hands.

This reference to *his* endorsement may seem confusing. After all, it seems that we too can endorse the project after it has been successful. How Williams sees the difference can be brought out by the use of his concept of *agent-regret*. When the agent looks back on what he did he is looking back on something he was responsible for. If he feels regret then what he feels or the expression he gives to that feeling is to be distinguished from what we might feel or express. And it is that agent regret that is being referred to in talking about whether Gauguin endorses what he did.

Williams is not saying that the end justifies the means, that the irresponsible and selfish actions of a Gauguin can be excused because of the great art he produced. On the contrary. The choice to engage in a ground project is itself a choice of an end rather than a means. The choice may be a difficult one if it involves turning away from definite and pressing human claims. But the ground project does not need to be defended on moral grounds, only the choice of it over other moral claims. What interests Williams is that by contrast with the choice to remain with his family, the justification for the choice to realise his gifts as an artist depends on an external contingency.

Whether or not he is doing the right thing cannot always be known to the agent. This is what Williams is suggesting about this example, and he knows that it will be especially distressing to philosophers who exalt the role of Reason, whether the reason be Practical or Theoretical. What Williams is saying is that a moral agent cannot always determine at the time he makes the decision whether he is doing the right thing. Moral luck is an embarrassment for the rule of reason; the justification for an action might not exist until after it can be determined whether or not the agent was successful.

'Moral luck' belongs to a tradition in moral philosophy of considering moral dilemmas that seem hard to resolve merely by the use of reason. Sometimes a dilemma has been cited by philosophers because they knew how it should be resolved and that resolution constituted an embarrassment to an opposing ethical theory or analysis. But the Gauguin dilemma is used by Williams not as a challenge to a moral theory but as a challenge to Reason itself. What he thinks is that no reasoning at the time Gauguin abandoned his family could have disclosed that he was making the right choice.

The Gauguin dilemma also needs to be contrasted with the kind of case cited by Sartre to illustrate how sometimes there is no decisive reason for doing one thing rather than another, for staying home and caring for your aging mother or for joining the Resistance. But Williams is saying more than that Gauguin was facing a terrible dilemma. What Williams is saying is that the nature of the dilemma could not be known until it became clear whether the project was going to succeed or fail. How the dilemma seems to the agent when he decides what to do may be quite different from how he sees it retrospectively, and the latter perspective is the one for Gauguin to take in considering whether or not he was justified in leaving his family.

What does luck have to do with it? To appreciate the problem we need to look at the example more closely. After all, we know a good deal about Gauguin's decision. In June 1885, when he and his six year old son, Clovis, left Copenhagen for Paris, Gauguin left his wife and his other four children behind. He was only to see them on two further occasions, once in May of 1887, when Mette, his wife, came to Paris to pick up Clovis as Gauguin was preparing to leave for Panama, the other time in March of 1891, when he visited his family in Copenhagen just before his first voyage to Tahiti.

Why did Gauguin leave Copenhagen? He left because he found life there intolerable. His wife and her family had only scorn for his painting. Respectable Danes found him uncouth, Mette's family questioned his suitability as a husband. And he and Mette quarrelled constantly. Worst of all, a one-man show of his paintings in Copenhagen failed miserably; few people even came to the exhibition, and nothing sold. Gauguin left for Paris and the centre of the art world, he left for an atmosphere much more congenial for a Post-Impressionist artist.

Why did married life interfere with Gauguin's project of realising his gifts as a painter? Gauguin was not willing to continue to live in an atmosphere he considered so hostile; and his wife, Mette, also was not willing to give up her creature comforts in order to live hand-to-mouth until Gauguin was able to support his family with his painting. He does not seem to have been too concerned that she and the family follow him to Paris (or wherever else his painting took him), and Mette showed little interest in doing so. As Gauguin was to observe on more than one occasion, she was quite happy with being a mother but quite averse to being a wife.

But then Gauguin did not think of the move as anything but temporary. He was going to Paris to prove to Mette and everyone else that he could support his family with his painting; he would become successful within a year or two and then send for his family to join him. Indeed, it was not until the death in 1897 of his favourite child, his only daughter Aline, that he stopped thinking of a reconciliation with his wife. She seems to have stopped thinking of it long before he did, but she continued to expect him to provide support for her and her family.

Armed with some knowledge of the situation, we can try to understand the role of moral luck. To understand it we need to consider what Gauguin was doing in leaving Copenhagen for Paris. When he left he thought of himself as taking a temporary leave to become a full-time artist in Paris where he would become successful enough to support his family. But he seems to have been wrong about its being only temporary because he did not rejoin his family when he did not become a commercial success. Not that he regretted his decision when he failed to find buyers for his work. Caught up in the bohemian conception of the artist, his commercial failure only encouraged him to find places to paint— Brittany, Martinique, Arles, Tahiti—where he could find the life that would produce his best work. He may have thought he was leaving to become a commercial success as an artist; but as I see it, he was really leaving to be an artist. I think that he was deceiving himself about why he was leaving in order to do what he really wanted to do—paint with the complete freedom to become the wild savage he saw as his real nature.

This characterization of what he was doing in leaving Mette benefits from hindsight. However much he might complain about his wife's bourgeois values, Gauguin should have known that material success, success that depended on acceptance by the very respectable people he scorned, was a fantasy. As a bohemian, he did everything he could to alienate those who might make him a success. And surely there was much about the way things worked out that appealed to him; he could continue to think of himself as a husband or father without having any of its burdens and responsibilities. From this point of view, he either knew better or was deceiving himself. The truth is that he was using the promise of commercial success as an excuse for getting out of a bourgeois marriage to become the savage he needed to become in order to realize his gifts as a painter.

It is hard to see how commercial success of his project could have redeemed his failures as a husband or parent. Even if he had been able to make enough money within a year or two of leaving Copenhagen to comfortably support his family this would not be the kind of case Williams has in mind. For one thing, Williams thinks of Gauguin as a success as a painter not as a commercial success; Williams does not think of the project of becoming a commercial success as a *ground* project. For another, Williams is not taking the position that the end justifies the means, that any gamble is worth taking if it is successful. As a gamble to support his family, Gauguin's decision to leave can be criticized on moral grounds (at the time it was made); we might say that the decision to leave was too risky. Gauguin would have been very lucky if he had been a commercial success. But that good luck would not have justified his decision to leave.

Let me pause to underscore the importance of the retrospective point of view in individuating an action. The very characterization of Gauguin's action, of what he was doing in leaving Copenhagen, depends on considerations that were not available at the time he made the decision. For Williams, the key consideration is the *success* of Gauguin's project; whereas, I have been stressing the importance of fitting his action into the pattern of self-deception that may become visible only after all his history becomes known to us.

Williams makes clear that in thinking about the person he is referring to as 'Gauguin' we are not to be 'limited by any historical facts.'[6] So, we should try to imagine that unlike the real Gauguin the one Williams has in mind left Mette not because he found living with her intolerable, but because he could not realize his gifts as an artist and continue to serve as a husband and father.

But why couldn't he realize himself as an artist while in the bosom of his family? The answer would seem to require the acceptance of the bohemian assumptions already implicit in Williams' talk of Gauguin's realizing his gifts as a painter, of his preferring to lead a life where his best painting would come, a life which will enable him really to be a painter. There is nothing bohemian about the assumption that someone's growth as a painter would be aided by his being part of an art world that included, among others, Degas, Manet, Monet, Pisarro, Cezanne and van Gogh. No doubt Copenhagen was a dreary place indeed compared to that other world. But we are not talking about where he needed to live but how he needed to live.

And the assumption needed here is that to be the artist he became he needed to live the part. But why was it necessary for him to be a savage in order for him to paint what he saw in his imagination, for example, as the Garden of Eden? Gauguin took as mistresses or *vahines* several young girls who offered themselves freely to him without expecting much in return, who had children by him without expecting anything from him as a husband or parent. Why was it necessary for him to live with these young concubines, in order for him to paint his many different versions of Eve and the Fall? These questions are rhetorical. I am not suggesting that Gauguin's art would have been the same if he had not lived as he did. But he could have gone there with his family, and he could have gone there in his imagination. In the absence of bohemian assumptions, I do not see how Williams is justified in supposing that Gauguin could realize his gifts as a painter only by abandoning his family.

How does luck enter into it? Perhaps we can better understand how Williams is thinking of Gauguin's decision if we try to answer this question. Williams sees Gauguin as engaging in a project, as Gauguin was engaged in a variety of other ventures such as selling stocks or imported tarpaulins, ventures that can be considered successes or failures on the basis of how much he sold and with what margin of profit. How is there something comparable to be found in the case of his project of becoming a painter? The one project we have discussed, that of providing for his wife and family with his art proved a dismal failure during his lifetime. But, as we have seen, that is not the project Williams has in mind, even if success seems to be such a determining factor in whether Gauguin was justified in gambling on the sale of his work after he left for Paris. Gauguin would just have taken a calculated risk; rather than continue to work under conditions he found hateful, he would have gambled that he could be a commercial success as an artist. The example is wrong because it does not incorporate the right kind of conflict between moral justification, on the one hand, and ground-project justification, on the other hand.

To understand the conflict we need to identify Gauguin's ground project and how the choice of it can be justified only retrospectively, in terms of its success or failure. Williams imagines Gauguin to leave to be a painter. What would count as success in that project (if, indeed, it can be considered a project at all)? Unless we use the very standards Gauguin himself was so conflicted about, success in the marketplace of art, *success* and *failure* are not terms that seem readily applicable to his venture.

Perhaps we are to think in terms of whether Gauguin really did want to be an artist. After all, many would-be artists have found that the bohemian lifestyle was what really attracted them. By contrast, Gauguin really did want to be a painter, even if his motivation was complicated by other desires, such as the desire to be acclaimed a great painter and to live as a savage. Williams would not count as an *external contingency* the fact that painting was a real object of Gauguin's desire; when he speaks of the success of Gauguin's project, he does not mean success in its turning out to be his project.

Success and failure are terms that do apply to some of the things Gauguin did, but none of them are the projects that Williams has in mind. Gauguin did succeed in creating the romantic image of himself that even Williams seems to have accepted as accurate, that of a highly sophisticated Frenchman who turns his back on civilization in order to realise himself as a painter. But he did not leave to create this image; and Williams makes clear that he has a different project in mind when he refers to Gauguin's leaving to pursue his art. Nevertheless, I wonder what Williams would think of a project where the agent's identity is so much a function of how others see him. By contrast, his project of living as a savage or Indian was not a success, just as his project of supporting his family with his art was not a success. Ironically, it is as a failed-savage or as a European-in-spite-of myself that his work derives much of its strength. None of these are what Williams has in mind; he is thinking only of Gauguin's realising his gifts as a painter.

Just what was Gauguin's project? Perhaps Williams thinks of it as a journey, an exploration of the artist's unconscious, his dreams and fantasies, a journey into his imagination. Is this the kind of journey that can be successful or unsuccessful? The answer would seem to depend on why the journey was being undertaken. In Gauguin's case the question doesn't make sense. He did not go on the journey to his unconscious in order to make great art; the great art was that journey. He did not first explore his unconscious and then incorporate what he discovered into his art; he explored his unconscious self in his art. Williams, as a hostage to bohemianism, might want to argue that the journey could not be carried out unless Gauguin was living his fantasies, but there would seem to be nothing to support this assumption.

But that does not matter to Williams. To make his point we have only to assume that the greatness Gauguin achieved was not possible without his becoming a savage. Whether or not this is true of the real Gauguin or explains why he left his family does not affect this point. It suffices to imagine Gauguin to act as he did because of his belief that he could not realise his gifts as an artist by continuing to live conventionally. In doing so Gauguin is taking a risk, gambling that his talents can flourish only under the conditions of bohemianism. And this explains what luck has to do with it. Whether or not he was justified in abandoning his family will depend on whether he wins his gamble.

What makes it a gamble is that Gauguin cannot know that the assumptions of bohemianism are true. He may have good reason for thinking that he has artistic talent but he is gambling that these talents can best flourish only when he no longer has any responsibilities to anyone but himself.

How will he know that his gamble paid off? We know how great an artist the real Gauguin became. But how could any artist, real or imagined, know whether he became great because he opted for living as a bohemian? The answer seems to be that he cannot know. That he succeeded does not by itself argue that he succeeded only because he turned his back on his family.

The argument for moral luck seems to be a gamble on the truth of bohemianism. We may never know whether it is right. But it might be. And isn't this all that Williams needs?

To answer this question we need to consider what the Gauguin we are imagining would be doing in leaving his family. The determination of what a real person is doing can be difficult. But this problem does not arise with someone whom we are inventing. All we have to do is say what he is doing. He is our creation. So he will be doing exactly what we say he is doing.

But it only seems easier to work with someone we have invented. The problem is that it is not enough to stipulate what he is doing; it also must be possible for us to imagine how he could be doing what he is said to be doing.

Recall what we can rule out as the artist's motivation. He is not to be leaving because his wife and family make it impossible for him to paint; otherwise the justification for his decision to leave would not depend on how things turn out. Nor is he to be leaving because he is unhappy in a conventional marriage and is using painting as an excuse for getting away from his marriage. Here too the decision to leave could be appraised at the time it was made and the artist's success would not be relevant to that appraisal.

The case we want is one where the artist does not want to leave his family. He and his wife get along well, he loves his children and wants to care for them. But he decides to abandon them because he believes that great art can be made only by not having a family. The decision is a most painful one, but in choosing to leave his family he is showing just how much painting means to him.

This artist is hard to take seriously. To see why this is so you have only to eavesdrop on the interior monologue he is conducting about his decision. "My painting is not going well. Perhaps it is because I am too happy. My wife is too supportive of my work, and I love her too much. I must make myself unhappy." He blames his lack of inspiration on his being so happy. But why? Someone as happy as he claims to be would not be so ungenerous as to blame his family for his own limitations.

He seems like the comic hero of a play, 'The Imaginary Bohemian,' satirizing the self-hatred of the bourgeoisie. The man rejects his life as husband and father not because it does not appeal to him but because it interferes with his realising his gifts as an artist. It is not hard to imagine this painter as a satirical creation. But it is hard to imagine him as a real person for whom painting is a ground project.

The moral life may frustrate the creative impulse. This is the idea we are being asked to take seriously. As luck would have it the attempt to bring to life the Gauguin who fits the requirement of Williams' philosophical position does not seem to have been successful. And perhaps there is an explanation for this failure. The idea that the moral life interferes with creativity is one in a long line of failed attempts at picturing morality as something that interferes with our doing or being what we really want to do or be.

There is another objection to how Williams sees Gauguin's dilemma. The person who chooses to carry out a ground project and then regrets having done so when the project is unsuccessful exhibits a failure of what Joan Didion refers to as 'moral nerve.'

> People with self-respect have the courage of their mistakes. They know the price of things. If they choose to commit adultery, they do not then go running, in an access of bad conscience, to receive absolution from the wronged parties; nor do they complain of the unfairness, the undeserved embarrassment of being named co-respondent. In brief, people with self-respect exhibit a certain toughness, a kind of moral nerve; they display what was once called character.[7]

What Didion says about the adulterer also applies to the Gauguin that Williams is asking us to imagine. If that Gauguin chooses to abandon his family to realise his gifts as a painter then he shows that he lacks self-respect when he regrets having made the choice because he did not succeed in realising those gifts. If he has self-respect then Gauguin accepts responsibility for the choices he makes: 'I chose to do something which would give meaning to my life,' he says. 'I knew that I risked a great deal in doing so, but I have no regrets about doing it just because it did not turn out successfully. What I wanted so badly I no longer want at all. But I regret nothing.'

What I am suggesting, following Didion, is that someone with character would not experience the kind of agent-regret so crucial to the Williams concept of moral luck. My point is not that Gauguin exhibits a lack of character by not being able to anticipate whether his project will turn out to be a success, a suggestion Judith Andre made in her paper on moral luck.[8] Rather, I am arguing that the lack of character is in the failure of moral nerve. By regretting the choice he made Gauguin would show a lack of self-respect; he would be rejecting the person who made the choice.

This completes my discussion of Gauguin and moral luck. It has led me to a discovery that I find surprising, that the very concept of moral luck is an expression of the idea that being moral is a burden or liability. Also surprising is that by emphasizing how the justification for Gauguin's choice may depend on how things turn out Williams ignores the importance of character. I am not sure how lucky I am to have made these discoveries about the assumptions behind the way Williams illustrates the concept of moral luck. But *je ne regrette rien.*

Notes

1. A letter from Gauguin to de Monfried in 1903, a month before Gauguin's death, quoted in Wayne Andersen, *Gauguin's Paradise Lost* (New York: Viking Press, 1971), p. 6.

2. Bernard Williams, "Moral Luck," [see chapter 2].

3. Williams, p. 37.

4. Williams, "Persons, Character and Morality," in *Moral Luck*, (Cambridge U. Press, 1981), p. 13.

5. Williams, "Moral Luck," p. 50.

6. Williams, "Moral Luck," p. 37.

7. Joan Didion, "On Self-respect," from *Slouching Towards Bethlehem* (New York: Farrar, Straus and Giroux), 1961, p. 145.

8. Judith Andre, "Nagel, Williams and Moral Luck" [see chapter 6].

Nagel, Williams, and Moral Luck*

Judith Andre

Bernard Williams and Thomas Nagel begin their discussions of "Moral Luck" by contrasting morality with luck.[1] Morality—at least as Kant articulates it—is the sphere of life in which, no matter what our circumstances, each of us can become worthy. Moreover, moral worth is the highest worth of all, and so there is a kind of ultimate justice in the world: each person is equally able to achieve that which matters most in life.

Nagel and Williams argue, however, that in practice we evaluate actions and agents partly on the basis of circumstances beyond the agent's control—on the basis of luck. Nagel argues that we ascribe *moral* value partly on such a basis, Williams that 'rational justification rests partly on luck. For Nagel the consequence is an incoherence within our moral conceptual scheme. Williams reaches a similar conclusion more slowly. Since rational justification is partly a matter of luck, rational justification is not synonymous with moral justification. If this is so, then our notion of rational justification is not synonymous with that of moral justification, and morality is not the unique source of value; and if not unique—he argues—not supreme. 'If the moral were really supreme, it would have to be ubiquitous: like Spinoza's substance, if it were genuinely unconditioned, there would have to be nothing to condition it' (Williams, p. 52). But this is fundamentally different from the concept of morality we (in some sense) have now: 'one thing that is particularly important about ours is how important it is taken to be' (Williams, p. 54). For Williams, when luck enters into judgments of justification, the judgment is non-moral but competitive with—and so destructive of—moral justification. For Nagel, luck does enter into moral assessment,

*From *Analysis* 43 (1983): 202–207.

although our intuitions say it should not. Each writer finds destructive inconsistency—possibly incoherence—within our concept of morality.

To these charges, two responses are possible. One is that we do not in fact justify actions as it is claimed we do, or at least *would* not if we were sufficiently reflective. A second possible response is to admit that we do justify actions partially on the basis of luck, accept the conclusion that we are not consistent Kantians, but reject the implication that our moral scheme is therefore incoherent. I shall make both of these responses here.

I will discuss first the four areas where, Nagel claims, luck partially determines 'moral' value. One is constitutive luck: 'the kind of person you are . . . your inclinations, capacities, and temperament'. Another is luck in consequences: 'luck in the way one's actions and projects turn out'. One drunken driver kills a child, but another gets home safely.

A third area is 'luck in how one is determined by antecedent circumstances'. This third area involves the classic conflict between believing we are determined and believing that we are morally responsible. So does Nagel's fourth area, which he calls 'luck in circumstance'. The person who became a Nazi prison guard might simply have been a bureaucrat, had his parents emigrated to Canada when he was young—yet we hold the guard morally responsible. This kind of example illuminates particularly well the difficulty in reconciling determinism and moral responsibility. Since we evaluate these two people differently on the basis of their different actions, we must be implicitly assuming some source of agency other than character (assumed to be identical in the two men) and circumstance (assumed to be beyond the control of either).

But compatibilism is not Nagel's primary subject. Since so much has been said on this issue already, and since Nagel does not advance that discussion, I would like to bracket the issue here.

The other areas, however—constitutive luck and luck in consequences—raise issues that can be discussed without entering the free-will-determinism debate. Take for instance the category 'luck in consequences'. Is the drunken driver who kills a child morally worse than the drunken driver who manages not to? Is successfully rescuing someone from a burning building morally better than trying unsuccessfully to rescue him? Or than accidentally harming him during the attempted rescue—perhaps by dropping him from a high ladder?

As I mentioned earlier, two kinds of response are possible. One is simply to deny the implication, to assert that these people do not differ in moral status. I'll make a more minimal claim here: the difference in moral evaluation substantially lessens upon reflection. The 'lucky' drunken driver has done something seriously wrong. Anyone who has lost a relative in an accident involving an 'unlucky' drunken driver will look with loathing upon *any* drunken driver. Reflection has the opposite effect upon our evaluations of lucky and unlucky careless drivers. If the carelessness is particularly common—taking one's eyes briefly off the road, for example—we're likely to say 'Anyone might have done that' and lighten our condemnation of the driver. In both cases, reflection at least narrows the apparent moral difference created by luck.

A variation of this response is to admit that luck does enter our moral evaluation, but to treat this as an inconsistency of which we could and should purge ourselves. Both Nagel and Williams claim that doing so would narrow the area of moral concern to the vanishing point (Williams, p. 53; Nagel, p. 66). If we were to exclude *everything* which Nagel calls luck—the kind of person one is, the circumstances which confront one, the choices one makes (if these are taken to be the result of antecedent circumstance), and the results of those choices—then Nagel and Williams are right. But in this paper I am bracketing the issue of determinism. Consistency in the remaining areas (constitutive luck and luck in consequences) would narrow but not erase the sphere of moral concern. Most people already make consistent efforts to separate moral judgment of someone from their appraisal of that person's 'constitution' (inclinations, capacities, temperament). Phrases such as 'Only God can judge her' reflect the belief that her internal intention to do the right thing—unknowable to the rest of us—is what really counts. As for luck in circumstances, it might be possible to learn to classify all careless drivers (lucky and unlucky) as morally identical.

However, a different kind of response is possible. Suppose that we do evaluate the lucky differently from the unlucky, and that we cannot (in some sense of 'cannot') change what we do. What follows from that fact? Although the remaining use of moral categories is clearly not Kantian, it does not follow that it is an inconsistent use. The word 'moral' is not nearly so precise as we sometimes feel—this is Nagel's and Williams' point—but it does not follow that the concept is internally incoherent.

The most obvious non-Kantian element in our moral scheme is the Aristotelian.[2] Part of being moral, for most of us, is being virtuous; and being virtuous involves more than doing the right thing. It involves as well the ability to see what the right thing to do is, and the *desire* to do that right thing. (Not just Kant's more abstract   desire-to-do-whatever-the-right-thing-turns-out-to-be.) Virtues, as Aristotle describes them, are possible only to those who have been reared in a moral community; a fortunate child-hood fosters adults who feel rightly as well as acting rightly. But people cannot choose their own upbringing, and emotions are not voluntary. (We do have indirect control over our emotions, as L. A. Kosman points out, but this is limited.)[3] For Aristotle it is better not to have to struggle to do the right thing. For Kant the presence or absence of inner struggle is morally irrelevant. The word 'moral' has a somewhat different sense in the two writers, but there is this in common: for both the adjective refers to an excellence of character such that the moral person is praiseworthy and emulable. He or she is a model for our children, and the kind of person which we would like our communities to foster. The Kantian concept, however, unlike the Aristotelian, is closely linked to Christian ideas of reward and punishment by an all-just, omniscient Judge. Even an atheist can ask what such a Judge *would* do; and of course the Judgment could only concern those matters over which the agent had control. Reward and punishment could not justly be allotted on the basis of upbringing or genetic endowment.

We use the concept of moral in both the Aristotelian and the Kantian sense. Many of our central concepts are hybrid: we can call someone 'evil', for instance, without imputing responsibility (for she may be criminally insane). Someone may be sadistic because of the way he was raised—but he's still sadistic, and it is not a contradiction to say this is a moral fault for which he is not to blame. Open-mindedness comes more easily to some than to others; it's still (when properly limited) a moral asset. Similar remarks could be made about selfishness, generosity, cruelty, bravery—and even about the spoiling of children. Through no fault of their own, they've been made defective. Of course our condemnation increases as the child becomes adult—blameworthiness is a specific kind of criticism which implies free choice—but selfishness and petulance in children are nevertheless character defects.

Is a moral framework which includes both Kantian and Aristotelian elements self-contradictory? It can look that way, as Nagel and Williams' examples make clear; but the appearance results from assuming that 'moral' can only have a Kantian sense, and then discovering cases where its application depends on circumstances beyond the agent's control. In its central sense, I contend, morality refers to excellence of character. Whenever we praise people as moral we mean they are worthy of praise and emulation; but only sometimes do we mean that they are worthy of reward.

Let me apply this to Nagel's 'luck in consequences'—the cases of the lucky and the unlucky bad drivers, of the successful and unsuccessful rescue attempts. Some people persistently misjudge, and in the process hurt other people. (We might call the agents 'morally accident-prone.') They are malformed in some way; something prevents them from correctly assessing the facts before they act. Impulsiveness, or heroic fantasies, or self-absorption—whatever its source, their ineffectiveness make them less than admirable, less than a model. But to the extent that its source is beyond their reach, they are neither blameworthy nor punishable. This accounts for some of the 'moral distance' between our evaluations of the drivers, too; some people know their limitations better than other people do.

Furthermore, we say that the unlucky driver is morally worse than the lucky one in part because we hold people responsible for the results of their actions. But 'responsible' has two kinds of application. One is what I've called the Christian-Kantian sense: the responsible party is subject to reward and punishment. The other sense is more prosaic: to be responsible is to have an obligation to rectify bad consequences. If I break your vase, I must replace it. I can be responsible in the second sense without being in the least blameworthy, although often the two coincide. We can also be blameworthy (for the risk we take) without in fact bringing about any bad consequences, and so without being obliged to rectify anything.

At this point one may ask, obliged on pain of what? Certainly there is moral defect if we fail to make good what we have destroyed when it is possible to make this good; furthermore, the defect is greater when the source of the damage is not just our action but our culpable action. But what about the cases where the damage cannot be repaired? Loss of life, most obviously, cannot be put right. There is at least a great sadness in having incurred a debt which one cannot meet, and therefore a feeling of inadequacy. As a result of that there is a sense of diminished worth. This is, however, distinguishable from moral fault in the sense of deserving punishment. If these considerations are right, then part of our sense of 'moral distance' between the lucky and unlucky driver is neither derived from nor inconsistent with Kantianism.

These same considerations apply, more simply and directly, to what Nagel calls 'constitutive luck'. Some people are generous, brave, and honest by inclination; others are not. The fortunate ones are so constituted by upbringing and biology. They may deserve no particular reward for what they are; but they are nevertheless worthy of admiration and imitation.

I think, then, that Nagel's claim of contradiction within our moral concepts is mistaken. What about Williams' related claim that the justification of actions (as, roughly, the right thing to have done) depends partly on luck? If that's true, he claims, then rational justification is not synonymous with moral justification, and hence moral justification is neither the unique nor the supreme source of personal value. His argument is intricate, and I will address only a few strands of it here. He describes in particular the cases of Gauguin and of Anna Karenina. Each abandoned a family in order to pursue a future good (artistic accomplishment, on the one hand; passionate love on the other). Williams claims that these undertakings turn out to have been justified only if the goal is realized. This is close to the kind of situation Nagel describes as luck in consequences, and it is open, I think, to the same analysis. First, it's at least reasonable to claim that consequences have nothing to do with our judgment of the cases. Many would simply condemn both Gauguin and Karenina; others would approve their actions. Even if, as Williams suggests, we ask whether their actions were reasonable (rather than moral) it's quite possible to assess the reasonableness of risk-taking.

Finally, however, if we suppose that Gauguin's success does affect our evaluation of his choice, we can account for that on the Aristotelian grounds mentioned earlier. The person who can correctly assess his or her chances of success is better-formed than the person who cannot.

Since considerations of luck enter without paradox into one kind of moral evaluation, they do not indicate a non-moral, competitive realm of evaluation. It is still possible to characterize the morally good life as that which should be sought, all things considered.

A final note. Not only does 'moral luck' pose considerably smaller problems than Nagel and Williams suggest, it is in fact part of our conceptual scheme which should, upon reflection, be kept rather than changed. First of all, it reminds us of moral questions different from those upon which we typically concentrate. 'What should I do in these circumstances?' is important; but 'What kind of person should I try to be, and help others to be?' is of equal importance. Secondly, 'moral luck' is sometimes illusory; we are sometimes to blame for results that at first *seem* beyond our control. We have more control over the kind of person we are than we sometimes think. I can, for instance, whittle away at the habits of self-deception which prevent me from seeing the world as it is. The 'morally accident-prone' can learn to be better; but they are unlikely to change if all our moral assessment is concentrated on intention and none on actual result.[4]

Notes

1. Thomas Nagel, 'Moral Luck' [see chapter 3]. Bernard Williams, 'Moral Luck' [see chapter 2].

2. Alasdair MacIntyre, *After Virtue* (Notre Dame: University of Notre Dame Press, 1981). Although I use the terms 'Aristotelian', 'Kantian', and 'Christian' here, I am not defending any particular historical view about the content of these traditions. Instead I use the terms roughly, as convenient labels for identifiably separate strands within our present ways of thinking.

3. L. A. Kosman, 'Being Properly Affected: Virtues and Feelings in Aristotle's Ethics,' in *Essays on Aristotle's Ethics*, Amelie Oksenberg Rorty, ed. (Los Angeles: University of California Press, 1980).

4. This paper received the 1983 Griffith Memorial Award from the Southern Society for Philosophy and Psychology, U.S.A.

7

Morality and Luck*

Henning Jensen

Thomas Nagel recognizes that it is commonly believed that people can neither be held morally responsible nor morally assessed for what is beyond their control. Yet he is convinced that although such a belief may be intuitively plausible, upon reflection we find that we do make moral assessments of persons in a large number of cases in which such assessments depend on factors not under their control.[1] Of such factors he says: 'Where a significant aspect of what someone does depends on factors beyond his control, yet we continue to treat him in that respect as an object of moral judgment, it can be called moral luck' (p. 59).

Here I offer a solution of the problems which led Nagel to frame his conception of moral luck and which concern whether our moral assessments may be determined, not just by the tendencies of actions and characters, but by their actual outcome. Nagel's conception of moral luck is based on a mistaken analysis of the relevant issues and should be discarded.

According to Nagel, the determination of our ordinary assessments by moral luck is such as to undermine, erode, or render illegitimate these assessments. Although he considers a number of ways in which moral luck determines our assessments, the main support for his contention that moral assessments are eroded by the influence of moral luck is drawn from his treatment of the topic of culpability as it relates to just one of these ways, namely, luck in the way one's projects and actions turn out. One of his examples concerns the moral assessment of a truck driver whose negligence in not maintaining his brakes in good condition contributes to the death of a child whom he runs over. That moral luck is relevant Nagel believes to be shown by the

*From *Philosophy* 59 (1984): 323–330.

fact that if the truck driver's negligence contributes to the death of the child, he will blame himself for the death, but, Nagel continues, 'he would have to blame himself only slightly for the negligence itself if no situation arose which required him to brake suddenly and violently to avoid hitting the child. Yet the *negligence* is the same in both cases, and the driver has no control over whether a child will run into his path' (p. 61). Throughout his discussion of this and other cases we find Nagel making the following claims concerning assessments of culpability: (1) these are not cases of a complete absence of all control; the agent has always made some contribution; (2) overall culpability corresponds to 'the product of mental or intentional fault and the seriousness of the outcome' (p. 63); (3) moral luck is involved because actual results beyond the agent's control influence our assessments of culpability. The foregoing account of how moral luck relates to our assessments of overall culpability is therefore quite incompatible, as Nagel himself insists, with the conception of morality which views morality as immune to luck and which is tied to the 'control condition', the idea that, Nagel's words, 'one cannot be more culpable or estimable for anything than one is for that fraction of it which is under one's control' (p. 60).

It is my contention that Nagel's conception of moral luck is based on a mistaken analysis of the relevant issues. My alternative account will provide a solution for the problems which led him to frame his conception of moral luck.

We need to begin by making some distinctions within the broad category of expressions of blame. Expressions of blame serve a large variety of purposes among which are to judge morally blameworthy, to reprimand, to reproach, to ascribe liability, and to induce shame, guilt or repentance. Within this variety I want to draw a distinction between two main purposes which may be served by expressions of blame. The first is that of judging someone morally blameworthy or deserving of blame. Such a judgment may be addressed to the person whose conduct is being assessed, it may be addressed to the world at large, or, if made by the speaker *in foro interno*, it may be addressed to no one at all. In all of these cases the primary intention of the speaker is to give an impersonal verdict applicable to anyone whose action is similar in relevant respects. A second main purpose which may be served by expressions of blame is that which is involved when an agent is not merely the 'subject of' expressions of blame, but is explicitly 'subjected to' such expressions. Whereas an agent may be judged morally blameworthy without realizing this, the appropriateness and success of expressions of blame such as reprimands, reproaches, and rebukes which 'subject' him to blame depend on his being cognizant of this.

In further clarifying the nature of these two main kinds of blaming expressions we might outline the nature of their justification. In order to judge that an agent is morally blameworthy for some act, we must be prepared to establish that he actually did the act in question and that he was at fault in acting. In most cases, the fault is ascribed to a defect of character. However, an agent may sometimes be blameworthy for an act which, though faulty, is not 'in character' in that it is not the sort of thing which he habitually does. As regards faultiness, whether of an agent or his act, the utilitarian will try to show that this heads up in tendencies to result in harmful consequences. Critics of utilitarianism will reply that, here as elsewhere, our ordinary moral consciousness includes the knowledge that certain considerations are morally relevant which are not grounded in utility. With respect to judging an agent morally blameworthy for some faulty act which he did, such critics will argue that, in addition to the harm in the form of painful states of feeling which may result from such an act, we must consider that such faulty acts may involve those injustices and wrongs which constitute injuries to mutual trust, to personal relationships, and to the very institution of morality.

We might now compare the foregoing account of the justification we give for verdictive judgments of moral blameworthiness with the account of the justification we give for our use of blaming expressions in which we subject an agent to overt blame. My account begins with the claim that the moral blameworthiness of an agent is a necessary condition for the use of blaming expressions which subject that agent to overt blame. The sufficient conditions are to be found in the prevention or alleviation of the two kinds of damage, noted earlier, which can result from faulty acts. The one concerns harmful consequences in the form of painful states of feeling; the other concerns the damage to mutual trust and personal relationships brought about by injustices and wrongs. And, it should be added, consideration of the latter kind of damage through injustices and wrongs should certainly precede our giving consideration to the former kind of harmful consequences. Alleviation of the kind of damage that occurs through injustices and wrongs is typically gained when the agent who is subjected to blame is thereby brought to a realization and acknowledgment of his fault and to a readiness to make whatever amends for it that he can. The agent is thus restored to a state of character from which, through fault, he had departed. And those affected by his faulty acts will have reason to resume their former attitudes of mutual trust and good will.

It should now be evident that the moral blameworthiness of an agent does not entitle others to subject him to overt blame. One can easily imagine a case in which a morally blameworthy person is not only contrite but extremely self-punitive, in which his act was faulty but not attributable to a character habitually faulty in this respect, and in which the situation including the faulty act is unlikely to recur. In such a case, the interests of morality might be better served by discouraging the wrongdoer from self-punitiveness and reminding him of his worth as a person than by subjecting him to blame. Indeed, anyone who subjected him to overt blame might himself be morally blameworthy for doing so. What is here at stake is the preservation of the integrity of persons and of their ability to function as moral agents. Although blaming expressions may have a restorative value for the faulty agent, they may be destructive if used excessively or inappropriately.

One further distinction is needed at this point before we can identify the kinds of blaming expressions which are such that their justification relates to actual results beyond our control. We need to distinguish between two main ways in which the control condition relates to our blaming expressions. The first concerns the kind of case in which an agent's faulty act is the cause of a harmful result but in which this result is beyond the risk created by the faulty action and hence beyond his control. In this kind of case the harm cannot be imputed to the agent because the respect in which his act was faulty was causally irrelevant to the production of the harm.[2] For example, let us take the case of a negligent truck driver who acts faultily in driving without having his brakes repaired and runs over a child. If the child darted in front of his truck in such a way that no one could have had time to apply brakes, then the respect in which his act was faulty was not causally relevant to the harm. His act was voluntary under the description of it as 'driving negligently without having had one's brakes repaired'. It was not voluntary under the description of it as 'killing a child who darts before one's truck before one could possibly apply brakes'. The harm in question was, we should say, utterly beyond his control and its occurrence can provide no ground for the kind of blaming expression which we have described as a verdictive judgment of moral blameworthiness. To suppose otherwise is to go against morality's concerns with action guiding and fairness. Further, since it was established earlier that moral blameworthiness is a necessary condition for those blaming expressions which subject an agent to blame, we may conclude that the occurrence of the kind of harm which is utterly beyond the agent's control can provide no grounds for those expressions which subject an agent to blame.

A second way in which the control condition relates to our blaming expressions concerns the kind of case in which an agent's faulty action creates a risk of harm within those possible results of his action which are causally related not only to his act but to the respect in which it is faulty. But whether one or other of these results actually occurs is beyond his control. This is of course the kind of case which is central to Nagel's example of the truck driver whose negligence contributes to the death of a child and whose 'overall culpability', Nagel claims, 'corresponds to the product of mental or intentional fault and the seriousness of the outcome' (p. 63). In this kind of case, I should maintain, the act is voluntary under the description of it as 'driving negligently without having had one's brakes repaired and, hence, creating a risk of killing someone'. It is not voluntary under the description of it as 'producing the actual result of killing someone rather than merely creating a risk of his death'. That one result, among those within the risk created by a faulty act, actually occurs rather than some other result is therefore beyond our control and would again appear to provide no grounds for moral assessment. But, Nagel retorts, we do blame more in the case of an actual harmful outcome. Therein lies the problem.

The solution to this problem and, in general, to the problems posed by Nagel's conception of moral luck requires the employment of two main distinctions which I have made and to which Nagel has given insufficient attention. These are: (1) the distinction between verdictive judgments of moral culpability or blameworthiness and blaming performances subjecting someone to blame; (2) the distinction between actual results which are in every sense beyond the control of the agent and actual results which are within the risk created by the faulty character of the agent's act, but are beyond his control in the qualified sense that, among the results within the risk, whether one result occurs rather than some other is beyond his control. In applying these distinctions, we may thus argue, *contra* Nagel, that the moral blameworthiness of a negligent truck driver who creates a risk of harm remains the same regardless of whether, through luck, his act has no harmful result. Further, Nagel's claim that we blame more in cases where faulty acts have a harmful result may now be reformulated as the claim that in some cases of this kind we not only do subject the agent to more blame, but ought to do so.

That we in fact do tend to subject him to more blame may be given a fairly straightforward explanation. That is, if actual harm occurs, the agent and others considering his act will have a painful awareness of this harm. This in turn may cause them to subject him to more blame and may cause the agent to have heightened feelings of blame and to blame himself more severely. However, that we not only do but *ought* to subject an agent to more blame is not explained by his account. Nagel of course regards this as an instance of that determination by luck which invalidates moral assessments. I want to argue, instead, that in cases in which we subject an agent to more blame when a harmful result follows from the faulty character of his act or to less blame if no such result occurs, our justification for doing so lies ultimately in a concern for the integrity of persons and their ability to function as moral agents.

How this concern relates to the justification of blaming performances subjecting agents to blame may be explained as follows. During an agent's lifetime the amount of actual harm produced by his faulty acts is likely to be much less than the harm which was potential but failed to occur. Within the compass of an agent's acts, one connection between his faulty acts and the amount of actual harm produced is provided by the character of his intentions. Acts which are negligent or even reckless are less likely to lead to harmful results than acts performed with a firm and deliberate intention to harm. Thus, at one end of the scale we find large numbers of negligent acts most of which have no harmful outcome and many of which are not even 'in character', that is, they may not be the sort of thing which the agent habitually does. At the other end of the scale, we find malicious acts which are extremely dangerous because of the likelihood of their producing harm and extremely reprehensible as indications of evil character. Now concerning the faulty acts at the end of the scale where less actual harm is produced, I want to argue that, at least in the case of agents who might be expected to subscribe to reasonable standards of care, the agent not only is but ought to be sub-jected to less overt blame for acts with no bad outcome. To subject an agent to as much blame for all of his negligent acts which have no bad outcome as for that far lesser number with a bad outcome is to require of him an unreasonably high standard of care which is likely to make him a moral perfectionist or even to destroy his ability to function as a moral personality. And it would make us all moral busybodies seizing upon all faults, regardless of out-come, as occasions for blaming performances. Not that negli-gence should be viewed with indifference. Some lesser degree of censure or punishment may no doubt be justifiable in many cases in which negligence leads to no harmful result.

The requirement that we impose a standard of care which is compatible with our concern for the capacity of persons to func-tion as moral agents serves to explain other variations in our blaming practices. Children are unlikely to have developed rea-sonable standards of care. Therefore parents, in seeking to incul-cate such standards, will be inclined to subject their children to more blame for faulty acts with no harmful result than they would impose on adults who had reasonable standards of care. Con-versely, we should be less inclined to subject persons who are known to be moral perfectionists to excessive overt blame.

At the other end of the scale, agents who perform extremely faulty acts with no harmful results will tend to be subjected to as much blame as those whose extremely faulty acts have harmful results. Initially, it might seem puzzling why cases at this end of the scale should be treated differently, but upon reflection the reasons for this will be clear. First, the extreme faultiness of the act is likely to indicate an extremely bad character and the dam-age to mutual trust and moral relationships which occurs when someone is seen to perform such an act—regardless of result—is very great. Second, as stated above, acts which are negligent or even reckless are less likely to lead to harmful results than acts performed with a deliberate resolve to harm. Thus at the lower end of the scale where faulty acts tend to have less harmful re-sults, we must not impose an unreasonably high standard of care which would render a person incapable of functioning as a moral agent. But at the other end of the scale, where extremely faulty acts tend to have very harmful results, our tendency to subject a person to as much blame for extremely faulty acts which have no harmful results as for those that do imposes no unreasonably high standard, but reflects instead our great concern for the damage to moral relationships which has nevertheless occurred as well as for the prevention of future harm. And, in such cases, our concern for the agent's moral integrity will not lead us to say that to subject the extremely evil person to as much criticism for those of his acts which have no bad outcome is to endanger his capacity to function as a moral agent, for that capacity is already very seriously impaired. It should be added that even the seriousness with which we ought to view extremely faulty acts does not impose upon us the unreasonably heavy burden of being strictly obliged to seek out every act of this sort for moral criticism.

Since Nagel believes that the notion of moral luck poses a threat to the Kantian conception of a good will that is immune to luck, it is of interest to note that the basic arguments which I have presented against Nagel's notion of moral luck are consistent with and implicit in Kant's moral theory. We are all familiar with Kant's conception of duty in the *Grundlegung* as including the requirement that, as he puts it, 'the ends of any person, who is an end in himself, must as far as possible also be my ends, if that conception of an end in itself is to have its full effect on me'.[3] But in a rather neglected passage in the *Metaphysic of Morals* Kant discusses the fact that one of my ends, which is at the same time a duty, is the 'preservation of the integrity of my morality'.[4] He goes on to argue that the removal of hindrances to morality and of those temptations which lead one to transgress one's duty therefore becomes, indirectly, a duty. Now if we combine the ideas in the above passages, it would seem to be implied that not only is it a duty for us to do whatever contributes to the preservation of the integrity of moral agents, but that it is, indirectly, a duty to remove hindrances to their integrity. Among such hindrances, I should suppose, would be the subjecting of an agent to excessive blame. It is worth noting that Kant's concern for preserving the integrity of persons adds a dimension to his theory which should help to counteract to some degree the tendency to regard him as defending an unduly harsh and rigoristic conception of duty.

We may now summarize the solution which has been provided for the problem which led Nagel to frame his conception of moral luck and which concerns how actual results beyond the agent's control are related to our moral assessments. Nagel's conception of moral luck supposes that actual results beyond the agent's control may directly determine our moral assessments of him. This, if it were the case, would indeed render moral judgments illegitimate and would run counter to morality's concerns with guiding action and with fairness. But this is not the case. My alternative account maintains that actual results beyond the agent's control do not determine our verdictive judgments of his moral blameworthiness. However, there are certain cases, such as those in which negligence is involved, in which a harmful outcome is not beyond the risk of harm created by the respect in which the act is faulty, but whether one or other of the possible results actually occurs is indeed beyond the agent's control. In such cases, actual results beyond the agent's control may, in this qualified sense, indirectly determine our subjecting the agent to more or less blame. However, this is to be attributed ultimately not just to luck, but to how subjecting an agent to blame in terms of actual results relates to a consideration which is fundamental to morality, namely, the preservation of the integrity of persons and their functioning as moral agents.

The perfectly good man will therefore be immune to luck at least in so far as he can neither be held morally blameworthy nor be justifiably subjected to blaming expressions. But none of us is perfectly good. Hence there will be certain cases which I have described in which we wil not be immune to the influence of luck in bringing us an actual outcome which renders us more vulnerable to being subjected to severer blame than we should have received had our luck been different. That this is the case appears upon reflection to be neither paradoxical nor undermining of morality. Thus it would avoid needless confusion to refer in this area to the influence of just plain luck, not moral luck.[5]

Notes

1. Thomas Nagel, "Moral Luck" [see chapter 3. Ed.] Page references in parentheses are to this article.

2. For a related analysis of the concept of fault see Joel Feinberg's article "Sua Culpa," in his *Doing and Deserving* (Princeton: Princeton University Press, 1970).

3. Immanuel Kant, *Foundations of the Metaphysics of Morals* in *Immanuel Kant: Critique of Practical Reason and Other Writings in Moral Philosophy*, Lewis White Beck (trans. and ed.) (Chicago: University of Chicago Press, 1949), 88.

4. Immanuel Kant, *The Metaphysical Principles of Virtue*, James Ellington (trans.) (Indianapolis: The Bobbs-Merrill Company, Inc., The Library of Liberal Arts, 1964), 46.

5. I am indebted to Joel Feinberg for his helpful comments concerning this paper.

8

Moral Luck*

Nicholas Rescher

Introduction

Before deliberating about specifically *moral* luck we would do well to undertake some preliminary deliberations about the nature of luck as such.

Even as "the best-laid plans of mice and men gang aft agley," so sometimes—no doubt more rarely—does the most haphazard effort yield a splendid success. Some people scheme, strive, and struggle to achieve their ends—and fail to make even a plausible start. Others have great benefits thrust into their hands fortuitously. Fortune is fickle, smiling on some and scowling at others without the least apparent rhyme or reason. Some are lucky and others unlucky. That is just how life goes.

The role of chance in human affairs was once the topic of extensive discussion and intensive debate among philosophers. In hellenistic Greece, theorists debated tirelessly about the role of *eimarmenê*, the unfathomable fate that remorselessly ruled the affairs of humans and gods alike, regardless of their wishes and actions.[1] The Church fathers struggled mightily to combat the siren appeal of the idea of *fortuna*, and Saint Augustine detested the very word *fate*.[2] The topic of good or bad fortune, along with the related issue of the extent to which we can control our own destinies in this world, was ardently controverted in classical antiquity and came to prominence again in the Renaissance. And the topic undoubtedly has a long and lively future before it, for it is certain that, as long as human life continues, luck will play a prominent part in this domain.

---

*From *American Philosophical Association Proceedings* 64 (1990): 5–20 [a revised version].

Almost invariably, luck, good or bad, powerfully affects our lives. A chance encounter at a sporting event leads X into the career that constitutes her life's work. By whim, Y decides to eat at a certain restaurant and meets the woman who is to be the love of his life—or eats the food that will lay him low with stomach poisoning. An unanticipated traffic jam leads Z to miss a flight that crashes. Luck holds us all in an iron grip. There is no getting around the fact that much of what happens to us in life—much of what we do or fail to achieve or become—is a matter not of inexorable necessity or of deliberate contrivance, but one of luck, of accident or fortune. As Pascal trenchantly put it: "You find yourself in this world only through an infinity of accidents" (*vous ne vous trouvez au monde que par une infinité de hazards*), seeing that: "Your birth is due to a marriage, or rather to a series of marriages of those who have gone before you. But these marriages were often the result of a chance meeting, of words uttered at random, of a hundred unforeseen and unintended occurrences."[3] As Pascal saw it, our very lives are a gamble. And his famous Wager argument is in fact an invitation to think about the big issue of life in this world and the next in the manner of a gambler.

One of the classical treatments of the role of luck in human affairs is the *Pocket Oracle* (*Oráculo manual y arte de prudencia*) by the Spanish moralist Balthaser de Gracián y Morales (1601–1658). First published in 1647, this book was a series of 300 pithy precepts, each accompanied by a brief commentary, setting out the guidelines of prudent action. It enjoyed a great popularity, was echoed by La Rochefoucault, and admired and translated into German by Schopenhauer.[4] Gracián's book depicted the human situation as an analogy with card games and formulated practical advice on this basis. His position in this regard stood as follows:

> In this life, fate mixes the cards as she lists, without consulting our wishes in the matter ("*Baraja como y cuando quiere la suerte,*" sec. 196).

> And we have no choice but to play the hand she deals to us. But the wise man bides his time and places his bets when conditions are favorable ("*Pero el sagaz atienda al barajar de la suerte,*" sec. 163).

He tests the waters, as it were, before getting in too deep, and if matters look inauspicious withdraws to play again another day ("*Conocer el dia aciago, que los hay. Nada saldrá bien, y aunque se varie el juego, pero no la mala suerte. A dos lances, convendrá conocerle y retirarse, advirtiendo si está de diá o no lo está,*" sec. 139).

The sagacious gambler never counts on luck's lasting and prepares for adversity amidst good fortune ("*Prevenirse en la fortuna próspera para la adversa . . . Bueno es conservar para el mal tiempo, que es la adversidad cara y falta de todo,*" sec. 113).

There are *rules* for coping with risks and the sagacious person can facilitate good fortune ("*Reglas hay de ventura, que no toda es acasos para el sabio; puede ser ayudado de la industria,*" sec. 21).

Of these rules the most important is to play well whatever hand fate may have dealt ("*La mejor treta del juego es saberse descartari: más importa la menor carta del triunfo que corre, que la mayor del que pasó,*" sec. 31).

Another cardinal rule is to know when to quit: the knowledgeable gambler never "pushes his luck" ("*Saberse dejar ganando con la fortuna es de tahúres de reputación . . . Continuada felicidad fue siempre sospechosa: más sequra es la interpolada y que tenga algo agridulce aun para la fruición: Cuanto más atropellándos las dichas, corren mayor ries go de deslizar y dar al traste con todo . . . Cánsase la fortuna de lievar a uno a cuestas tan a la larga,*" sec. 38).

Thus one crucial rule is not to deem oneself as destined for domination. To think oneself to be the ace of trumps is a fatal flaw ("*No ser malilla. Achaques es de todo lo excelente que su mucho uso viene a ser abuso,*" sec. 85).

In this way Gracián analogized the conduct of life to card play and reinterpreted the guidelines of good card sense as principles of life. Life and playing cards are both games of chance, as it were, and the precepts for effective operation in both contexts are fundamentally akin.

Gracián's perspective struck a responsive note among his fellow Spaniards. Gambling has long been a prominent facet of Spanish life. (The *Lotería National*, established by Carlos III in

1763, is the oldest surviving national lottery.) Official estimates indicate that money spent in gambling currently amounts to some 15 percent of family income, making Spain a world leader in this regard.[5] Spaniards widely view gambling not as a human weakness or vice, but as a plausible opportunity for improving one's condition. As they see it, life is precarious; in all of our doings and dealings we cannot count on things going "according to plan!" Planning, prudence, foresight, and the like can doubtless help to smooth life's path, but they are far from sufficient to assure a satisfactory outcome to our efforts. Chance, accident, and luck—fortune, in short—play a preponderant and ineliminable role in human affairs. In all of our doings and undertakings we humans give hostages to fortune. The outcome of our efforts does not lie in our control: fortune (chance, contingency, luck) almost invariably play a decisive part.[6]

Luck unquestionably deals with different people very differently. But fortunately, there are many different sorts of human goods—riches, intelligence, good looks, an amiable disposition, artistic talent, and so on. Mercifully, a person dealt a short suit in one department may well get a long suit in another: one can be unlucky at the gaming table of worldly fame and still be lucky in love. In a way, money is the most democratic of goods. In contrast to good looks or intelligence or a healthy constitution, one does not have to be born into money, but can, with fortune's aid, acquire it as one goes along.

Luck marks the deep conflict between the actual and the ideal in this world. The most needy and deserving people do not, in general, win the lottery (and if they did, there would, ironically, be no lotteries for them to enter). Luck is the shipwreck of utopias—the rogue force that prevents ideologues from leveling the playing field of life. Only before God, the just law, and the gravedigger is the condition of all alike and equal. Rationalistically minded philosophers have always felt uneasy about luck because it so clearly delimits the domain within which people have control over their lives.

One way of reading the lesson urged by skeptics from classical antiquity to the present day is as follows: that no matter how conscientiously we "play by the rules" in matters of factual inquiry, there is no categorical assurance that we will answer our questions correctly. Even in science there is an ineliminable prospect of a slip between evidence and generalization. Moreover, there can be epistemic windfalls: cases where we "play it fast and loose" as far as the rules are concerned and still get our answers right. Then too there is in the epistemic side the issue of "serendipity"—the finding of areas of our questions or solutions to our problems by pure lucky chance rather than by design, planning, contrivance, and the use of methods. In managing our information as in managing other issues in this life, luck can become a determinative factor.

Admitting that an element of unplannable unforeseeability pervades all human affairs,[7] Renaissance humanists often inclined to the optimistic view that rational endeavor can prevail against the slings and arrows of outrageous fortune. For example, Poggio Bracciolini (1380–1459), in his tracts *De miseria humanae conditionis* and *De varietate fortunae*, championed the efficacy of rational virtue: "The strength of fortune is never so great that it will not be overcome by men who are steadfast and resolute."[8] Fortune as such is no more than the product of the interaction between human reason and nature's forces—both products of God's endowment of his world. Others took a much less sanguine line. Therefore in Chapter 25 of *The Prince* (1513) Machiavelli after surveying the cruelties and haphazards of the politics of his day, set more pessimistic limits to human endeavor by assigning half of what happens in this domain to the intractable power of *fortuna*, though her rogue force might be partially tamed by prudently installed dikes and embankments.

What Is Luck?

What is luck? In characterizing a certain development as lucky for someone, we preeminently stake two claims:

1. That as far as the affected person is concerned, the outcome came about "by accident." (We would not claim that it was lucky for someone that his morning post was delivered to his house—unless, say, that virtually all of the mail was destroyed in some catastrophe with some item of urgent importance for him as one of a few chance survivors.)
2. That the outcome at issue has a significantly evaluative status in representing a good or bad result, a benefit or loss. (If X wins the lottery, that is good luck; if Z is struck by a falling meteorite, that is bad luck; but a chance event that is indifferent—say someone's being momentarily shaded by a passing cloud—is no matter of luck, one way or the other.)

Accordingly, the operation of luck hinges on outcomes on what happens by accident rather than by design. Luck requires that the favorable outcome in view results not by planning or foresight but "by chance"—by causes impenetrable to us, or as the 1613 *Lexicon Philosophicum* of Goclenius put it, "not by the industry, insight, or sagacity of man, but by some other, altogether hidden cause" (*non ab hominis industria et acumine iudicioque dependens, sed a causa alia occulta*). Luck is a matter of our condition being affected, be it for good or ill, by developments that are neither intended nor foreseen, but lie substantially outside the domain of our control. However note that happy or unhappy developments can remain a matter of luck from the recipient's point of view even if its eventuation is the result of a deliberate contrivance by others. (Your secret benefactor's sending you that big check represents a stroke of good luck for *you* even if it is something that *he* has been planning for years.)

Luck fares rather mixedly in European languages. Greek *tuchê* is too much on the side of haphazard. In Latin, *fortuna* comes close to its meaning, with the right mixture of chance (*casus*) and benefit (be it positive or negative). But German has the misfortune that *Glück* means not only luck (*fortuna*) but also *happiness* (*felicitas*). The French *chance* (from the Latin *cadere* reflecting "how the dice fall") is a close equivalent of luck, however. And the Spanish *suerte* is also right on target. On the other side of the coin, several languages have a convenient one-word expression for specifically bad luck (French *malchance*, German *Pech*)—considering the nature of things, a most useful resource, which English unaccountably lacks. (Despite its promising etymology, *misfortune* is not quite the same, because it embraces any sort of mishap, not merely those due to accident but also those due to one's own folly or to the malignity of others.)

Often—in lotteries, in marrying an heiress, or in escaping unscathed from an explosion thanks to the shielding of somebody else's body—one person's good luck can be attained at the cost of another's ill.[9] But good luck can also be victimless. If by some lucky stroke the world escapes an apocalyptic epidemic—or a nuclear war—everyone is lucky without any price paid by some unfortunates.

The core of the concept of luck is the idea of things going well or ill for us due to conditions and circumstances that lie wholly beyond our cognitive or manipulative control. Luck pivots on incapacity. In the affairs of an omniscient being who *knows* all outcomes or an omnipotent being that *controls* all outcomes, there is no scope for luck. (God is exempt from the operation of luck.)

A physical system is said to be chaotic when its processes are such that minute differences in an initial state can engender great differences in the result, with diminutive local variations amplifying into substantial differences in eventual outcomes. (The weather is a fairly good example.) This sort of situation is pervasive in human affairs. Very small differences in how we act or react to what occurs about us can make an enormous difference in the result. A tiny muscle spasm can lead us to grasp and breathe in the germ that kills. The slightest change in timing can make the difference between buying a winning or a losing ticket in a lottery. Chaos (in this somewhat technical sense) pervades our human affairs and means that "luck"—that is, the impetus of *chance* on matters of human weal and woe—is destined to play a major role in our affairs.

Yet luck inheres even more prominently in cognitive than in physical limitations. Even in a causally (or, for that matter, theologically) deterministic world, we can appropriately characterize as happening "by chance" *from our human point of view* those eventuations whose embedding in the world's causal (or rational) structure lies altogether beneath the threshold of any observations and discriminations that we could possibly manage to make. For then their rationalization (however real) could play no possible part in our deliberations and determinations. Accordingly, ontological determinism notwithstanding, such eventuations would figure in our thinking as matters of fortuitous chance. Their results are matters of "luck" *for us*, because (by hypothesis) no planning or foresight on our part can play even the slightest determinative role in the matter.

Can Luck Be Managed?

This aspect of incapacity is crucial. For one must avoid the tempting but catastrophic mistake of considering luck a harnessable force or agency in nature—or a power or talent of some sort that people can manage or manipulate.

The idea that luck is a somehow personified power or agency whose services can be enlisted and whose favor can be cultivated or lost is an ancient belief, reflected in classical antiquity by the conception of the goddess Fortuna (Greek Tuchê), often depicted on ancient coins as the bestower of prosperity, equipped with a cornucopia. Philosophers (especially Cicero) and theologians (especially the Church fathers) eloquently inveighed against this superstition—generally in vain. To be sure, the diffusion of Christian belief in an all-powerful deity countervailed against a mystical belief in luck. And post-Cartesian philosophy, with its increasing faith in scientific reason, reinforced this tendency among thinking people. Nonetheless, as with other ancient superstitions such as astrology, the practice of seeking to win her favor by giving homage to "lady luck" has never been altogether extinguished.

The belief in an unlucky day (Friday the 13th),[10] a luck-producing object (a rabbit's foot), or a luck-controlling force (one's lucky star), turns on the idea that luck is something that can be promoted or influenced. But all this is mere superstition. It withdraws luck from the domain to which it belongs—that of uncontrollable chance or circumstance—and domesticates it to the more familiar and comfortable realm of the regular and manageable. But alas, if luck could be manipulated, then it would cease to be what it *ex hypothesi* is; namely, *luck*. If luck could be managed, we would not have the proverb, "You can't beat a fool for luck."

Though (virtually by definition) we cannot control or manipulate the chance element in human affairs, we have certainly come to *understand* it better and thus to accommodate ourselves to it more effectively. The bachelor male who moves from a job in a factory that employs only men into an office heavily staffed with unmarried women thereby obviously improves his chances of finding a wife and thus securing domestic bliss—or its opposite. The person who buys a lottery ticket at least creates the opportunity to win; one who does not has no chance. Luck is not a force or agency that we can manipulate by way of bribery or propitiation. But it is something we can control within limits, by modifying the way we expose ourselves to it.

There is certainly little, if any, point in "cursing one's luck" when ill fortune befalls us. There is no sensible alternative to acknowledging the futility and wastefulness of rage and resentment—as opposed to a constructive determination to work to shape a world where the likelihood of misfortunes and disasters is diminished. The workings of luck are beyond our reach; whether we will be lucky or unlucky is something over which—virtually by definition—we can have no control. But the scope or room for luck is something we can indeed influence. The student who works hard does not rely on luck to pass the examination. The traveler who maps the journey out in advance does not rely on luck to produce a helpful and knowledgeable person to show the way. Foresight, sensible precautions, preparation, and hard work can all reduce the extent to which we require luck for the attainment of our objectives. We can never eliminate the power of luck in our affairs—human life is unavoidably overshadowed by the threat of chaos. But we certainly can act to enlarge or diminish the extent of our reliance on luck in the pursuit of desired ends. There is everything to be said for striving to bend one's efforts into constructive lines and then—win, lose, or draw—to take rational satisfaction in this very fact of having done all one could. (Admittedly, there will be circumstances when this is pretty cold comfort—as when one finds oneself on a tumbril headed for the guillotine. But that is just life!)

What is regrettable about the superstitious management of luck—keeping track of one's unlucky days, carrying a rabbit's foot, thanking one's lucky stars, planning by odd numbers, and all the rest—is that it is counterproductive. It diverts time, energy, and effort away from the kind of effective planning and working that has some real chance of improving one's lot. For to some extent, a wise person is indeed in a position to manipulate luck—not via occult procedures but by thoughtful planning and sensible action.

In various contexts, the prudent person can pick and choose the risks that are incurred. There are, above all, three ways in which we can influence the element of luck in our lives:

1. *Risk avoidance.* People who do not court danger (who do not try to cross the busy roadway with closed eyes) need not count on luck to pull them through.
2. *Insurance.* People who take care to make proper provisions against unforeseeable difficulties by way of insurance, hedging, or the like need not rely on luck alone as a safeguard against disaster.
3. *Probabilistic calculation.* People who try to keep the odds on their side, who manage their risks with reference to determinable probabilities, can thereby diminish the extent to which they become hostages to fortune.

Note, however, that in the main these represent means for guarding against bad luck and its consequences. The prospects we have for courting good luck are fewer, though there are indeed things we can do to put ourselves in its way. (Only by buying a ticket for the lottery can we possibly win it; by improving our qualifications we can increase the chances of securing a good job.) But the fact remains that, in this real world of ours, good luck can be managed only within the most narrow of limits.

To be sure, in one important regard a "superstitious" feeling that luck is "on one's side" in one's present endeavors can make a difference. This has no bearing—obviously—when one is involved in a position of pure chance (like playing the horses), but such a presentiment can certainly influence outcomes in circumstances where one's mental attitude counts because a feeling of confidence can affect performance. When a sales representative is dealing with "a difficult customer" or a tennis player with a "tough opponent," the feeling that today is one's lucky day—that on this occasion success will come one's way even "against the odds"—can make a real difference for one's prospects. But, of course, this is less a matter of actual luck than of psychology.

We Americans are imbued with the can-do spirit. The attitude of fatalistic resignation is alien to us. We enthusiastically agree with the old Roman (Plautus) who said that sagacious people make their own luck or fortune ("*Sapientis ipse fingit fortunam sibi*"). And the fact that this is unquestionably an unrealistic *assertion* does not prevent it from being a sensible *attitude.* For when we toil in the way of our cognitive deficiencies we generally cannot be certain what will happen if we really make the effort and try. And so by making these confident efforts we increase the prospects of producing excellent though otherwise unexpectable results.

People can, accordingly, come to grips with luck in some promising ways. Perhaps most important, they can do this by taking sensible measures to shield themselves against the consequences of bad luck. Be it in lotteries or in business, in romance or in warfare, one can manage one's affairs so as to reduce reliance on luck alone to yield a favorable issue. For example, only the commander who maintains a strategic reserve is in a good position to take advantage of an unexpectedly created opportunity. Napoleon's well-known tendency to entrust commands to marshals whose records showed them to have "luck on their side" did not (in all probability) so much betoken superstition as a sensible inclination to favor those who had a demonstrated record for the sagacious management of risks in warfare. Chance favors the prepared—those who are so situated as to be in a position to seize opportunities created by chance.[11] Those on the lookout for unanticipated openings can best take full advantage of them when they occur.

Nevertheless it is necessary and important to bear in mind that one cannot rationally manage and manipulate particular, genuinely stochastic outcomes, for that would be a contradiction in terms: if they were responsive to causal manipulation, those eventuations would not really be matters of chance at all. The idea of the rational management of chance eventuations is an absurdity—which does not alter the circumstance that the rational management of the *opportunities* that chance may bring our way is a very real talent.

The issue of the extent to which society should make up for the vagaries of luck in their impact on the fortunes of its members is an interesting question of social philosophy.[12] One widely respected ethicist tells us that in the just social order bad luck will be redressed in various regards "since inequalities of truth and natural endowment are undeserved, these inequalities are to be somehow compensated for."[13] Presumably this would be done by improvising the lot of the unfortunates rather than by leveling everyone else down to their condition. If so, clearly, being born in the right place and time—in a society willing and able to afford this vast compensatory project—would itself be a massive stroke of luck. But should we even try somehow to compensate people for their unasked for deficiencies in intelligence, talent, good looks, ambition, and "drive," or for their psychological hardships, medical disabilities, or difficult children? Even raising these questions brings a smile, because the list is in principle unending. Luck's complexity and scope in human existence is too large for manipulability. There is simply no way of leveling the playing field of life. Indeed, efforts in this direction are in good measure inherently self-defeating. In trying to compensate people for ill luck, we would surely create more scope for luck's operation. For whatever forms of compensation we adopted—money, increased privileges, special opportunities—are bound to be such that some people are in a better position to profit by them than others, so that luck expelled by the front door simply reenters by the back. Moreover, it is by no means clear that everyone would welcome such compensation. Many of us would look joylessly on the agents of the Commissariat of Equalization coming to inform us of our awards for having an obnoxious personality or—to take a more philosophical example—for being egregiously devoid of common sense.

Although social utopians would fain compensate for bad luck in this world, philosophers—characteristically less sanguine—have generally looked elsewhere for compensation: to the next world with the Church fathers, the unending long run with Leibniz, or the noumenal order with Kant. Throughout, recourse to a transcendental order betokens a sober recognition in the unavoidable role of luck in this world's scheme of things.

Bismarck said that God so arranged matters that fortune favors children, fools, and the United States of America. But of all the world's people, it is perhaps those of Spain who rely most heavily on luck. As we saw earlier[14], gambling has long been a prominent facet of Spanish life, perceived not as any weakness or vice but as a reasonable tactic for improving one's condition.

Can One Have Moral Luck?

To all appearances, luck comes to bear not only on the factual issue of what happens to us in life, but also upon normative issues of moral appraisal.[15] For one thing, insofar as the moral status of an action depends on its consequences, these can often be ruled by matters of mere accident. (For example, it may be a matter of pure chance whether someone eats a poisoned apple put maliciously under a tree.) For another, whether or not a malign individual (a vandal, say, or an embezzler) is able to practice this vice, will depend on the existence of opportunities, which can also be a matter of pure chance.

The impact of luck on moral issues occurs particularly at three levels. First off, there is that of particular actions.

Particular Actions. Consider the case of the lucky villain who burgles the house of his grandfather, whom he knows to be absent on a long journey. Unbeknownst to him, however, the old gentleman has meanwhile died and made him his heir. The property he "steals" is therefore his own—legalistically speaking, he has in fact done nothing improper: a benign fate has averted the wrong his actions might otherwise have committed. In his soul or mind—in his intentions—he is a wicked thief, but in actual fact he is quite guiltless of wrongdoing under the postulatedly accurate description of his act as one of "taking something that belongs to oneself."

By contrast, consider the plight of the hapless benefactor. To do a friend a favor, he undertook to keep her car for her during an absence on a long journey. At around the expected time, the car is reclaimed by the friend's scheming identical twin—of whose existence our good-natured helper had no inkling. With all the goodwill in the world he has, by a bizarre act of unhappy fate, committed the misdeed of giving one person's entrusted property over to another. In intention he is as pure as the driven snow, but in actual fact he has fallen into wrongdoing.

Such cases illustrate how particular actions of a certain moral orientation can misfire because of the intervention of fortuitous circumstances. In fact, considerations of exactly this sort lead Kant to put such moral accidents on the agenda of ethical theorizing. For him, they furnish decisive indications that consequentialism will not do—that we must assess the moral status of actions on the basis not of their actual *consequences* but largely on the basis of their *intentions*. As Kant sees it, *moral* status and stature are wholly determined by what one wittingly tries to do and not by one's success, by actual performance. And there is much to be said for this view. But things can also be said against it. This becomes clear when we turn to the next item.

Courses of Action. Consider the case of the night watchman of a bank who abandons his post to go to the aid of a child being savagely attacked by a couple of men. If the incident is "for real," we see the night watchman as a hero. However, if the incident is a diversion stage-managed as part of a robbery, we see the night watchman as an irresponsible dupe. And yet from *his* point of view there is no visible difference between the two cases. How the situation turns out for him is simply a matter of luck.

In this way various courses of action acquire an appraisal status depending largely or wholly on how matters turn out— whether this is something that lies largely or wholly outside the agent's sphere of control. Human life is paved with such pitfalls. This seems to underscore the Kantian position.

But does it actually do so? To clarify the matter further, let us now shift attention from action to character and consider moral qualities.

Moral Qualities. Character traits—moral ones included— are dispositional in nature, relating to how people *would* act in certain circumstances. For example, candor and generosity represent morally positive dispositions, dishonesty and distrust negative ones.

But note that a person can be saved from the actual consequences of malign dispositions by lack of opportunity. In a society of adults—in a mining camp, say, or on an oil rig—the child molester has no opportunity to ply this vice. Again, the very model of dishonesty can cheat no one when, Robinson Crusoe-like, he lives shipwrecked on an uninhabited island—at any rate until the arrival of the man Friday.

Perhaps all of us are to some extent in this sort of position— are moral villains spared through lack of opportunity alone from discovering our breaking point, learning our price. As Schopenhauer somewhere observed, the Lord's Prayer's petition, "Lead us not into temptation," could be regarded as a plea for matters so to arrange themselves that we need never discover the sorts of people we really are.

But what, then, of the moral position of the individual who is venial by disposition and inclination, but has the good fortune to be able to stay on the good side of morality because the opportunity for malfeasance never comes his or her way? As one recent discussant insists, "if the situation never arises, he will never have the chance to distinguish or disgrace himself in this way, and his moral record will be different."[16] But then, must morality not let such a blackguard off the hook, seeing that the issue of opportunity lies beyond the agent's control and: "It seems *irrational* to take or dispense credit or blame for matters over which a person has no control . . ."[17] Plausible though this may sound, it gets the matter wrong. The difference between the would-be thief who lacks opportunity and his cousin who gets and seizes it is not one of moral condition (which, by hypothesis, is the same on both sides); their moral *record* may differ, but their moral *standing* does not. From the vantage point of one who "sees all, knows all" through a vision that penetrates into a person's depths, the moral status of the two individuals would be the same. The morally lucky culprit is lucky not in that his or her moral condition is superior, but simply because he or she is not unmatched. Lacking the occasion to act, one cannot be found out. We frail and vulnerable humans may indeed be lucky in enjoying a destiny that does not involve having one's weaknesses exposed, one's limits tested, one's vices exhibited. But the luck involved relates not to our moral condition but only to our image: it relates not to what we are but to how people (ourselves included) will regard us. The difference at issue is not moral but merely epistemic. (With the merely would-be wrongdoer who lacks opportunity we cannot, of course, deplore the *act*, which never occurred, but we can and must, by hypothesis, deplore the moral condition of the individual.)[18]

From the moral point of view, how people think and how they are decided and determined to act counts every bit as much as what they actually manage to do. The person who is prevented by lack of opportunity and occasion alone from displaying cupidity and greed still remains at heart an avarious person and (as such) merits the condemnation of those right-thinking people who are in a position actually to know this to be so—if such there are. Morality encompasses more than action: it is a matter of inner condition of which actual action is the overt expression.

This helps to explain why it is that, although the coward can excuse himself by pleading his nature, his naturally timorous disposition, the immoralist cannot comparably plead her natural inclinations and tendencies, and expect her innate cupidity, avarice, lecherousness, or the like to get her off the moral hook. For in such a case it is exactly her disposition that condemns her. (The fact that she did not come by her disposition by choice is immaterial; dispositions just are not the sort of thing that comes up for selective choice.)

After all, it makes no sense to say things like, "Wasn't it just a matter of luck for X to have been born an honest (trustworthy, etc.) person, and for Y to have been born mendacious (avaricious, etc.)?" For it is just exactly those dispositions, character traits, and inclinations that constitute these individuals as the people they are. One cannot meaningfully be said to be lucky in regard to who one is, but only with respect to what happens to one. Identity must precede luck. It makes no sense to envision a prior featureless precursor who then has the good (or bad) luck to be fitted out with one particular group of character traits rather than another. In person theory as in substance theory there is no appropriate place for bare particulars that, having a priori a nondescript (propertyless) prospect identity, can then be filled out with properties a posteriori.

People's moral attributes do not come to them by luck but emerge from them on nature as free individual agents. Holding people responsible for their moral character (rather than seeing this as something added fortuitously *ab extra*) is an inherent part of the fundamental moral presumption involving treating a person as a person. To see this as an extraneous adulation that may or may not come one's way by luck is simply to cease to treat people as people.

The moral status of people as agents is a matter of the "interior" dimension (their intentions and inclinations); it is in significant measure a matter of how "they would act if." And here, to be sure, we have no choice—given the difficulties of epistemic access—to forming our judgments of people on the basis of what we observe them to say and do. But all that is mere *evidence* when the moral appraisal of human agency is at issue. The "morally lucky" villain is not *morally* lucky (by hypothesis, he is a villain); he is lucky only in that his reprehensible nature is not *disclosed.* The difference is not moral but epistemic; it is a matter of not being found out, of "getting away with it." It is precisely because both one's *opportunities* for morally relevant action and (unfortunately for utilitarianism) the *actual consequences* of one's acts lie beyond one's own control that they are not determinants of one's position in the eyes of morality.

Of course, the point cuts both ways. The virtuous person can be preempted from any manifestation of virtue by uncooperative circumstance. Here is the moral heroine primed for benign self-sacrifice, prepared at any moment to leap into the raging flood to save the drowning child. But fate has cast her into an arid and remote oasis, as devoid of drowning children as Don Quixote's Spain was lacking in damsels in distress. To be sure, we would be unlikely to *recognize* this heroism in either sense of the term. On the one hand, we would be unlikely to *learn* of it. And on the other, we would, even if evidence did come our way, be ill advised to *reward* it in the absence of circumstances that brought it into actual operation. (For one thing, we would not be confident that it is actually strong enough not to break under the pressure of an actual need for its manifestation.)

But what then of one's inclinations, disposition, and character? Are not these too issues outside our control? This issue must be faced, though here with telegraphic brevity. The salient point is that, even after all the needed complications and qualifications are made, the fact remains that these personality features are not merely things regarding which we happen to "have no choice"—they are by their very nature things to which the idea of choice does not apply. Putting these factors outside morality's reprobation with the standard excuse that the agent "has no control" over them involves a category mistake because the whole control issue is irrelevant here from the angle of moral concern—seeing that, although in some (morally irrelevant) sense one's inclinations, disposition, and character merely fail to be "matters within one's *control*," these factors are not things that lie outside oneself but, on the contrary, are a crucial part of what constitutes one's self as such.

The role of luck in human affairs has the consequence that the lives we actually lead, including all the actions we actually perform, need not in fact reflect the sorts of persons we really are. In the moral domain, as elsewhere, luck can obtrude in such a way that—be it for good or for bad—people simply do not get the sort of fate they deserve. And this specifically includes our moral fate too—for good or ill we may never be afforded the opportunity of revealing our true moral colors to the world at large.

What does all this mean? Does it mean (as Kant thought) that morality is not of this world—that moral appraisal requires making reference to an inaccessible noumenal order that stands wholly outside this empirical sphere of ours? Surely not!

Most recent discussions of "moral luck" fail to appreciate that the opportunity-deprived immoralist's good luck appertains not to her *moral status* but merely to her *reputation.* The prime consideration from the moral point of view are things not apparent to the naked eye: character, disposition, and intention. The moral significance of acts lies in their serving as evidence in this regard. And the moral bearing of luck enters in because its operation can deflect the evidential linkage by disrupting the normal, standard import of actions.

We must form our moral judgments not on the basis of what happens *transcendentally* in an inaccessible noumenal order, but rather on the basis of that most prosaic of all suppositions; namely, that things happen as they *generally and ordinarily* do, that matters take the sort of course that it is only plausible to expect.

Moral evaluation as we actually practice it generally reflects the *ordinary* course of things. *Ordinarily,* breaking and entering is a wicked thing to do. *Ordinarily,* leaving one's post to help someone in need is a good thing. *Ordinarily,* driving drunk increases the chance of harm to others. *Ordinarily,* mendacious people cause pain when they scatter lies about them. *Ordinarily,*

people ultimately get to manifest their true colors. Moral appraisals are *standardized* in being geared to the situation of the ordinary common run of things. Admittedly luck, be it good or bad,
can intrude in such a way as to prevent matters from running in
the tracks of ordinariness. And then things go wrong. Moral acts
that normally lead to the good can issue in misfortune. But that
is just "tough luck." It does not—or should not—affect the issue
of moral appraisal.

People who drive their cars home from an office party in a
thoroughly intoxicated condition, indifferent to the danger to
themselves and heedless of the risks they are creating for others,
are equally guilty in the eyes of *morality* (as opposed to *legality*)
whether they kill someone along the way or not. Their transgres-
sion lies in the very fact of their playing Russian roulette with the
lives of others. Whether they actually kill someone is simply a
matter of luck, of accident and sheer statistical haphazard. But
the moral negativity is much the same one way or the other—even
as the moral positivity is much the same one way or the other for
the person who bravely plunges into the water in an attempt to
save a drowning child. Regardless of outcome, the fact remains
that, in the ordinary course of things, careless driving puts
people's lives at risk unnecessarily and rescue attempts improve
their chances of survival. What matters for morality is the ordinary tendency of actions rather than their actual results under
unforeseeable circumstances in particular cases.

One recent writer flatly denies this (after all, some philosophers will deny anything!). He writes: "Whether we succeed or fail
in what we try to do [in well-intentioned action] always depends to
some extent on factors beyond our control. This is true of . . . almost any morally important act. What . . . [is accomplished] and
what is morally judged is partly determined by external factors.
However jewel-like the good will may be in its own right, there is
a morally significant difference between actually rescuing someone from a burning building and dropping him from a twelfth
story window while trying to rescue him."[19] The difference our au-
thor speaks of is indeed there. But only because of a lack of spec-
ificity in describing the case. Preeminently, we need to know *why*
it was that our rescuer dropped the victim? Was it from carelessness or incompetence or a sudden flash of malice? Or was it because despite all due care on his part, Kant's "unfortunate fate"
intervened and a burnt-out timber gave way under his feet.[20] If
so, then Kant's assessment surely prevails. Where a moral agent's

success or failure is differentiated only and solely by matters of pure luck, then there is patently no reason for making different *moral* appraisals one way or the other. To say this is not of course to say that we may not want to differentiate such situations on *nonmoral* grounds; for example, to reward only *successful* rescues or to punish only *realized* transgressions as a matter of social policy *pour encourager les autres.*

It is imperative in this regard to contemplate Bernard Williams's example of the person who abandons a life of service to others to pursue his art, a decision whose moral justification (according to Williams) will ultimately hinge on how good an artist he turns out to be, which largely depends not on effort but on talent and creative vision, issues at the mercy of nature's allocation over which he has no control.[21] But what earthly reason is there for seeing the *moral* situation of the talented Gaughin as being in this regard different from that of the incompetent Ignaz Birnenkopf and to excuse the former where we would condemn the latter? The impropriety of an abandonment of a moral obligation is not negated by the successes it facilitates on other fronts. Kant's point that the talented and untalented, the lucky and the unlucky should stand equal before the tribunal of morality is well taken, and Hegel's idea that great men stand above and outside the standards of morality has little plausibility from "the moral point of view."

The Kantian idea goes straight back to the Greek tradition. Greek moralists were generally attracted to the following line: how *happy* we are will in general be a matter of accident, is chancy business; pleasure is bound to depend on chance and fortune, on the fortuitous opportunities that luck places at our disposal. If fate treats one adversely enough, then one may simply be unable to realize the condition of affective happiness (as counterdistinguished from rational satisfaction). Chance plays a predominant role here—circumstances beyond one's control can be decisive. But our virtue is something that lies within our own control and thus reflects our real nature. And this holds quite in general for the achievement of well being along the lines of the Greek *eudaimonia.* One is entitled to take rational satisfaction in a life lived under the guidance of sound values irrespective of how circumstances eventuate in point of happiness. One's affective *happiness* lies in the hands of the gods, but one's moral *goodness* is something that lies in one's own power. Moral appraisal is a nature for the guidance of life. Its rules and principles are—and have to be—geared to the realities of this world, to the normal (standard, typical) course of things. Rational evaluation is a matter of rules and principles, and in the moral case they have to be attuned to the structural, normal course of things.

Here Kant is surely right in following the lead of the Greeks. Morality as such is impervious to luck: no matter how things eventuate, the goodness of the good act and the good person (and the badness of the bad act and the bad person) stands secure from the vagaries of outcomes. But Kant's *analysis* of this situation went wrong. If morality prescinds from luck, this is not because morality contemplates the *ideal* situation of a *noumenal* sphere, but because morality contemplates the *normal* situation of the *ordinary course of things* in this mundane sphere of our quotidian experience, a course from which the *actual* sequence of events can and often does depart.

There is, to be sure, some good reason for viewing the failed and the successful rescue in different lights. For, by hypothesis, we know that the person who brings it off successfully has actually persevered to the end, whereas the person whose efforts were aborted by a mishap might possibly have abandoned them before completion for discreditable motives such as fecklessness, folly, or fear. We recognize, after all, that an element of uncertainty pervades all human activities and an uncharacteristic flash of inconstancy might possibly deflect someone in process of performing a worthy act. But if we did somehow know for certain—as in real life we never do—that, but for circumstances beyond one's control, the agent would indeed have accomplished the rescue, then we will have no basis for denying moral credit. Our reluctance to award full credit has its grounding in considerations that are merely epistemic and not moral. I submit that in this regard Kant's perception was quite right.

Thus consider a somewhat variant case—that of the brave woman who leaps into the raging waters (or the flaming inferno) to save a trapped child. Only after the fact does she learn that it was her own. Had she known it all the time, she would indeed have gotten full marks for motherly solicitude, because under the circumstances we would have to presume that this, rather than disinterested humanitarianism, provided the motive. But once we establish that she had no way of realizing this at the time, we have to award her full moral credit.

To be sure, with a little novelistic imagination we can all envision bizarre circumstances in which the exercise of the standard virtues (truth telling, kindness) repeatedly produces disastrous effects. But their status as virtues is geared to the standard course of things—how matters *standardly* and *ordinarily* go in their actual world. Because morality is geared to the world's ordinary course of things, heroic action is not a demand of morality but a matter of supererogation. (And this, of course, is the Achilles heel of Kant's analysis.)

The salient point is that the person who defaults on a valid obligation in pursuit of a greater good has to be judged by the nature of the action irrespective of ultimate consequences. In giving the money you entrusted to me to any needy cousin, the negative moral status of my action is not affected by whether this actually manages to save the person's life.

It is in fact not difficult to construct examples that illustrate the advantages of the present normalcy-oriented approach as compared with Kant's noumenal perspective. Consider the case of Simon Simple, a well intentioned but extremely foolish lad. Thinking to cure Grandmother's painful arthritis, Simon bakes her for 20 minutes at 400° Fahrenheit in the large family oven. He labors under the idiotic impression that prolonged exposure to high temperatures is not only not harmful to people but actually helpful in various ways—curing arthritis among them. His *intentions* are nothing other than good. Yet few sensible moralists would give Simon a gold star. For he should know what any ordinary person knows: that broiling people medium well by prolonged exposure to temperatures of 400° is bad for them. We base our moral judgment on the ground rules of the ordinary case, and Simon's good intentions simply do not get him off the hook here. (That is just another aspect of his bad luck.)

The artist who abandons his family to follow his guiding star, the father who sacrifices his child to the demands of his god, the statesman who breaks his word to his associates for the national good do not "violate pedestrian morality in the name of a higher *moral* good"—they allow extramoral objectives to override moral considerations. We may or may not decide to excuse them in so acting, on the basis of "everything considered" deliberations. We may, in the end, conclude that they acted "rationally" (i.e., for good and sufficient reasons). But we must not deceive ourselves into thinking that they acted morally after all—that their moral status as such is somehow safeguarded by their luck in realizing larger objectives of some sort.

The person who defaults on a valid moral commitment (a promise, say, or an obligation of some sort) is not excused by a fortunate issue of this fault. A transgressor whose unforeseeable consequence turn out to have a fortunate issue for those concerned (a *felix culpa*) is still a transgressor. And the same holds for the morally virtuous act gone awry through the intervention of an unbound fate. Insofar as moral assessment is consequentialistic, it is geared to the normal, standard, foreseeable consequence that we have to look and not to the fortuitous issue of the individual case.

What has been said here about the relationship of luck to morality holds for the relationship between luck and practical rationality as well. Even if performing a certain action is in fact conducive to realizing your appropriate ends (if, say, ingesting yonder chemical substance will actually cure your illness), it is nevertheless *not* rational so to act if you have no knowledge of this circumstance (and all the more so if such information as he has points the other way). Even when we happen by luck or chance to do what is, under the circumstances, the best thing to do, we have *not* acted rationally if we have proceeded without having any good reason to think that our actions would prove appropriate—let alone if we had good reason to think that they would be inappropriate. The agent who has no good reason to think that what she does conduces to her appropriate ends is not acting rationally. And this deficiency is not redeemed by unmerited good fortune, by luck's having it that things turn out all right. Rationality in action is not a matter of acting *successfully* toward our ends, but one of acting *intelligently*, and given the role of chance in the world's events, these are not necessarily the same.

For the moral point of view, the crucial thing is to earn an E for effort. Whether our circumstances are straightened or easy, whether our childhood is protected or brutalized, whether our chances in life are many or few—all this is not a matter of our own choosing but lies "in the lap of the gods." But what matters from the angle of morality is what we make of the opportunities at our disposal, such as they are, however meager. Of these to whom little is given, little can be expected, and of those to whom much is given, much. Our horizons for moral action may be narrow or wide—that depends on the visissitudes of facts. For the moral point of view, however, it is—to reemphasize—effort that counts. Those who confront a steep slope cannot be expected to make heading comparable to that of those who find an easy path before them. Situations and circumstances are realities of luck, but the rational evaluation of moral blame or credit is of course designed to take this into account.

In sum, although the role of luck may be decisive for the *consequences* of our actions, it is not so for their evaluative status, be it rational or moral.

Do People Deserve Luck?

Can someone have deserved or undeserved good luck? Of course. Good luck often comes to the unworthy; ill luck, to those who deserve better. But if genuine *luck* is at issue (with its admixture of real fortuitous chance), then it would always be a mere superstition to contemplate the matter in retributively causal terms—to think that people come by their good or bad luck because they somehow deserve it. Under normal circumstances, what ultimately matters for the moral enterprise is not achievement but endeavor. And it is exactly this that prevents luck from being a crucial factor here. Luck, be it good or ill, generally comes to people uninvited and unmerited. Life is unfair—and luck is, above all, the reason why. The key lesson here is once again Kant's. We would do well to see luck and fortune as extraneous factors that do not bear on the moral assessment of a person's character. What actually happens to us in life is generally in substantial measure a product of luck and fate, of "circumstances beyond our control."

It is crucially important, then, to recognize the role of luck in human affairs—for good and ill alike. For otherwise one succumbs to the gross fallacy of assimilating people's character to their actual lot in life. The recognition of luck, more than any other single thing, leads us to appreciate the contingency of human triumphs and disasters. "There but for some stroke of luck go I" is a humbling thought whose contemplation is salutary for us all. One cannot properly appreciate the human realities so long as one labors under the adolescent delusion that people get the fate they deserve. During every century of the existence of our species, this planet has borne witness to a measureless vastness of unmerited human suffering and cruelly unjust maltreatment of people by one another. Only in exceptional circumstances is there any link between the normative issue of the sorts of people we are and the factual issue of how we fare in this world's course of things. The disconnection of the two factors of fate and desert, which luck so clearly signalizes, is a fact of life, a perhaps tragic but nevertheless characteristic and inescapable feature of the human condition. But from the specifically moral point of

view, it is *desert* that is determinative and fate is ultimately—
and mercifully—irrelevant. With respect to responsible rational
agents we do—and must—take the stance that however much
their fortune may depend on matters of chance and circumstance, their *moral condition* is something that lies in their
own hands.

Notes

This essay is a revised version of a paper delivered in Atlanta in
December 1989 as Presidential Address to the Eastern Division of the
American Philosophical Association and published in its *Proceedings*
for that year. In revising it for publication here I have profited by some
suggestions from the editor for allowing more closely to the concerns of
this anthology.

1. Some earlier Greek speculations about the impetus of *tuchê*
(chance) on people's prospects for the good life are treated in Martha C.
Nussbaum, *The Fragility of Goodness* (Cambridge, 1986).

2. He abhorred the word as being literally unintelligible. *"Abhor-
remus praecipue propter vocabulum, quod non in se vera conservit in-
telligi" (De civitate dei*, v. 9). For Augustine all that occurred was part of
God's plan. What we call *chance* is simply a matter of human ignorance.

3. *"Trois Discours sur la condition des grands,"* in *Oeuvres com-
plètes*, ed. Louis Lafuma (Paris, 1963), p. 366.

4. For a brief account of Gracián, see the article by Neil McInnes
in *The Encyclopedia of Philosophy*, vol. 3 (New York: Macmillan, 1967),
pp. 375–376. For a fuller treatment, see Alan Bell, *Balthasar Gracián*
(Oxford, 1921).

5. *The Economist* (August 29, 1987), p. 49. At present, the
largest-ever lottery is *el gordo* ("the fat one") held in Spain with a prize
well in excess of $100 million. In 1988, Spain's 38 million inhabitants
gambled away more than $25 billion—over $650 per capita (*New York
Times* [May 14, 1989]). To be sure, the phenomenon is not confined to
Spain. In 1793, the construction of the "Federal City" in the District of
Columbia was promoted by a "Federal Lottery" in which George Washington himself bought at least one ticket.

6. On the perspective, Spanish philosophers took the prominence
of fortune in human affairs to betoken the limits of human power, setting
the stage for a fundamentally pessimistic appreciation of the power of
human reason for guidance in this sublunary sphere. We find this attitude prominent not only in the great figures of the Golden Age of Spanish

literature, who were more or less contemporaries of Gracián (in particular Quevedo and Calderón), but also much later—in Unamuno's insistence that human reason is inadequate and unsatisfactory as a guide to life, and in Ortega y Gasset's rejection of the utility of scientific reason as directrix of human affairs. The idea that life is too chancy and fortuitous a thing to be manageable by rational means runs as a recurrent leitmotif through the history of Spanish thought. Gracián's recommendation of the gambler's perspective fell on fertile ground.

7. *Nam rerum humanorum tanta est obscuritas varietasque, ut nihil dilucide sciri possit* (Erasmus, *Encom. Moral.*, XLV).

8. For an illuminating discussion, see Antonino Poppi, "Fate, Fortune, Providence and Human Freedom," in C. B. Schmitt et al., eds. *The Cambridge History of Renaissance Philosophy* (Cambridge, 1988), pp. 641–667. (The quotation is from p. 653.)

9. As one German writer puts it, often "the guardian angels of those who have luck are the unlucky" (*Die Schutzengel derer, die Glück haben, sind die Verunglückten.*) Hans Pichler, *Persönlichkeit, Glück, Schicksal* (Stuttgart, 1967), p. 47.

10. *"El martes ni te cases ni te embarques"* (Neither marry nor journey on the Tuesday), runs a Spanish proverb.

11. When the New York Mets won the 1969 World Series despite being generally viewed as the inferior team, some attributed this outcome to "mere luck." As reported by Arthur Daley in the *New York Times*, Branch Rickey rejected this imputation with the sage observation that "luck is the residue of design." (James Tuite, ed., *Sports of the Times: The Arthur Daley Years* (New York, 1975), p. 285; I owe this reference to Tamara Horowitz.

12. The question is interestingly discussed in Richard A. Epstein, "Luck," *Social Philosophy and Policy* 6 (1988): 17–38.

13. John Rawls, *A Theory of Justice* (Cambridge, Mass., 1971), p. 100.

14. See p. 144 and note 5 above.

15. Compare Thomas Nagel, "Moral Luck" [chapter 3]. See also Bernard Williams's essay on the topic [chapter 2] and Norvin Richards, "Luck and Desert" [chapter 9].

16. Nagel, "Moral Luck," p. 65.

17. Ibid., p. 61.

18. To be sure, the law—for very good reason—deals only with realizations; the merely would-be lawbreaker lies beyond its condemnation. But morality and law simply differ in this as in other regards. To take the Williams and Nagel law on "moral luck" is in fact to take an overly legalistic view of morality.

19. Nagel, "Moral Luck," p. 58.

20. "Even if it should happen that, by a particularly unfortunate fate or by the niggardly provision of a stepmotherly nature, this [good] will should be wholly lacking in power to accomplish its purpose, and if even the greatest effort should not avail it to achieve anything of its end, and if there remained only the good will (not as a mere wish but as the summoning of all the means in our power), it would sparkle like a jewel in its own right, as something that had its full worth in itself" (Immanuel Kant, *Foundations of the Metaphysics of Morals*, sec. 1, para. 3).

21. Williams, *Moral Luck*, pp. 38ff.

Luck and Desert*

Norvin Richards

... the intuitively plausible conditions of moral judgment
threaten to undermine it all.[1]

One 'condition of moral judgment' is that matters beyond a
person's control cannot bear on what he deserves. For example, to
be born in Pakistan cannot make you deserve to fare less well
than if you had been born somewhere else. Nor can you deserve
credit for winning a lottery through sheer luck, or blame for
bleeding when you are cut. Those are all matters beyond your
control, and thus beyond your responsibility: a connection so
fundamental that Nagel can say 'It seems *irrational* to take or dispense credit or blame for matters over which a person has no control . . .'.[2]
     And yet, Nagel also argues, 'If the condition of control is con-
sistently applied, it threatens to undermine most of the moral assessments we find it natural to make.'[3] For one thing, says Nagel,
we take the consequences of a person's behaviour to bear on just
how bad a thing he has done, and thus on how harsh a response
he should receive—even though the consequences may be determined by something beyond his control! Consider the driver who
roars through a school zone at 70 m.p.h., oblivious to the children darting a few feet from his path. If he is lucky enough to pass
through without hitting anyone, he is guilty of reckless driving,
and will be criticized accordingly. But what if a child chooses precisely the wrong moment to dash after a ball, and ends up crushed
beneath our driver's wheels? Then it will be *manslaughter* he has

*From *Mind* 65 (1986): 198–209.

committed, a far worse thing to have done, and we will take him
to deserve much harsher treatment.

What makes the difference, though, is something beyond
the driver's control: his luck in what the children do. So here, Nagel would argue, we give luck the very power we deny it can have:
the power to make a person deserve harsher or milder treatment.
And, says he, we could not stop doing so without abandoning an
equally fundamental tenet that those who do more harm deserve
harsher treatment than those who do less.

Similarly, "The things we are called upon to do, the moral
tests we face, are importantly determined by factors beyond our
control. It may be true of someone that in a dangerous situation
he would behave in a cowardly or heroic fashion, but if the situation never arises, he will never have the chance to distinguish or
disgrace himself in this way, and his moral record will be
different."[4] If his record *is* different, through his good or bad luck
in never having been put to the test, we will treat him differently.
Indeed, such a discrimination is so basic that " . . . our ordinary
moral attitudes would be unrecognizable without it. We judge
people for what they actually do or fail to do, not just for what they
would have done if circumstances had been different."[5] Thirdly,
according to Nagel, there is 'the phenomenon of constitutive
luck—[luck in] the kind of person you are . . . your inclinations,
capacities, and temperament'.[6] It is because of your set of inclinations and capacities and your temperament that you act as you
do. Thus, in holding you responsible for your actions, we allow
your good or bad luck in having that set and temperament to affect your deserts.

In sum, the practice of moral judgement appears to Nagel to
be a paradoxical one. On the one hand, it requires that matters
beyond one's control can have no bearing on one's deserts. On the
other, it requires that they have *enormous* bearing after all. The
paradox is not dispelled, it seems to me, by observing that our
practice has both Kantian and Aristotelian elements, as Judith
Andre has done in her otherwise illuminating article.[7] At most,
that only explains why our practice is paradoxical in the way
Nagel claims it is.

I want to argue instead that it is not paradoxical after all,
and to offer a different explanation for the several ways in which
luck appears to bear on deserts. Central to my argument will be a
claim that what a person deserves for a particular deed can differ
from the criticism we are actually entitled to level against him for

doing it. I think, that is, that our epistemic position regarding the matters which determine an agent's deserts is so imperfect that (for example) someone can have acted much more culpably than anyone has grounds to realize. If he has, no one is entitled to criticize him as harshly as he deserves. For criticism should reflect not a pretended omniscience but one's actual grasp of what has been done.

A culprit may thus be lucky or unlucky in how clear his deserts are. And we must allow his luck to make a difference in how we treat him, if we are not to change our practice into one in which we pretend omniscience. But in doing so we do not contradict the contention that his luck cannot affect what his deserts *are*. So, we do not act paradoxically, as Nagel contends, but only reflect our epistemic shortcomings, and the agent's good or bad fortune in those.

I

My case for this conclusion requires me to speak of an agent's character. By this I mean his set of preferences, in so far as these are relatively stable over time: the fact that he prefers company to solitude, or telling the truth to being misleading, and so on. Such a preference can be fortunate or unfortunate in the actions it makes one more likely to perform and the subsequent consequences for oneself and others.

Now it is scarcely radical to say that when we are concerned with what a person deserves, we are interested in his behaviour *as a display of character*. It is easy to understand the standard excuses in that light. Having harmed someone, I urge that I was not malicious but only ignorant: i.e., that I am not someone for whom the harm was a positive attraction, but only someone who did not realize it would occur. Ideally, I hope this ignorance will not itself show me to be insufficiently averse to harm of the sort I have done. Or, in a different case, I might plead that I acted under duress: that I did this harm only to avoid another, a more innocent weighting of outcomes than might have appeared. Still another time, my plea might be provocation: that I am not a bully or a hothead but only someone whose aversion to violence can be overcome.

One reason to be concerned about the character enacted in a bit of behaviour is that character, by definition, is relatively stable. *Qua* display of character, the deed involves a taste or level of aversion which may be indulged again, in any number of ways, if the current episode is not made unrewarding for the agent. Whatever measures we do take to protect ourselves from future indulgences may be more or less unpleasant for him. It would be unreasonable for the measures to do him more harm than they protected others from suffering at his hands. But the more dangerous his future indulgences are, the more costly to him those protective measures may reasonably be. Thus, behaviour which enacts a particular trait calls for, or 'deserves', protective measures in proportion to the risk of future harms at which it puts other people.

The fact that a person does deserve a particular sort of response does not settle how he should be treated by those who wish to give him what he deserves, however. For they are not omniscient: they have only their *grasp* of his deserts to enact, and they are obliged to be careful in a matter this important. So, for example, his acting in a way which deserves their rebuking him does not entitle them to rebuke him, since their grounds for believing him to have done so may be inadequate. The rebuke could be epistemically irresponsible, even though deserved.

Moreover, *matters beyond the agent's control* bear on how clearly we see what he deserves—and, thus, on the legitimacy of our treating him in that way. His luck in those matters affects how we ought to treat him, not by changing what he deserves, but by changing the grounds on which we are obliged to judge. For example, it may be a person's good luck that there are no eyewitnesses to her misdeed. Jealous of your new carpet, she empties her wineglass over it—just as the ring of a telephone distracts the only person who would have seen her do so. A moment later, she slips quietly into the next room. Much later, you discover the stain—and have no grounds for blaming her for it. Were you to treat her as (in fact) she deserved to be treated, you would be acting quite irresponsibly, and her *luck* has made this the case.

I think we can also imagine matters differently, so that adding an eyewitness *would not* strengthen your grounds for inferring that this woman deserves whatever such people do deserve. Perhaps you enter the room before she has time to depart, while she is still smiling down at the spreading stain and before she removes the random droplets which splashed her shoe. Bad luck for her—again, not in that your arrival changes what she deserves, but in that it changes the legitimacy of your treating her as she deserves.

I think that Nagel's first sort of luck, luck in the consequences of one's actions, plays this same role. Like luck in the presence or absence of eyewitnesses, it sometimes affects our grounds for seeing what a person deserves, and, thereby, the legitimacy of our treating him in that way. Other times, we are as clear *without* the tell-tale consequences: we do not always need *success* to see what was intended, any more than we always need an eyewitness.

This would not be an inconsiderable role for luck in consequences to play. But neither would it be a paradoxical one. It would not amount to allowing luck to affect deserts, but only to recognizing that we are not omniscient about such matters, and that we must be responsible in our inferences about them.

Consider, for example, the reckless driver. Sometimes, if a driver harms no one, there is room for the belief that his speed and degree of attention are adequate: that he is sufficiently alert to avoid accidents if the need arises, that his speed is safe for a person of his skills, and so on. Even if these contentions are quite false, so that in fact his driving enacts a very dangerous level of unconcern and his behaviour deserves a very harsh response, the matter may be debatable so long as he does no actual harm. For such a driver, it is only when he hits someone that it becomes plain he *is not* sufficiently attentive, that his speed *is* too fast for him, that he *is not* giving sufficient weight to the risk of harm to others when he drives as he does. It is only when his luck—and his victim's—runs out, that we have sufficient grounds for treating him in the way he has deserved to be treated all along.

On the other hand, on other occasions the accident is superfluous, in the same way as an eyewitness can be superfluous. That is, the accident does not strengthen our grounds for believing his driving to be reckless, is not crucial to the legitimacy of our treating him as he deserves. Instead, common sense about human reaction time, the limitations of human eyesight, and the nature of local conditions is enough: we are entitled to conclude that anyone driving that way, in that place, at that time, is driving recklessly. If so, we need not wait for the tragic impact, to be entitled to treat him as he deserves.

In short, if we ought to treat a certain driver differently from one whose identical recklessness ends in manslaughter, that will not be because the two deserve different treatment. It will be because (a) their behaviour does not make their equal deserts equally clear and (b) our treatment should reflect our understanding of those deserts. The agent's luck in the consequences of his actions can affect our understanding of his deserts, and, thereby, the way we ought to treat him. It does not affect the character he enacted, however. So, it does not affect his deserts, for those are determined by the character enacted.

II

But isn't this way of dealing with luck in consequences self-defeating, since Nagel also maintains that what character one *has* to enact is also beyond one's control? If the 'kind of person you are . . . your inclinations, capacities and temperament' is determined by matters beyond your control, and your deserts are determined by which such features you enact, then (once again) your deserts appear to be determined by something beyond your control. This time, their ultimate determinant is whatever made you the person you are.

This argument succeeds, I think, if one's character is *to no extent* one's own artefact. But if the individual makes any contribution whatever to the sort of person he is, that contribution can be the basis for his deserving praise or blame for what he does. Nagel leaves room for such a contribution. Speaking of such qualities as conceit, he says "To some extent such a quality may be the product of earlier choices; to some extent it may be amenable to change by current action. But it is *largely* a matter of bad fortune."[8]

Of course, he could be wrong about this. It could be that one's character is shaped *entirely* by forces beyond one's control. If so, the practice of attributing responsibility is undermined, with no need for us to refer to the other sorts of luck Nagel brings to our attention. But he does not argue for this traditional determinism/incompatibilism, appearing instead to want to offer a different puzzle.

It could also be that although one's character is only 'largely' one's good or bad fortune, and partly also one's own doing, in assigning deserts we take the wrong part seriously. For example, it could be that two individuals who had the same character, one through no fault of his own and the other far more as the result of his own contributions, would be taken to deserve the same response for enacting this character. But, in fact, where we do see such differences we do not take the deserts to be the same—because we do not allow luck to affect deserts. Where we do not see such differences, we do take the deserts to be the same. Since our evidence about such matters is far from perfect, no doubt we sometimes do not treat people as they deserve when we follow our grasp of the situation. That is not the same as allowing their luck in our grasp to affect what their deserts *are*, however, but only the result of deserts turning on something difficult to discern.

III

Thirdly, according to Nagel, one's *opportunities* for agency are also matters of luck. Perhaps you would have saved a drowning swimmer, had you been near by when he began to struggle. But you were miles away at the time, caught in a traffic jam on the freeway. You never even knew a rescue was needed, until the next day's newspaper. So you missed your chance to be a hero, and, thus, your chance to deserve the praise bestowed on the woman who *was* at the right place at the right time. Her luck and yours brought you different opportunities to act and, it seems, different opportunities to deserve to be treated in a certain way by your fellows.

What if you were to complain about this, insisting that you should be praised for the heroism you would have performed, and praised just as highly as the heroine is for her actual heroism? Nagel thinks this would not be merely immodest and insecure of you, as it might be if you demanded praise which actually was your due. Rather, your demand would be deeply confused, because the praise is *not* your due: 'We judge people for what they actually do or fail to do, not just for what they would have done if the circumstances had been different.'[9]

Of course, if Nagel means by this that we *do not* judge people for what they would have done, he is mistaken. Suppose you had been abandoned in a time of need by someone you took to be a friend. Suppose that in talking this over with a third party, it struck you how much more steadfast *he* would have been than the swine who deserted you. Might not this realization prompt you to praise your friend quite warmly? Or suppose you were convinced that a repairman would have stolen your wallet had he not realized he was under scrutiny. Might not that be a sufficient basis for treating him rather harshly? In both sorts of cases, it seems that someone can deserve to be treated in a certain way, not because of what this person has done but because of what it is plausible to think he *would* do, if given the opportunity.

Still, actual agents do differ from potential ones in their deserts, as Nagel urges. The difference is that only the actual hero is praiseworthy *for saving the swimmer*, only the actual Nazi is blameworthy *for the behaviour at Belsen* which he performed. It would be ludicrous to say the potential hero deserves our warm response *for that deed*, with which he had nothing to do, or that the potential Nazi deserves a harsh response *for what happened at Belsen*. However, I will argue, this difference in deserts is much less significant than Nagel thinks.

My central contention will be that if the potential agent is as much like the actual one as we are imagining, then there will be something else in his behaviour which will call for the same response. If so, his luck in not doing a *particular* deed will not affect the treatment he deserves. He will deserve the same sort of encouragement or reconditioning, but he will deserve it for a different enactment of virtuous or vicious character. His luck will thus affect not what he deserves but the time at which he deserves it and, once again, the clarity with which he can be seen to deserve it.

Let us focus upon the following pair of actual and potential miscreants: "Someone who was an officer in a concentration camp might have led a quiet and harmless life if the Nazis had never come to power in Germany. And someone who led a quiet and harmless life in Argentina might have become an officer in a concentration camp if he had not left Germany for business reasons in 1930."[10]

We are imagining here an *émigré* who shares the traits of character which the other man enacted in being a concentration camp officer—so that only the *émigré*'s geographical good luck prevented his playing that same role. Perhaps, for example, both men have an extremely strong desire to please persons in authority, and little or no aversion to the suffering of anyone they consider inferior.

To call the *émigré*'s desire to please authorities 'extremely strong' is to rank it relative to his other desires. For him, the chance to please an authority is a greater attraction in an alternative than most of the other things he considers attractions. So he is quicker to notice what he takes to be signs of their wishes, adopts courses he takes to please them with greater alacrity, and pursues those courses more persistently in the face of what are for him temptations to do otherwise.

Similarly, to say he is not very averse to suffering in those he considers inferior is to rank that aversion relative to his others. For him, their suffering is not much of a mark against a course of action, but is something more easily overridden than other aversive features. So he is not very alert about their suffering, perhaps fails to notice it entirely, is not much deterred from a course by realizing that it threatens this harm, persists in such courses, and so on. Finally, since we are speaking here of the *émigré*'s character, we are describing features which are relatively stable over time.

Now, I have already suggested that it is not the harm a person does that determines his deserts, but the features of character which he enacts. Thus, it is someone's *indifference to my suffering* that calls for attempts to change him, or to deny him future opportunities to harm me, or to show him that such behaviour will be costly in the future. The harm he actually does me in his indifference is only a sign of how indifferent he is and how dangerous his indifference is: the same reactive measures may be appropriate even though he has done me very little harm.[11]

If all that is right, and if each of the *émigré* and the concentration camp officer enacts the character described, then each will deserve the same response to those enactings. For each will have enacted the same dangerous, stable features of character, calling for the same protective and re-educative responses. The *émigré*'s behaviour will have been less striking, perhaps, and we will then be less clear that it does call for this response. But his deserts will be the same, just as the deserts of the *lucky* reckless driver do not differ from those of the unlucky one. Once again, the reason we should treat the two differently is not because they deserve different treatment, but because (a) their behaviour does not show their deserts equally clearly and (b) we should treat people according to our understanding of their behaviour.

But, isn't it possible that the *émigré* has the requisite character to be a camp officer but *never* enacts it, in any way? So that he never deserves these responses after all, by virtue of his good luck in never having this part of his character called into action? Nagel appears to think of character in such a way:

A person may be greedy, envious, cowardly, cold, ungenerous, unkind, vain, or conceited, but behave perfectly . . . an envious person hates the greater success of others. He can be morally condemned as envious even if he congratulates them cordially and does nothing to denigrate or spoil their success. Conceit, likewise, need not be displayed. It is fully present in someone who cannot help dwelling with secret satisfaction on the superiority of his own achievements, talents, beauty, intelligence, or virtue.[12]

In fact, however, the paragraph does not describe people who never enact the traits in question, but only people who do not enact these in particular ways. To dwell with secret satisfaction on one's own superiority is a conceited action, albeit a different one from bragging. And envy can play a role in one's 'cordial congratulations'—making the words ring false, the handshake last a bit too long, and the smile be a bit too broad. *Qua* enactments of conceit and envy, on my view these call for the same protective and reeducative responses as the more blatant displays. Since their call is so much more muted, however, it might well be pretentious to respond to them as if it were clear. If so, we should treat such actions differently, although not because their agents deserve a different response.

Moreover, the idea of unenacted character is a mistaken one, it seems to me. One's character is the relative weight various matters have for one in one's actions, in what comes to one's notice, and in the hesitations and bearing with which one acts, no less than in whether one acts in a recognizably conceited way (for example). Character is not a control-box determining what matters shall have which weight, but the fact that they *do have* that weight as one moves through the world.

Even if we do grant that the *émigré* will enact the character in question, though, he will not enact it by serving as an officer in a concentration camp. Can we conclude that, in him, the character will not be so unfortunate as it was in the German? If so, on the view I have offered his enactings of the character will not deserve so harsh a response, for they will not indicate something so threatening. His deserts would then have been changed by his having had this character *in Argentina* rather than in Germany: something which might have been a matter of luck. However, I do not think it does follow from the *émigré*'s not serving in a camp that the traits are not so bad a thing in him. Indeed, a trait whose enactings are not spectacularly painful for others stands a greater chance to persist. It is less likely to draw the outraged reactions which can make a man change. The *émigré* is likely to live an entire life in which he takes the pleasures of authorities too seriously and the pain of certain others too lightly. That will be a stunted life, as well as a damaging one.

IV

I have agreed with Nagel that our verdicts in judging people turn on matters beyond those people's control, and that our practices would be very different if they did not do so. Unlike him, however, I do not think this amounts to our paradoxically allowing luck to affect deserts. Instead, I have argued, to a very large extent people are lucky only in our *verdicts*, not in what they deserve, and their luck must affect our verdicts because it affects our grounds for reaching them.

This way of accommodating Nagel's paradox has carried certain philosophical commitments: to one analysis of character and another of desert, and to the belief that one's character is to some extent one's own artefact. This is not the place to defend these commitments against every objection they might provoke. However, there is one possible misgiving so deep as to require comment. It amounts to a doubt that I have been talking about *desert* at all. Clearly, if it *is not* desert I have striven to prove independent of luck, then even if my strivings have been successful they will not have proved *desert* unparadoxical.

The reason for doubting that it is desert I have been discussing, when I have discussed seeing actions as enactments of character, is the purpose I gave for looking at them in that way. The idea was that, as an enactment of character, an action makes future behaviour more likely, thereby calling for re-educative and protective responses against that future behaviour. But this focus on the future is the mark of utilitarian thinking; whereas, traditionally, a person's *desert* is supposed to have nothing to do with the consequences of treating him any particular way. Desert is supposed to flow from the nature of the deed; in my way of talking, it does so only in so far as deeds indicate future deeds by being symptoms of patterns in the agent's behaviour.

Now, personally, I am not convinced that my way of talking does not describe desert. It may be that when someone has the intuition that a particular deed just calls for a harsh response, this is nothing more than a commendably quick realization of how dangerous the agent is. But let us suppose that nothing like this is true and that it is *not* desert I have defended against paradox but something else altogether. Two possibilities arise.

First, it may be possible for the objector to recast my chief line of argument so as to defend desert. Essentially, I have argued that desert is a function of character enacted; that it is our *understanding* of the character enacted that depends on the agent's luck in such matters as his opportunities and the harm he actually does; and that this is quite different from allowing his deserts themselves to depend on his luck. Perhaps the same could be said by someone who did not share my views as to why we should care about the character enacted. Such a person wants to say instead that to enact some character-traits is *intrinsically* worse than to enact others, and thus deserving (in itself) of a harsher response. Perhaps it might still be argued, that is, that the agent's luck does not affect the wickedness of the character he enacts but only how clear we are about it—and, thus, does not affect his deserts but only our grasp of those deserts, which is all we have to implement.

Alternatively, it may be that no such variation can be developed. Perhaps our grasp of intrinsic wickedness has nothing to do with the agent's opportunities to act or the harm he actually does, so that variations in these cannot explain why we should treat certain agents differently. Or, perhaps there is some other obstacle. If so, my efforts do not show that desert is unparadoxical and cannot be adapted to do so. However, they would then show something equally interesting, in my opinion. They would show that we can avoid paradox if we shift to the way of thinking which I have set out: an argument for doing so, regardless of whether that amounts to a reconstrual of desert or an abandoning of it.

Still, it might be objected that this new way of thinking is seriously incomplete: that some of our deepest feelings about deeds in which harm is done have no place in it. For although we do sometimes criticize others or feel ashamed of ourselves for actions *qua* dishonest, or cowardly, with little interest in how much harm was actually done, on other occasions it is just the reverse. If you had crushed some poor child with your automobile, *that* is what would prey on your mind, and you would get no relief from our saying that no one could have seen her dart from that shadow. If the neighbour girl had dropped your baby so that its neck broke, that would change for ever your feelings about her—

no matter how clear it was that no one could have held that tiny, slippery, wriggling body.

Now, it is true that these are reactions to the harm done rather than to the character expressed in doing it, and, thus, that they do not connect with desert as I have analysed it. That is not a flaw in the analysis but a virtue, however, for the reactions are not judgements that a harsh response is deserved! Your feelings about the neighbour girl obtain even though you know it *was not* her fault your baby died. Running over the child is terrible for you even though you know you could not have helped it.[13] One can even feel a similar revulsion toward inanimate objects—the rope the lynch-mob used, the ripper's knife—even though it is plainly absurd to think of such objects as morally responsible for the awful uses to which they were put and thus to deserve our reactions to them. Indeed, to construe such reactions as judgements about desert, and thus to want an analysis of desert to cover them, is to miss what is most intriguing about them: the fact that we feel at least somewhat justified in having such feelings despite recognizing that they *are not* deserved.

What place can be found for the idea that we sometimes ought to have such feelings even though they are undeserved? Perhaps they could be understood and evaluated as displays of the character of those who have them. For example, it seems plausible to say that the girl who caused your baby's death ought to be distressing for you to encounter because (a) the sight of her should remind you of the event and (b) the memories should be very painful ones for you. So, your inability to tolerate her in your sight would express your quite appropriate feelings about your baby's death. Were she just another person to you, despite her intimate connection with the tragedy, that would mean it was not the tragedy for you that it should have been.

Her having acted faultlessly is irrelevant to all this, of course. That is why the soap which made the baby slippery ought also to arouse strong feelings in you. The idea is not that we are called to protect ourselves from such objects and people, or to re-educate them, as we are when they display bad character and deserve harsh treatment. Instead, what calls for our response is our own abhorrence of the harm done. The difference between these two sometimes makes us uneasy about the reaction which seems somehow right and which we are inclined to say we 'cannot help having', for in having it we may also feel that we are being *unfair.*

I have not meant to give a full account of these special reactions, however. The point has been that to give them no place in an account of desert is not to give a flawed account of desert, because they are not reactions to it. If so, they do not provide a reason for dissatisfaction with the suggested way of escaping Nagel's paradox.

Notes

I am grateful for the comments of Scott Hestevold and for suggestions from the editors of *Mind*.

1. Thomas Nagel, "Moral Luck" [See chapter 3. Ed.] All future references are to this chapter.

2. P. 61.

3. P. 59.

4. P. 65.

5. Pp. 65–6.

6. P. 60.

7. "Nagel, Williams, and Moral Luck" [See chapter 6. Ed.].

8. P. 65.

9. P. 66.

10. Pp. 58–9.

11. Similar views about desert can be found in Hume's *Enquiry Concerning the Principles of Morals* (see, in particular, Sec. V, part II); in Richard Brandt's "A Utilitarian Theory of Excuses," *Philosophical Review*, 1969 (see, in particular, pp. 353–8); and in Michael Bayles's "Character, Purpose, and Criminal Responsibility," *Law and Philosophy*, 1982.

12. P. 64.

13. 'The lorry driver who, *through no fault of his*, runs over a child, will feel differently from any spectator . . . ' (Bernard Williams, "Moral Luck" [chapter 2], p. 43, my emphasis).

Crime and Moral Luck*

Steven Sverdlik

Does our moral thinking embody any recognition of what has been called "moral luck"?[1] Discussion of this question has tended to focus largely on the moral concepts of praise and blame. In this particular domain the issue then is the following: can the operations of factors beyond an agent's control affect how praiseworthy or blameworthy a person is for a given action? Examples in this vein are along these lines: if A goes through all the steps that A regards as necessary to kill B, will A be more blameworthy if B actually dies? The element of luck involved is clearly brought out if one considers the various sorts of factors which could intervene to save B's life: for example, if A fires a rifle at B and the bullet is deflected by a cigarette case in B's pocket, or a bird suddenly darts in the way. Similar cases could be generated for acts involving recklessness or negligence. For example, if A runs a traffic light and then hits B's car, is A any more blameworthy than if A runs the light and luckily hits nothing? With respect to acts that involve an intention to inflict harm, the problem of moral luck amounts to the question of whether a complete *attempt* to commit a crime or to do wrong is morally equivalent to *success* in committing the crime or doing the wrong. (Obviously talk of "successful negligence" is absurd.)

There is no doubt that common sense is some what perplexed by this question. My own impression is that people unfamiliar with philosophy will reflexively hold that the actions are indeed different, but that they will quickly retract their statement when they realize its implications. The most important of these implications is presumably its denial of the proposition that a person can only be held responsible for conditions under his or

*From *American Philosophical Quarterly* 25 (1988): 79–86.

her control. If we do admit that the attempter and the successful criminal are unequal in blameworthiness then we seem to be allowing that a person's moral responsibility can be affected by, e.g., the unforeseeable and uncontrollable flight of a stray bird. It is notorious, however, that the law typically punishes success more severely, and that it punishes the unlucky negligent person more severely, as well. It is not surprising, therefore, that there have been philosophers who have asserted that in the sorts of cases mentioned there is a difference in the *moral* responsibility of the agents. That is to say, there are theorists who hold that there is not only, as we might say, legal luck, but moral luck as well.[2]

In the present paper I try to show that the thesis that there is moral luck is riddled with difficulties and is much harder to defend than has been realized. I do not directly address the arguments of the defenders of the position.[3] Instead, I present a set of problem cases for the position and I conclude that there is no defensible way for the moral luck theorists to handle them. I limit myself to what seems like the simplest case, that of intentional wrongdoing, and I venture no opinion as to whether my conclusion can be extended to cases of recklessness or negligence. Nor do I consider intentional conferring of benefits.[4] However, my negative arguments tend to show that, at least in the case of intentional wrongdoing, there is no difference in moral responsibility between the person who attempts to do wrong and the person who succeeds.

A few more preliminary remarks will be helpful. First, just to fix terminology, let us call the position defended by the proponents of the idea of moral luck the "non-equivalence" theory and the position I am defending the "equivalence" theory. Since one is the contradictory of the other, any arguments tending to show that one is false thereby tend to show that the other is true. Second, to maintain the equivalence theory is to hold that *other things being equal* a complete attempt is morally equivalent to its successful conclusion. Neither theory implies that attempt and success are the only factors affecting blameworthiness or responsibility. Obviously there are other factors like provocation and motive. The dispute is about whether when all these other factors are held constant the mere fact that an attempt succeeds can make a difference in a person's blameworthiness. Third, a proponent of the equivalence theory need not deny that attempts often produce harm; indeed they may produce just as much harm as successes.[5] The dispute, rather, is this: *if* a success produces more harm than the complete attempt, is this fact alone sufficient to augment the blameworthiness of the agent? Fourth, the remarks thus far have suggested that the factor that is the subject of disagreement is apparently the (additional) *harm* that ensues when an agent is successful in wrongdoing or crime. There is no doubt, though, that "harm" is a complex concept and that different crimes produce different sorts of harm. For example, there is bodily injury, death, ruined reputation, confinement and so on. The list obviously widens when largely social harms, such as those involved in treason, are included.[6] I here offer no account of the concept of harm because I think any such account would be neutral with respect to the issue between equivalence and nonequivalence theories. My examples will all stick to one type of harm—death—in order to simplify discussion. (I assume that there is a resolution to the paradox which maintains that death is not a harm to a person, on the grounds that in being dead there is no one *to be* harmed.[7]) Fifth, it should be emphasized that I restrict my attention to what I called "complete" attempts: that is, where the agent believes that he or she has done everything necessary to assure that the harm occurs. It is well known that the law will accept behavior that falls somewhat short of this point as being an attempt. (It is also well known that distinguishing a legal attempt from "mere preparation" like searching for one's intended victim is a crux in the criminal law.) Again, to simplify matters, I will use the standard example of firing a gun with the intention of killing the person aimed at. In this sort of example the issue is whether, other things being equal, a person's moral responsibility will vary depending on whether the intended victim dies or not. Finally, I have a confession to make: I assert that the cases I consider tend to show that the non-equivalence theory is untenable because of its absurd consequences. But I admit that these consequences may be no *more* absurd than the thesis that the unforeseeable flight of a bird between me and my victim will affect my moral responsibility. And this thesis is explicitly affirmed by the non-equivalence theorists. But, if the consequences I point out are no more absurd than this proposition then it still may at least be true that a *set* of absurd consequences has more probative force than one alone. This is how I would interpret the force of the following cases.

Consider a case of what the law calls "transferred intent" (or "transferred malice"). *A* intends to shoot *B* fatally but in fact accidentally kills C instead. This is to be distinguished from a case of mistaken identity where A kills C thinking that in fact C is B. In order to avoid irrelevant complications, suppose that A was in no way reckless or negligent before firing the gun, and that the interposition of C was completely unforeseeable. I think that most people's reaction in such a case is to say that A is equally blame-worthy if B is killed or if C is. The equivalence theory has a simple and plausible explanation of this reaction, *viz.*, that the attempt to kill B (which involved, as it turns out, killing C instead) is morally equivalent to killing B successfully. What is the non-equivalence theorist going to say about this case? Is killing B morally equivalent to attempting to kill B but accidentally killing C?

It might be thought that the non-equivalence theorist can maintain that the two acts are equivalent. But so far as I can see such a theorist must deny that they are equal in blameworthi-ness. Certainly the non-equivalence theorist cannot argue that the two cases are equivalent on the grounds that in both cases A is attempting to kill B. To argue in this way would be to maintain that the morally relevant feature of the two cases is the intention with which A acts, but this would be to abandon the non-equivalence view. That theory is premised on the view that the *outcome* of an act has relevance, otherwise attempts and suc-cesses would be equivalent. In other words, to say that the two cases are morally equivalent on the grounds that A had the same intention in both cases is in effect to take up the equivalence theory.[8]

There is another suggestion that might be made. Could the non-equivalence theorist argue that the two cases are equivalent on the grounds that the harm is the same? This is attractive be-cause presumably the motive for espousing the non-equivalence theory in the first place was that successful wrongdoing involves more harm than an attempt to produce it. If more harm is suffi-cient to establish more blame then it is plausible to hold that if the harm is equal then the blame is equal. The connection be-tween the former proposition and the latter is not logical, but it seems reasonable to assert both if one is going to assert one of them.

Unfortunately, though, the position now arrived at is deeply counterintuitive. After all, if A succeeds in killing B then A has intentionally inflicted this harm, but if A kills C then the harm that results is produced accidentally. The non-equivalence theorist would therefore be committed to the barbaric view that all harms of the same magnitude involve equal blameworthiness: if I accidentally kill a person then I am just as blameworthy as when I intentionally do so. Surely this "strict liability" position is one that no one seriously wishes to hold.

Therefore, it seems that the non-equivalence theorist cannot hold that a person is as blameworthy in a case of transferred intent as he or she is in a case of successful attempt. This seems like a difficulty for the theory since, as I mentioned, we tend, even on reflection, to think that the cases are equivalent. There is a further point of perhaps greater interest. The non-equivalence theory seemed to get its impetus from the fact that successful attempts often involve more harm than unsuccessful ones. But we just saw that it cannot be harm *as such* that is operating to distinguish the cases since blameworthiness can vary while harm remains constant. (Presumably the converse holds as well.) Therefore, what needs to be done is to reformulate the non-equivalence theory in such a way as to take account of this fact. But it remains to be seen whether a non-problematic reformulation is possible.

It seems that the most plausible reformulation is the following. Other things being equal, an attempt to do wrong in which the *intended* harm takes place makes the agent more blameworthy than an attempt to do wrong in which the intended harm does not take place. The non-equivalence theory is now using the occurrence of the intended harm to distinguish attempt and success, and is not using the idea of harm as such. Notice that on this theory cases of transferred intent are not as blameworthy as cases of successful wrongdoing. I now want to suggest that this theory has a problem case of its own with which it has no satisfactory way of dealing.

Consider a case where *A* attempts to kill *B* in a certain manner. To stick to our simple case: suppose that *A* intends to kill *B* by firing a bullet into *B*'s head. Suppose, however, that *B* does not die as a result of the wound that *A* inflicts, although *A* thinks that *B* is dead. Further, suppose that *B* dies later because of some subsequent event that takes place, and which would not have killed *B* if *A* had not shot him or her. To simplify matters it would be best to suppose that the further event is natural. For example, suppose that *A* shoots *B* in a field and leaves *B* lying there, thinking him or her to be dead. As it happens *B* is not dead, and is, perhaps, not even close to death. But a number of hours pass and a storm gathers. Lightning strikes the unconscious body of B and B dies. Let us suppose that the formation of the storm was completely unforeseeable at the time that A shot B.

Is A as blameworthy in such a case as A would have been if B had died instantly as a result of the gun-shot wound? The equivalence theory says yes. If A is just as responsible when the attempt fails altogether then *a fortiori* A is as responsible when the act succeeds in an unforeseen way. What does the non-equivalence theory say about a case where the result was intended but the manner was not? The theory as stated above is indeterminate with respect to this question. I will consider three possible suggestions meant to deal with such cases.

One tack is to require that the harm intended must occur in the manner intended if there is to be a difference in blameworthiness. On this view A is not as blameworthy when B is finally killed by the lightning as compared to the case where B dies instantly from the gun shot wound, because the former case involves a harm occurring in a manner not intended. There is thus a difference of opinion with the equivalence theory here. I think this proposal can be pretty quickly disposed of. Suppose that A makes a bomb and sets the timer on it to go off at 9:00 a.m. A then sets the bomb in a train station and because of some minor defect in the timer the bomb explodes at 9:15. A intended the result that in fact takes place, mass carnage, but A had intended that it occur at 9:00 a.m., not 9:15. Can the fact that the harm took place in such a trivially different manner really make any difference in A's blameworthiness?

On the other hand, one might suggest that the intended manner is morally irrelevant, at least so long as this does not involve any variation in the amount of harm produced. On this view, if A intends to produce a harm to B in a certain manner then A is just as blameworthy if the intended harm occurs to B in some non-intended way, so long as the non-intended manner involves the same amount of harm as the intended. This thesis would entail that with the terrorist just described the blameworthiness is the same in either case, so long as we make the reasonable assumption that the bomb's sitting in the train station for an extra fifteen minutes involves no additional harm. Notice that this second version agrees with the conclusion that the equivalence theory reaches about the two cases. The disagreement concerns the premises.

In order to see the difficulty with this suggestion it is necessary to move beyond the largely formal considerations that have been central to the discussion thus far. We have been taking cases two at a time and asking whether the agent is equally blameworthy in both cases, and what rationale the different theories under investigation would give for their answers. We have not asked how *much* blame would be appropriate, nor have we asked about *what* the agent is being blamed for. But at this point the latter question has a good deal of importance. Throughout this paper I have used the terms "blameworthy" and "morally responsible" interchangeably. I have assumed that for our purposes the two are synonymous. It is interesting to note that both terms are similar in one respect, *viz.*, that they or their relatives can be applied to acts or to resultant states of affairs. Thus, we say that A is to blame for the forest fire, or that A is to blame for leaving a campfire burning. Again, we say that A is responsible for B's death, or that A is responsible for killing B. (We also say that A is responsible for attempting to kill B.)[9]

The critical point now is this: what, on this version of the non-equivalence theory, is the person being blamed for in the two cases? There seems to be no problem when A harms B in the intended manner: we can say that A is to blame for B's death. But can we say this in the case where A causes B's death, but in an unforeseeable manner? The non-equivalence theory, in this version, holds that the agent is equally blameworthy in either case (with the proviso about no collateral harm, which is inoperative in the case of A's shooting B in the field). It would seem, therefore, that the theory is impelled to say that in the case of unforeseen manner the agent is also to blame for the result, i.e., the death. The serious problem with this suggestion is that A produces B's death by the sheerest *coincidence.* It is true that A intended to kill B, and carried out all the steps A thought necessary to do so. Still, B's death is connected only fortuitously with A's action, even if it is true that B would not have died but for A's action. It is a subtle question whether one could say that A "accidentally killed" B, but one is certainly justified in saying that A's act led to B's death by an unlucky coincidence. It does seem true to say that A "accidentally caused" B's death. We see once again that there is a tendency in the non-equivalence theory to revert to strict liability for harm, that is, to hold people responsible for harm that they produce, no matter how fortuitously. This, I submit, is a very

serious difficulty which undermines the appeal of this version of
the theory. It is true that this version of the non-equivalence
theory does not always hold a person responsible for harm produced fortuitously, but it does do so in the sort of case under
discussion.

Before moving on to the third version of the non-equivalence
theory I would like to pause and consider some further questions
that might arise about the second version. This version, again, is
that a) other things being equal, an attempt to do wrong in which
the intended harm takes place makes the agent more blameworthy than an attempt to do wrong in which the intended harm
does not take place, and b) the manner in which the harm comes
about is morally irrelevant so long as it does not differ in harm-
fulness from the manner that was intended. I have objected that
this theory, when applied to the shooting in the field case, has the
consequence that A is morally responsible for B's death, which in
fact resulted by chance from A's act. It might be asked whether
the non-equivalence theorist can say instead that A is to blame for
the act of attempting to kill B. The answer, I think, is that this
would again mean that the theory is collapsing back into the
equivalence theory. If in this case A is blamed for the act, why not
as well when A succeeds in killing B instantaneously? And if A is
blamed in both cases for the act then why isn't A equally blameworthy when the act occurs but the death doesn't? It would
seem, in other words, that talk of blame for acts is inherently favorable to the equivalence theory. It is true, that many act de-
scriptions have results built into them, e.g., "to murder."[10] But it
also seems to be the case that whenever we find such terms we
can always paraphrase them in a way that pares off the result and
leaves an action: e.g., "fired a gun at." Indeed it would seem that
the equivalence theorist will say that talk of responsibility for results or states of affairs is merely a *facon de parler*. Whenever
there is talk of responsibility for, e.g., a death, what there is really
responsibility for is the act which caused the death. Omissions
must for our purposes be counted as actions, but since the relevant meaning of "omits" is "intentionally omits," there does not
seem to be anything objectionable in taking "act" this broadly.

It might also be asked whether it is true in the field case that
A *caused B's* death. After all, suppose that B would not have died
from the shot alone, and that the lightning bolt was also a necessary condition of B's death. Can one really say in that case that
A caused B's death?[11] It seems that the answer must be yes. One

way to see this is to alter the case slightly and suppose that *A* foresaw the lightning and meant to take advantage of it, stunning *B* in such a way as to leave him or her vulnerable to the bolt that would be fatal. In this case surely we wish to say that *A* caused *B*'s death, and yet exactly the same sequence of events would take place after the firing of the gun if *A* intended to kill *B* straightaway and had no idea that the storm was coming. The mental states of *A* cannot alter the fact of there being causal connections in the subsequent events. If *A*'s act is causally connected to the death when *A* has an intention then *A*'s act is also causally connected to the death when *A* has no such intention. I do not deny that one might well wish to speak in one case of the act's being "the" cause of the death, and in the other (where the lightning's intervention was unforeseen) of the act's being merely "a" cause. My point is that in both cases the act is causally connected with the death, and that the existence of an intention has no bearing on this fact.

To conclude discussion of the second version: The non-equivalence theorist faces a dilemma with respect to cases of intended harm but unintended manner. The theorist can either make the manner fully relevant in the sense that any divergence from the intended manner makes a difference to blameworthiness (the first version). On the other hand, the theorist can hold that divergence in manner is largely irrelevant (second version). The problem with the first version is obvious. The second version's problem, I have said, is its commitment in this sort of case to a kind of strict liability for harm. In the problem case for the second version—the field case—the equivalence theorist does not disagree with the conclusion that the non-equivalence theorist reaches. But the non-equivalence *must* say that *A* is responsible for *B*'s death whereas the equivalence theorist *can* say this, but can *also* say that *A* is responsible for attempting to kill *B*. And, of course, the latter way of putting the point seems more faithful to the theory's guiding intuition.

Let us turn, then, to a third version of the non-equivalence theory. Once again we take as constant the claim that other things being equal, the occurrence of an intended harm makes a difference to blameworthiness. And it is added that the manner which actually ensues must be foreseeable at the time of action, otherwise one is not as responsible as would otherwise be the case. That is, one is not as blameworthy when the intended harm results in an unforeseeable manner as when it occurs in a foreseeable manner. In this version of the non-equivalence theory *A* would *not* be as blameworthy when the lightning finally does *B* in as when *B* dies immediately as a consequence of *A*'s gun shot. This version again represents a disagreement with the equivalence theory since, as we saw, the manner of the harm's occurring is irrelevant to that theory. The third version, incidentally, is roughly the position found in the criminal law. [12]

I am of the opinion that the doctrines and distinctions of the criminal law are deserving of the utmost respect by the moral theorist, but I am convinced that there is a reason for thinking that the foreseeability test is unacceptable as a means of distinguishing cases from a moral point of view.

The point is that what is unforeseeable may make only the most insignificant difference in the result. For instance, *A* shoots at *B* and a bird unforeseeably intervenes. Yet the bullet may deflect off the bird and hit *B* in a place just slightly different from the spot *A* was aiming at. *A* may have aimed at *B*'s forehead but the bullet instead strikes *B* in the chest. Can this variation in trajectory make any difference in *A*'s blameworthiness? Or, again, to revert to an earlier case: the malfunction in a bomb's timer may be quite unforeseeable, yet it is hard to accept that an explosion's occurring fifteen minutes later than planned can make a difference, all else being equal, in a terrorist's blameworthiness. Sometimes a person might intend to produce a state of affairs in a certain manner and yet believe that the state of affairs *might* come about in some other, unintended way. But it is also possible that a person intends to produce a state of affairs and does not believe that it could come about in some other way because, for example, the steps to be taken are believed to insure that events will take place in a given way. The difficulty is seeing why this difference makes a difference inasmuch as the divergence could consist in the fact that, e.g., a bomb goes off at 12:15 rather than 12:00. The difficulty here is related to the one mentioned in regard to the first version, namely, an insignificant factor's making a moral difference. Nor will it do to suggest that "foreseeability" be understood in an objective fashion. The bomb's timing malfunction could be objectively quite unforeseeable and yet it still is hard to accept that this in itself could make the terrorist less blameworthy if the bomb goes off fifteen minutes late.

It is time to take stock of the arguments. I have presented two sorts of cases that present problems for the non-equivalence view. The first is "transferred intent." The initial difficulty for the theory is that it seems driven to hold that *A*'s killing of *C* is less blameworthy than A's killing of the intended victim B—a result at odds both with the equivalence theory and, I think, with common sense. The case also shows that the non-equivalence theory is not based on the idea that harm as such makes a difference between attempt and success, but rather on the idea that the difference between the cases is due to the occurrence of the harm *intended* by the agent. But this position still needs clarification in the light of a second kind of case where the intended harm takes place, but in an unintended way. The equivalence theory has a clear way of dealing with such cases, but the non-equivalence theory is caught between Scylla and Charybdis. On the one hand it can require that the actual manner be the intended one, or that the actual manner be foreseeable. In either case, trivial differences from the manner intended will entail a difference in blameworthiness. On the other hand, if the actual manner is irrelevant (so long as it involves no harm additional to that intended) then people will sometimes be blamed for harms that result from their actions in the most bizarre and fortuitous fashions. I will not claim that the equivalence theory definitely jibes with common sense: the non-equivalence theory gets much of its impetus from the fact that the two are at odds to some extent. But I do claim that the equivalence theory avoids the difficulties mentioned. It has, in addition, a certain intuitive appeal of its own as is evidenced, for example, in the case of transferred intent. In matters of this kind these considerations may be sufficient to tip the scales of reflective opinion in favor of the equivalence view.

There are two observations I wish to add in closing. The first, which I hope is unnecessary, is the following. To be committed to the equivalence theory is *not* to hold that harm is a completely irrelevant consideration in one's blameworthiness. I take no position on the matter here, but everything I have said is consistent with the proposition that harm is relevant when considering the blameworthiness of general *types* of actions.

Second, I want to discuss briefly one consideration which might explain why a successful attempt *seems* to involve more blame than an unsuccessful one. (There are also other considerations.[13]) It has been suggested that whenever blame is called for there is also usually an obligation to make reparations. An agent in such a case then has two obligations: to submit to just censure and to make reparations. Oftentimes the unsuccessful attempter will have only the first of these obligations, hence, the common misimpression that the successful wrongdoer is more

blameworthy.[14] Of course, the obvious problem with this suggestion is that it seems to stumble on the sort of case here discussed,
that of murder. In successful acts of killing, the person harmed
can't be compensated for the harm, although relatives can be to
some extent. I can't but think, however, that a related suggestion
has a certain plausibility even in the case of successful murder.
Perhaps the psychology of one's reaction to a murder is this: one
feels a certain level of indignation constituting one's blame for the
act, and one feels as well a demand that, as always, victims of
harm be compensated. Yet, one realizes, the victim can't be compensated and one's indignation increases, partly because one
feels that it is grossly unjust to be able to evade a duty to compensate by extinguishing one's victim. It would be as if murder
"paid," to some extent, from a moral point of view.

This train of thought seems understandable, but quite questionable rationally. It has a certain plausibility when an act of killing is a further act following, say, a rape and is intended to avoid
the obligation to compensate. But a murder is not usually so intended, and therefore it is illegitimate to treat it as if it were.
There is a further difficulty in the usual case where a murder is
not intended to evade the duty of compensation. It is hard to see
how augmenting the blame rectifies the injustice, since increased
blame does the victim no good; yet it was, so to speak, on behalf
of the victim that the blame was increased.[15]

Notes

1. The phrase is Bernard Williams': see the article with this title
in [chapter 2]. Thomas Nagel commented on Williams' paper when it was
first delivered and accepts his conclusions, although not all his arguments. See "Moral Luck" [chapter 3]. There is a rather different discussion reaching the same conclusion in Peter Winch's "Trying" in his
Ethics and Action (London: Routledge and Kegan Paul, 1972).

2. All three writers mentioned above accept this view.

3. I heartily endorse the remarks Holly Smith directed at Nagel in
"Culpable Ignorance," *The Philosophical Review*, vol. 92 (1983), pp.
569–70. There are other criticisms in Judith Andre, "Nagel, Williams
and Moral Luck" [see chapter 6]; Norvin Richards, "Luck and Desert"
[chapter 9].

4. This issue is addressed, albeit inconclusively, in Michael Slote, "Desert, Consent, and Justice," *Philosophy and Public Affairs*, vol. 2 (1973), pp. 323–47, esp. pp. 327–36.

5. Lawrence Becker argues that this is typically the case in the area of harms cognized by the criminal law. "Criminal Attempts and the Theory of the Law of Crimes," *Philosophy and Public Affairs*, vol. 3 (1974), pp. 262–94.

6. A useful discussion of this matter is contained in Michael Davis, "Harm and Retribution," *Philosophy and Public Affairs*, vol. 15 (1986), pp. 236–66, esp. pp. 241–52.

7. Joel Feinberg discusses, *inter alia*, whether killing harms the victim in "Harm and Self-Interest," *Rights, Justice, and the Bounds of Liberty* (Princeton: Princeton University Press, 1980), esp. pp. 59–68.

8. It might be retorted by the non-equivalence theorist that it is only in cases of transferred intent that the intention is the relevant feature, whereas in other cases it is the harm that results. But this is obviously *ad hoc*.

9. On this point, with respect to blame, see Smith, *op. cit.*, p. 564. With respect to responsibility see my paper "Collective Responsibility," forthcoming in *Philosophical Studies*. It has been denied that a person is said to be responsible, in the relevant sense, for his or her actions. See George Pitcher, "Hart on Action and Responsibility," *Philosophical Review*, vol. 69 (1960), pp. 226–35, esp. 227–31; P. H. Nowell-Smith, "Action and Responsibility" in *Action Theory*, ed. by M. Brand and D. Walton (Dordrecht, Holland: D. Reidel, 1976), pp. 311–22, esp. 314–19. See also the response to Pitcher by H. L. A. Hart in *Punishment and Responsibility* (Oxford: Oxford University Press, 1968), pp. 224–25. Neither Pitcher nor Nowell-Smith, however, denies that one can be *blamed* for one's actions. It would seem that Nowell-Smith confuses the claim that A is morally responsible (blameworthy) for his or her action with the claim that A is *causally* responsible for his or her action. The latter certainly does seem odd unless one accepts "agent causation." It should be added that I am using the words "blameworthy" and "to be blamed for" interchangeably with each other and with "responsible." It is true that "blame" (as well as "responsible") has a non-moral, causal meaning, but my usage of these terms is never intended in the present paper to have this meaning.

10. See Joel Feinberg, "Action and Responsibility" in his *Doing and Deserving* (Princeton: Princeton University Press, 1970), pp. 133–34.

11. This question is due to David Ring.

12. Wayne R. LaFave and Austin W. Scott, Jr., *Criminal Law*, second edition (St. Paul, Minn.: West Publishing, 1986), pp. 287–92, esp. 289. I am indebted for this reference to Fred Moss, who also helped me by discussion to formulate my thinking on these matters.

13. See the passage in Holly Smith, *op. cit.*, pp. 569–70, and Richards, *op. cit.*, p. 178. Smith and Richards agree in their suggestion that the difference in reaction in the two types of cases (i.e., attempt and success) may not be fully a *moral* reaction. Cf. the remarks of the sage legal scholar David Daube: "I remember a discussion with a leading classicist. I put it to him that it was understandable if a mother whose kid was run over by a motorist, *however blameless*, might not want to see him socially. He replied that he would have nothing to do with such a woman. This is surely over-intellectual; and passing strange coming from an expositor of Greek tragedy," (my emphasis). *Ancient Jewish Law: Three Inaugural Lectures* (Leiden: E. J. Brill, 1981), p. 50.

14. See W. D. Falk, "Intention, Motive and Responsibility," *The Aristotelian Society*, supplementary volume 19 (1945), p. 254, note. Compare Andre, *op. cit.*, pp. 205–06.

15. It is true that if Feinberg ("Harm and Self-Interest") is correct, then not only a) is death a harm, but b) it is possible *further* to harm a dead person (by, e.g., neglecting the terms of his or her will). And if that is possible, then presumably c) it is possible to *benefit* such a person. (Feinberg does not address this issue.) If such *post mortem* benefitting is possible then it would seem d) to be possible to compensate a victim of murder. If all these steps are granted then my contention that a plausible but unreasonable train of thought underlies the non-equivalence thesis even in the case of murder would have to be abandoned. But I think it is manifest that these are very big steps to take and no one, to my knowledge, has ever fleshed them out in such a way as to make plausible the conclusion that the victims of murder can be compensated for the wrongful deaths inflicted upon them. (Michael Davis very briefly suggests that some limited forms of compensation can be given to people wrongly (i.e., mistakenly) executed by the state in "Is the Death Penalty Irrevocable?," *Social Theory and Practice*, vol. 10 (1984), pp. 143–56, esp. p. 150.)

I am indebted to an anonymous referee of *American Philosophical Quarterly* for a detailed set of comments which have stimulated a number of revisions.

11

Morality and Bad Luck*

Judith Jarvis Thomson

I

There is a cluster of meta-ethical problems that have been familiar to all of us since we started thinking about philosophy: the cluster of problems about morality that are generated by Determinism. Suppose we grant first that every event has a cause, and second that for an event to have a cause is for that event to *have* to occur once its cause has occurred, and third that causality is transitive. Then, human acts being events, they too have causes, and thus have to occur once their causes have occurred; and causality being transitive, there is for each of us a time before our birth after which whatever we will do, our doing of it will have to occur. So whatever we do, we have to do, and cannot refrain from doing. This conclusion—The Determinist Thesis: Whatever we do, we have to do, and cannot refrain from doing—makes trouble for morality in the following way among others. It is intuitively plausible to think that your doing such and such, whatever the such and such may be, is not to your discredit unless you could have refrained from doing the such and such. (You killed Zelda? How terrible of you to have done that! But then we learn that what happened was this: you were forcibly injected with a drug that made you flap your arms wildly, but Zelda was in the way and you knocked her off a cliff. Now we do not think it was to your discredit to have killed Zelda.) But if we conjoin the thesis that your doing such and such is not to your discredit unless you could

---

*This is a revised version of the Second Metaphilosophy Address delivered at the Graduate Center of the City University of New York in April 1988. From *Metaphilosophy* 20 (1989): 203–221.

have refrained from doing the such and such with The Determinist Thesis, the result is that nothing a person does is to his or her
discredit. That strong result may be reformulated as follows: The
Strong Result: Whatever we do, our doing of it is not to our discredit. This is familiar territory. What is new is what has been
thought to be a new way of getting, not quite all the way to The
Strong Result, but near enough to it to be worrisome. What I have
in mind is something Bernard Williams and Thomas Nagel drew
attention to in their articles on what they call "moral luck".[1]

They too, like the Determinist, would have us take a closer
look at causality. Much of human action consists in causing
things: a breaking is a causing of a break, a killing is a causing of
a death. For example, person P shot person Q in the foot; if the
wound caused infection, and the infection caused Q's death, then
P has not only shot Q in the foot, P has killed Q. More generally,
there are many pairs of activities X and Y such that if we engaged
in X, and our engaging in X caused an outcome of a certain kind,
then we have not merely engaged in X, we have engaged in Y. But
sometimes, Williams and Nagel remind us, it is merely a matter of
luck—good or bad—that the agent's engaging in X caused an outcome of the appropriate kind; then it was merely a matter of luck
that the agent who engaged in X, also engaged in Y. But how, they
ask, could it be to a person's discredit that he or she engaged in
Y where it was merely a matter of luck that he or she did? It is
very plausible to think it could not.

An example will help. Alfred is a careful driver. Among other
things, he never backs out of his driveway without looking. This
morning, as always, he backed out of his driveway, watching carefully as he went. But this morning, alas, a small child had crept
into a low pile of leaves at the foot of Alfred's driveway, and in that
he could not see it, Alfred ran over it and killed it. It was mere bad
luck for Alfred (to say nothing of its having been bad luck for the
child) that the child had crept into that pile of leaves, and mere
bad luck for Alfred that his backing out of his driveway caused
the child's death. Surely it is not to Alfred's discredit that he
killed that child.

So far so good. Now for another story. Bert is normally a
careful driver. Among other things, he hardly ever backs out of
his driveway without looking. This morning, however, he backed
his car out without looking because of the exciting news he was
listening to on the radio. That is a bad business, and it is to Bert's
discredit that he did. Moreover, he was unlucky: a child ran into

the path of his car. Because, and only because, Bert was not look-ing, he did not see it, so he ran over it and killed it. I stress: if Bert had been looking, he would have seen the child and stopped short. But he was not looking so he did not stop short. How could it be to Bert's discredit that he killed a child where it was merely a matter of luck that he did?

Something fishy just happened, and we should stop over it. Surely Bert is to blame for that child's death! Bert backed his car out without looking, and it was by acting wrongly in that way that he caused the child's death. Alfred also caused a child's death, but *he* did so through no fault of his own, and therefore he is not to blame for the death he caused. We do, I am sure, want to say that while it is not to Alfred's discredit that he killed a child, it *is* to Bert's discredit that *he* did.

In fact there was something false assumed in that rhetorical question I just asked. I asked "How could it be to Bert's discredit that he killed a child where it was merely a matter of luck that he did?" But it was not merely a matter of luck that Bert killed the child. It was mere bad luck for Bert that a child ran into the path of his car; but it does not follow from that, and by hypothesis is not true in the story, that it was mere bad luck for him that he killed the child. For I said, in telling the story, that it was because, and only because, he was not looking that he did not see the child and therefore ran over it and killed it. If he had not behaved wrongfully, if he had been looking, he would have seen the child and stopped short. That is why Bert is to blame for the child's death—unlike Alfred.

Nagel would I think say this. "Granted: it wasn't *mere* bad luck for Bert that he killed the child. But it was mere bad luck for him that the child ran into the path of his car, and it was there-fore in part bad luck for him that he killed a child." I think he would draw our attention to a third story. Carol too is normally a careful driver. Among other things, she hardly ever backs out of her driveway without looking. This morning, however, she backed her car out without looking because of the exciting news she was listening to on the radio. That is a bad business, and it is to her discredit that she did. But Carol was lucky: no child ran into the path of her car, and nothing untoward happened as she backed out. I think Nagel would say: "The difference between Bert in the second story and Carol in the third story is entirely a mat-ter of the bad luck Bert had and she did not have." And I think Nagel would go on to say: "So Bert's acts (his backing out without looking *and* killing a child) can shed no more discredit on him than Carol's act (her backing out without looking) sheds on her. For surely if Bert did more than Carol did only because of the bad luck he had and she did not, then he is no more discredited by what he did than she is by what she did."

I think we feel considerable sympathy with this idea—it does seem very plausible.

Down this road lie some generalizations. Let us first take note of the fact that luck may work the other way. Bert backed his car out without looking, and it was bad luck for him that a child ran into its path, so it was in part a matter of bad luck for him that he killed it. Suppose Successful-villain tied a child up, placed it at the foot of his driveway, and then backed down towards the child, intending to run over it, and did run over it. It was not bad luck for Successful-villain that the child was tied up, lying in the path of his car; and it plainly cannot be said to have been even in part a matter of bad luck for Successful-villain that he ran over the child. Not because this was good luck; rather because it was neither. If I shoot a man in the head, there is no luck at all in its being the case that my shooting him causes his death, so that I have thereby killed him.

All the same, we may suppose that Unsuccessful-villain (like Successful-villain) tied a child up, placed it at the foot of his driveway, and then backed down towards the child, intending to run over it; and we may suppose also that nature, or God, was kinder to the child in Unsuccessful-villain's case than in Successful-villain's—the child Unsuccessful-villain wished to kill made a superhuman effort and burst its bonds so as to be able to get out of the path of the car in time. This *was* luck. Unsuccessful-villain may think it was bad luck, in that he had wanted to kill the child, though we may view him as having had good luck; and in any case it was certainly good luck for the child.

So the difference between Successful-villain and Unsuccessful-villain does not lie in Successful-villain's having had bad luck, but in Unsuccessful-villain's having had bad or good luck, according to your view of the matter. But how could this difference make a difference as to the discredit which their acts shed on them? I am sure Nagel would say: "Surely it is no more to Successful-villain's discredit that he tried to kill a child and succeeded than it is to Unsuccessful-villain's discredit that he tried to kill a child without success. For it was mere luck (good or bad) that distinguishes them from each other."

The following generalization emerges. Take any person, who engaged in an activity or set of activities X. And suppose that person's engaging in X caused an outcome of kind O. We can always imagine a second person who also engaged in X, but whose engaging in X did not cause an outcome of kind O. Perhaps it was luck (good or bad) that the first person's engaging in X caused an O, perhaps it was instead luck (good or bad) that the second person's engaging in X did not cause an O. Either way, it is no more to the first person's discredit that he or she both engaged in X and caused an O than it is to the second person's discredit that he or she merely engaged in X and did not also cause an O.

More simply: take any person, who engaged in an activity or set of activities X. It is no more to that person's discredit that he or she both engaged in X and did cause this or that outcome by engaging in X than it is to that person's discredit that he or she engaged in X.

Now many people hold a view of human action which can be expressed very roughly as follows: whatever a person does, his or her doing of it is either itself a purely mental act, or is a causing of something by some purely mental act or set of purely mental acts—whether of commission or omission. On this view, if you formed the intention of turning on the lights, and therefore did so, your turning on the lights was your causing the lights to go on by a set of purely mental acts, among which was your forming the intention of turning the lights on. Again, if your job was to feed the baby, and you would have fed it if you had not forgotten, but you did forget and it therefore died, then you killed the baby, and your killing of the baby was your causing its death by your failing to advert to your duty to feed it. If this idea about what people do is correct, then given our generalization, it follows that whatever we do, our doing of it is no more to our discredit than are those purely mental acts by which we do it—that is, The Weak Result: Whatever we do, our doing of it is no more to our discredit than are those purely mental acts by which we do it.

The Weak Result plainly is weaker than what I earlier called The Strong Result. The Strong Result, which we got to from Determinism, says that nothing at all that we do sheds any discredit on us. The Weak Result says only that nothing that we do sheds any *more* discredit on us than is shed on us by our purely mental acts.

I think it pays to stress that these two results were reached by different routes. What the Determinist draws our attention to is the fact that the causal relation licenses modal conclusions; and with that in hand, in conjunction with a very plausible view about what sheds discredit, we find ourselves zipping right through quickly to The Strong Result. What Nagel and Williams draw our attention to is the fact that it is not essential to a cause that it have such effects as it does have; and with that in hand, in conjunction with a very plausible generalization about what sheds discredit, together with a more or less plausible view about human action, we find ourselves getting, not all the way to The Strong Result, but anyway to The Weak Result.

What they do have in common, however, is the notion "discredit".

II

Let us begin by focussing on that notion. I have been pretending it is clear, but it is not.

I mentioned the notion "blame" in passing earlier on; we might well think that that is the notion "discredit" that is at work in The Strong and Weak Results.

The word "blame" turns up in a number of different ways in English, but I think its single most familiar kind of occurrence is in a certain kind of ascription of blame to a person for an unwelcome entity, typically an event or state of affairs. Who is to blame for this child's death? Who is to blame for the kitchen floor's being covered with mud? Bloggs is, we say. Very roughly, (Blame-1a) A person P is to blame for an unwelcome event or state of affairs just in case P caused it by some wrongful act or omission for which P had no adequate excuse.[2] So, for example, as I said earlier, Bert is to blame for the death he caused since he caused it by backing his car out without looking, which was a wrongful act for which he had no adequate excuse; by contrast, Alfred is not to blame for the death he caused since although he did cause the death, he did not cause it by a wrongful act or omission.

We sometimes say that a person is to blame for *being* such and such, where his or her being such and such is unwelcome—as, for example, in "Bloggs is to blame for being without a pencil". But a person's being such and such is a state of affairs, so this kind of occurrence of "blame" is a sub-kind of the kind for which I offered (Blame-1a) as analysis. Thus Bloggs is to blame for being without a pencil just in case he is to blame for the state of affairs that consists in his being without a pencil—that being true just in case he caused that state of affairs by a wrongful act or omission for which he had no adequate excuse.

A rather different way in which "blame" sometimes occurs is in a certain kind of ascription of blame to a person for *doing* such and such, where his or her doing it is unwelcome—as, for example, in "Bloggs is to blame for spitting at Cloggs". If a person P is to blame for *being* such and such just in case P is to blame for the state of affairs which consists in P's being such and such, then isn't a person P to blame for *doing* such and such just in case P is to blame for the event which consists in P's doing the such and such? If that were right, then this kind of occurrence of "blame" would also be a sub-kind of the kind for which I offered (Blame-1a) as analysis. But I think that that is not what people have in mind when they say such things as "Bloggs is to blame for spitting at Cloggs". When they say that, what I think they have in mind is not that Bloggs caused his spitting at Cloggs by some wrongful act for which he had no adequate excuse, but rather that Bloggs' spitting at Cloggs was itself a wrongful act for which he had no adequate excuse. I think, that is, that the analysis of this kind of occurrence of "blame" is: (Blame-1b) A person P is to blame for doing such and such, where P's doing the such and such is unwelcome, just in case P's doing the such and such is a wrongful act or omission for which P has no adequate excuse.

I do not suppose it matters much whether we say that what I have so far drawn attention to are two notions "blame", or one notion "blame" which is ascribed in two different ways. In order to stress a contrast I am shortly going to point to, I will say that there is one notion "blame" here, ascribed by sentences of the two different forms.

Now The Weak Result has nothing to say about whether, and if so in what degree, an unwelcome event or state of affairs, such as a child's death, or a person's being without a pencil, sheds discredit on a person. What The Weak Result attends to is the degree to which our doings of things shed discredit on us. So perhaps we can anyway construe the word "discredit" in it in accordance with (Blame-1b)?

The fact is that we can't. In the first place, the argument for The Weak Result says that once we have taken account of how much discredit Bert's having backed his car out without looking sheds on him, no further discredit is shed on him by his having killed the child he thereby killed. But Bert is not merely to blame for backing his car out without looking, he is also to blame for killing the child, for both of these—his killing of the child as well as his backing his car out without looking—were wrongful acts for which he had no adequate excuse.

More important, second, the argument for The Weak Result invites us to attend to the *degree* to which this or that act sheds discredit on a person, and the notion "blame" we have just singled out does not come in degrees. No doubt some acts are worse than others; no doubt some excuses are better than others; but a person's having no adequate excuse for a wrongful act does not itself come in degrees—either a person acted wrongfully without an adequate excuse or he or she did not, and there's an end on't.

There is, alas, a second notion "blame" which does come in degrees. Who is to blame for the kitchen floor's being covered with mud? "Bloggs", I say. "Ah", says Cloggs, "don't blame Bloggs for it". That's a funny business. One would have thought I had already blamed Bloggs for the kitchen floor's being dirty when I said he was to blame for it. So what can Cloggs mean by saying "Don't blame Bloggs for it"? Well, Cloggs may mean that Bloggs is not to blame for it in the sense we have pointed to. (Perhaps Cloggs thinks that Bloggs did not even cause it.) But it is of interest that Cloggs may mean something else. He may mean something like "Don't look askance at Bloggs", "Don't think *ill* of Bloggs". Here we may suppose Cloggs quite agrees with me that Bloggs caused the mess by a wrongful act or omission for which he had no adequate excuse, but nevertheless thinks the wrong was minor, not something that gives good reason to think Bloggs a bad person.

I said "alas" because I think that is a terrible way to talk. There is high praise and weak praise, and you can damn a person with faint praise; but blame is not symmetrical with praise, and there is no high blame or weak blame or faint blame. No matter: this is a fairly common use of the word and we know what people have in mind who talk the way I imagined Cloggs to do. Something like the following captures this use: (Blame-2) A person P is to greater or lesser blame for doing (or being) such and such, where his doing (or being) the such and such is unwelcome, just in case P's doing (or being) the such and such is stronger or weaker reason to think P a bad person.[3] I call this a second notion "blame" since it differs from the first in coming in degrees.[4]

Now it is surely this second notion "blame" that lurks behind that word "discredit" in the argument for The Weak Result. Bert and Carol backed their cars out without looking; Bert thereby caused a child's death, and thus killed a child, and Carol did not. The argument to The Weak Result says that what Bert did sheds no more discredit on him than what Carol did sheds on her. It is very plausible that we should take this to mean: what Bert did gives no stronger reason to think him a bad person than what Carol did gives to think her a bad person. Indeed, it is very plausible that that is *true*. For their negligence was the same, and the difference between them issues entirely from a piece of luck Carol had that Bert did not have.

Again, Successful-villain successfully murdered a child, and Unsuccessful-villain merely attempted murder. Here too I think we feel there is no difference in this respect: the facts we have been told about them give us equally strong reason to think they are bad people. For the difference between them issues entirely from a piece of luck Unsuccessful-villain's victim had and Successful-villain's victim lacked.

In short, I think that—modulo such concerns as we may well have about the view of action which it rested on—we should agree that The Weak Result is true. Neither of Bert and Carol is as bad as the two villains are: laziness, occasional inattention to the requirement to take simple precautions against doing harm, that is one thing, a readiness to commit murder is quite another. But other things being equal, Bert is no worse a person than Carol is, just as Successful-villain is no worse a person than Unsuccessful-villain is.

And it should be stressed also that The Weak Result is entirely compatible with its being the case that a person P is to blame—first notion "blame"—for the bad outcomes P causes, and for causing those outcomes. What Bert did gives no stronger reason to think he is a bad person than what Carol did gives to think her a bad person; but Bert is to blame—first notion "blame"—for a child's death, and for killing a child, whereas Carol is not. Similarly for Successful-villain, by contrast with Unsuccessful-villain.

III

Nagel supposes that something paradoxical comes out in the considerations that supported The Weak Result. On the one hand, following Kant, we think we are not "morally at the mercy of fate" (as Nagel puts it): surely it is irrational to rest moral assessment on what is, from the point of view of the person being assessed, mere good or bad luck. On the other hand, good or bad luck does have an effect on our moral assessments. Here is a passage he quotes from Adam Smith: "But how well soever we may seem to be persuaded of the truth of this equitable maxim [that one cannot be morally at the mercy of fate], when we consider it after this manner, in abstract, yet when we come to particular cases, the actual consequences which happen to proceed from any action, have a very great effect upon our sentiments concerning its merit or demerit, and almost always either enhance or diminish our sense of both." How are we to square our thought that we are not morally at the mercy of fate with the fact that "the actual consequences which happen to proceed from any action, have a very great effect on our sentiments concerning its merit or demerit, and almost always either enhance or diminish our sense of both"? Nagel tells us there is a paradox here, a paradox deeply embedded in our moral thinking.

Should we agree? Smith said "the actual consequences which happen to proceed from any action, have a great effect upon our sentiments concerning *its* merit or demerit" (my emphasis). Thus: Smith's Thesis: The actual bad consequences of an act incline us to think it worse than we would otherwise have thought it according as those consequences are worse. Is that thesis true? Well, what thought exactly does it attribute to us?

One possible interpretation is this: our thought is that the act itself is a "worse thing to happen" than it would have been had it not had those bad consequences. (Compare the fact that your fall downstairs was a worse thing to happen than it would have been had it not caused you a broken leg.) I am sure that under this interpretation of it, Smith's Thesis is true. Bert's backing his car out (which he did without looking, and which caused a death) really was a worse thing to happen than Carol's backing her car out (which she also did without looking, but which caused nothing untoward). And Alfred's backing his car out (which he did with all due care, but which caused a death) was as bad a thing to happen as Bert's backing his car out, and a worse thing to happen than Carol's backing her car out.

But this really is an uninteresting interpretation of Smith's Thesis, for under this interpretation of it, there is nothing in it that conflicts with our thought that we are not *morally* at the mercy of fate. After all, the fact that Alfred's backing his car out caused a death says nothing morally interesting about him.

On some views the evaluative notion "worse thing to happen" is not even, itself, a moral notion. Why not? Because it has nothing to do with *blame*.

We do not need to settle whether an evaluative notion has to licence conclusions about blame if it is to be not merely evaluative but also moral. Whether or not that is true, it is plausible to think it *is* thoughts about blame, or anyway thoughts that licence thoughts about blame, that Smith's Thesis should be understood to attribute to us. So understood, Smith's Thesis attributes to us thoughts about particular acts, but the thoughts about the acts have implications about their agents—so understood, the thesis says: Smith's Thesis (Blame Interpretation): The actual bad consequences of an act incline us to think its agent more to blame than we would otherwise have thought him or her according as those consequences are worse. But is this thesis true? Suppose (i) we hear that Bert was negligent and caused a death, whereas though Carol was also negligent she caused nothing untoward. We may well think that shows Bert was more to blame than Carol in that we think it shows Bert was more negligent than Carol. Not just that his negligence was worse in that it had worse effects but that he acted more carelessly. If that were true—and in the real world of actual cases (as opposed to the world of carefully constructed hypothetical cases) it is likely to be—then Bert really would be more to blame than Carol, and there would be nothing paradoxical in our thinking this of him.[5] But suppose (ii) we hear in addition that Bert was no more negligent than Carol, and that the difference between them lies in the bad luck he had and she did not. *Now* do we believe Bert more to blame than Carol?[6] I am sure we do not. Bert of course is to blame for a death (first notion "blame"), and Carol is not; but Bert is no more to blame than Carol (second notion "blame"), for given (ii), it is plain that Bert's history gives no more reason to think him a bad person than Carol's gives to think her a bad person.

"But don't we regard Bert with a moral indignation that would be out of place in respect to Carol? And doesn't that show we think him more to blame—in *some* sense of blame—than we think her?" Blame is often said to connect in some way with the "reactive attitudes". Well *do* we regard Bert with an indignation that would be out of place in respect to Carol? Even after we have been told how bad luck figured in his history and good luck in hers? I do not find it in myself to do so. And if we do, why is that a sign of a paradox in our moral thinking as opposed to a mere confusion on our part? After all, there is no good reason to regard Bert with an indignation that would be out of place in respect to Carol. Bert will of course feel markedly worse than Carol will, and it is right that he do so, for he caused a death whereas she did not—Alfred too will feel markedly worse than Carol will, for Alfred too caused a death[7], whereas she did not. Won't Bert feel worse than Alfred will? I should hope so, for Bert caused the death he caused by negligence and Alfred did not. But where is *blame* in all of this? For Bert's history really does give no more reason to think him a bad person than Carol's gives to think her a bad person.

A second of Nagel's grounds for supposing that there is a paradox in the offing here issues from a recognition that there is luck, not merely in the outcomes of our acts, but in the situations we find ourselves in, in response to which we act. On the one hand, following Kant, we think we are not "morally at the mercy of fate." On the other hand, there is what comes out when we remember that "It may be true of someone that in a dangerous situation he would behave in a cowardly or heroic fashion, but if the situation never arises, he will never have the chance to distinguish or disgrace himself in this way, and his moral record will be different" (p. 65). Nagel's example is this. Ordinary German citizens of Nazi Germany were faced with opportunities, and called on to make choices, that citizens of other countries were not. If an ordinary German citizen failed the test he was forced by circumstances to take, and acted badly, then his "moral record" is different from that of, say, a Canadian, who *would* have acted as badly if he had been forced to take the same test, but who was lucky enough not to have been forced to take it. The Canadian is (as Nagel puts it) "not similarly culpable". How are we to square the thought that we are not morally at the mercy of fate with the fact that the German's moral record is different from the Canadian's, and that they are not similarly culpable?

For my own part, I find this Canadian rather hard to get a grip on. What on earth is supposed to fix it about him that he would have acted as badly as the German did had he been forced to take the same test?

So let us take a simpler pair. Here are Judge Actual and Judge Counterfactual. Both are corrupt: both would accept a bribe if a bribe were offered and it was large enough. But neither has ever been offered any bribes. (They look so noble in their robes.) The defendant in a suit before Actual now offers Actual a large bribe, and Actual happily accepts it. If the defendant's suit were being tried before Counterfactual, he would have offered Counterfactual the same bribe, and Counterfactual would have accepted it equally happily, but by the luck of the courthouse draw, the suit is tried before Actual, and nobody offers Counterfactual a bribe.

The moral records of Actual and Counterfactual are different: one took a bribe and the other did not. Moreover, they are not similarly culpable: one is guilty of bribe-taking and the other is not. But do we regard Actual with a moral indignation that would be out of place in respect to Counterfactual? I hardly think so.

No doubt we will punish Actual and not punish Counterfactual, for we attach a penalty to bribe-taking and not to being a judge who would take a bribe if offered one; but that is for very good reasons that have nothing to do with the relative badness of those who actually, as opposed to merely counterfactually, take bribes. (Similarly for the difference in the punishments we will impose on Bert and Carol.) Would you have God throw Actual into a deeper circle of hell than Counterfactual? That would be rank injustice in Him, even if there is chance in nature and He did not cause the courthouse draw to come out as it did.

I fancy that a paradox is not a mere conflict of inclinations: it is a conflict of inclinations that for good reason survives a closer look. I think that this one does not.

IV

I suggested in section II that—modulo such concerns as we may well have about the view of action which it rested on—we should agree that—The Weak Result: Whatever we do, our doing of it is no more to our discredit than are those purely mental acts by which we do it—is true, given we take the word "discredit" in it to stand for the second notion "blame". What happens if we take the word "discredit" in—The Strong Result: Whatever we do, our doing of it is not to our discredit—also to stand for that second notion "blame"? What happens is that The Strong Result surely turns out to be false.

Here is Successful-villain, who murdered a child. "Ah", says the Determinist, "Successful-villain's killing of that child *had* to occur, Successful-villain could not have failed to kill it." Friends of the argument to The Strong Result would have us conclude that it is therefore not to Successful-villain's discredit that he killed the child. Can we take them to mean that Successful-villain's having killed the child is no reason at all to think him a bad person? Not if we are to suppose them to be right, for a man's committing murder *is* reason, excellent reason in fact, for thinking him a bad person.

The point to take note of here comes out particularly clearly if we look at a different result some people get to from Determinism. What I called The Determinist Thesis—The Determinist Thesis: Whatever we do, we have to do, and cannot refrain from doing—is a thesis about events, for it says that whatever a person does, the event that consists in his or her doing of it has to occur. Causal considerations take us equally well to a second determinist thesis, namely The Second Determinist Thesis: Whatever features we have, we had to have, and couldn't not have had. So, for example, if a person P has the features "is brown-haired" and "is left-handed", P had to have those features, and couldn't not have had them. And from here, one can as well pass to a second strong result, this one about features, namely The Second Strong Result: Whatever features we have, our having of them is not to our discredit. Can we take that to mean: whatever features we have, our having of them is no reason to think us bad people? Hardly. Suppose David has the following features: he is arrogant, a bully, a coward, devious, full of envy, and so on down through the alphabet of vices. The Second Strong Result says that his having those features is not to his discredit. But it certainly is excellent reason to think him a bad person. Surely it would be crazy to say "I can quite see that David is arrogant, a bully, a coward, and all the rest, but I wonder whether there's any reason at all to think him a bad person."

What I think the friend of these ideas would reply is this: "*Of course* David is a bad person. It's just that he couldn't have not been, so it's not to his discredit that he is." Indeed, the friend of these ideas must say this, for being a bad person is a feature of a person, and The Second Strong Result tells us that it is not to our discredit that we have such features as we do have. But "It's not to David's discredit that he is a bad person" cannot be true if it is taken to deny the second notion "blame" of David—for a man's being a bad person is excellent, indeed conclusive reason to think him a bad person.

Similarly for Successful-villain. The fact that he murdered a child just plain is reason to think him a bad person. If anyone says that his murdering of the child is not to his discredit, what is said cannot be true if it is taken to deny the second notion "blame" of him.

What emerges, then, is that while—modulo such concerns as we may well have about the view of action which it rested on—The Weak Result: Whatever we do, our doing of it is no more to our discredit than are those purely mental acts by which we do it—is true if the word "discredit" in it stands for the second notion "blame", The Strong Result: Whatever we do, our doing of it is not to our discredit, is false if the word "discredit" in it stands for the second notion "blame".

V

What happens if we take the word "discredit" in The Strong Result to stand for the first notion "blame"? To interpret The Strong Result in that way is to interpret it as saying that we are not to blame for any of our doings, where—according to (Blame-1b)—*that* means that none of our doings is itself a wrongful act or omission for which we have no adequate excuse. Thus, for example, Successful-villain's killing of the child he killed is not to his discredit since either his killing of the child was not a wrongful act or omission, or he had an adequate excuse for killing it.

A similar interpretation is available for The Second Strong Result: Whatever features we have, our having of them is not to our discredit. If we take the word "discredit" in The Second Strong Result to stand for the first notion "blame", then we are interpreting it as saying that we are not to blame for having any of the features we do have, where—according to (Blame-1a)—*that* means that our having such features as we do have was not caused by any wrongful act or omission of ours for which we have no adequate excuse. Thus, for example, David's being arrogant, a bully, and all the rest (indeed, David's being a bad person) is not to his discredit since he did not cause himself to have those features by a wrongful act or omission for which he had no adequate excuse.

In so far as we are inclined to feel that Determinism makes The Strong Result and The Second Strong Result true, I am sure that that is because we are interpreting those results in these ways, *and* because we feel that if Determinism is true, then none of a person's acts are wrongful acts for which he or she had no adequate excuse. (From here on, for brevity, I ignore acts of omission.)

Perhaps we feel that if Determinism is true, then none of a person's acts are wrongful at all, by way of a general principle typically expressed as " 'Ought' implies 'can'," or as we might put it here, " 'Wrongful' implies 'can refrain' ". If you do a thing, then according to The Determinist Thesis, you could not have refrained from doing it; it follows by the general principle, that your doing of it was not wrongful.

However a little reflection makes us see the reason there is to feel uncomfortable about this conclusion. Here is Edward, who is a really nasty character. Among other things he did yesterday was this: he tortured a baby to death for fun. *Fun!?* Where is the fun in torturing babies to death? Well, that is one of the many nasty things about Edward, the very fact that he does find doing this fun. So he did it. Can we really say with a straight face that Determinism shows us that Edward's doing this was not wrongful?

So perhaps instead we feel that while a person's acts may well be wrongful compatibly with the truth of Determinism, if Determinism is true then everyone always has an adequate excuse for what he or she does. Edward's torturing the baby to death was wrongful all right, but he had an adequate excuse for doing it.

But a little further reflection makes us see the reason there is to feel uncomfortable about this conclusion too. How *could* a man have had an adequate excuse for torturing a baby to death for fun?

There is of course an interplay between these two notions. The more inclined we are to think that a person's doing a thing was wrongful, the less inclined we are to think he or she had an adequate excuse for doing it. It seems perfectly plain that Edward's torturing a baby to death for fun was a wrongful act, and we therefore find it hard to see how he could have had an adequate excuse for it.

The interplay works the other way too. That is, the more we are inclined to think that a person had an adequate excuse for doing a thing, the less inclined we are to think his or her doing of it was wrongful. We learn that you killed Zelda. "How terrible", we think. Then we are told that this is how it happened. You were forcibly injected with a drug that made you flap your arms wildly, but Zelda was in the way and you knocked her off a cliff. That being so, you did have an adequate excuse for killing Zelda, and now we are disinclined to think that your killing of Zelda was a wrongful act. Similarly, if Determinism really does yield that Edward had an adequate excuse for torturing that baby to death for fun, we really would be the less inclined to think his act wrongful.

And in any case, if Edward did have an adequate excuse for torturing that baby to death for fun, it would follow from that fact that he was not to blame for doing it. If Edward is not to blame for torturing a baby to death for fun, then surely nobody is to blame for anything—first notion "blame"—and The Strong Result is true.

VI

The time has come to take a closer look at that notion "adequate excuse". When we give it a closer look, what I think comes out is that those two notions "blame" are related, and that it is not a mere linguistic accident that the same word "blame" is used to ascribe both.

It is a fair question exactly what I meant by the phrase "adequate excuse". A short answer to the question what I meant by it is this: completely exonerating or exculpating excuse. But what is a completely exonerating excuse? I suggest that it is an excuse that completely negates [8] the second notion "blame". The following thesis suggests itself: The Connection Thesis: A person P is to blame for doing such and such under the first notion "blame" if and only if P is in some measure to blame for doing the such and such under the second notion "blame". Thus P is to blame for doing such and such under the first notion "blame" if and only if P's doing the such and such gives some reason to think P a bad person. Consider Alfred again. He ran a child down, and it was mere bad luck for him that he did. He is not to blame (first notion) for killing that child, for his killing of it does not give any reason at all to think him a bad person. Bert also ran a child down, and it was not mere bad luck for him that he did: he was driving negligently. He is to blame (first notion) for killing that child, for his killing of it does give some reason to think him a bad person—though, given The Weak Result, Bert's killing of the child gives no more reason to think Bert a bad person than Carol's equally negligent driving gives to think Carol a bad person.

If The Connection Thesis is correct, then we should reject The Strong Result, construed as denying that the first notion "blame" ever applies to anyone. Here is Edward, who tortured a baby to death for fun; it cannot be thought that he had an adequate excuse for doing that, since his having done it *does* give us reason, excellent reason, to think him a bad person. Similarly for Successful-villain. Similarly, as I said, for Bert. That Bert did not kill the child intentionally, that he killed the child only by negligence, certainly mitigates: Bert's killing of the child does not give strong reason to think him a bad person. But it does give some reason to think this, and that is what marks him as not having an adequate excuse, and thus as having been to blame (first notion) for killing the child.

More generally, we would be entitled to pass from The Determinist Thesis to the result that no one is to blame (first notion) for doing anything only if the fact—supposing it a fact—that the present was unalterably fixed by the past meant that everyone always has an adequate excuse. Thus only if the fact that the present was unalterably fixed by the past meant that nothing anyone does gives any reason at all to think him a bad person. But that has got to be false.

It is common enough in discussions of the bearing of Determinism on morality for people to want to say "Well look, while some excuses surely do negate blame, not just any excuse does." And then it is common to start making lists of the excuses that do negate blame. For example: ignorance, compulsion, coercion, and so on. We feel uncomfortable about this response so long as we think the list of blame-negating excuses is a mere arbitrary clutter. Why isn't universal causation also a blame-negating excuse? That is why it is helpful to attend to the relation between the two notions "blame": doing so brings out the what is in common to those blame-negating excuses that makes them negate blame, namely the fact that they do negate the second notion "blame".

VII

And what of punishment and the unfavorable reactive attitudes that many people feel to be out of place if Determinism is true? Thinking of a man as a bad person does carry in train regarding him with disapprobation, mistrust, and the like; and—in light of the relation between the two notions "blame"—thinking of a man as deserving of punishment for what he did (he being to blame for doing it) does presuppose thinking of him as deserving of disapprobation, mistrust, and the like. Are we right to feel that Determinism makes all this be out of place? Answering this question would require looking into the deep question I have bypassed, namely what causality itself is. I said that what the Determinist draws attention to is the fact that the causal relation licenses modal conclusions; what modal conclusions, exactly?

I have only two comments to make, and neither bears directly on that question. In the first place, it pays to remind ourselves of how tightly wedged into an array of characterizations of people "bad person" is. I invited you to suppose that David has the following features: he is arrogant, a bully, a coward, devious, full of envy, and so on down through the alphabet of vices. And I said it would surely be crazy to say "I can quite see that David is arrogant, a bully, a coward, and all the rest, but I wonder whether there's any reason at all to think him a bad person." Are we to conclude from Determinism that David is not a bad person (for Determinism shows that unfavourable reactive attitudes are out of place), and therefore that David is not arrogant, a bully, and all the rest? That no one has any of these features at all? And if we do draw this conclusion from Determinism, shouldn't it be concluded, not that this shows there is a paradox at the heart of our moral thinking, but rather that we are confused about what causality is?[9]

Second, what confronts us here is not the same as what confronted us in section III above. What was at stake there was the idea that we regard the man who has bad luck in what his wrongful act causes (Bert), and the man who has bad luck in the circumstances he finds himself in (Judge Actual), with *more* disapprobation than we do those who lack that bad luck but are otherwise the same (Carol and Judge Counterfactual). Nagel and Williams pointed to something of great interest in pointing to the fact that luck does figure in our lives in these ways; I suggested, however, that when we take seriously that mere luck *is* what makes the difference, then we do not feel this difference in degree of disapprobation. But nothing in those contrasting pairs of cases shows that disapprobation is altogether and everywhere out of place. As I said, The Strong and Weak Results are reached by entirely different routes.[10]

Notes

1. Bernard Williams, "Moral Luck" [chapter two]; Thomas Nagel, "Moral Luck" [chapter three].

2. I said "very roughly", for surely the unwelcome outcome has to have been "within the risk" imposed by the wrongful, unexcused, act or omission—perhaps we can even say that the wrongful act or omission has to have been wrongful precisely in that it imposed a risk of the very kind of unwelcome outcome the act did in fact have. For you are not to blame for an unwelcome outcome of an act of yours if the outcome was caused by the act via a freakish, entirely unpredictable causal route. (This constraint has an obvious bearing on the limits of luck in blame: it shrinks them.)

In passing, there is of course a still simpler way in which "blame" turns up in English, as in such contexts as "The drought was to blame for the famine". Here I think we simply mean the drought caused the famine. But I think we never simply mean "caused" in ascriptions of blame to people.

3. Other options, which might well be preferable, are:

A person P is to greater or lesser blame for doing (or being) such and such, where P's doing (or being) the such and such is unwelcome, just in case P's doing (or being) the such and such is reason to think P a more or less bad person,

or

A person P . . . is reason to think P of more or less bad character,

or

A person P . . . is reason to think P has a more or less serious character flaw.

The differences among the possible formulations of (Blame-2) will not matter for our purposes.

4. It is arguable that there is yet another, third, notion "blame", which (like the second) comes in degrees. What I have in mind is that people sometimes say that person P is more to blame for outcome O_1 than person Q is for outcome O_2 (sometimes here $O_1 = O_2$), and perhaps mean by this that P made a larger causal contribution to O^1 than Q did to O_2 (compare "The drought was more to blame for the famine than the bad soil was")—or perhaps that P's wrongful act made a larger causal contribution to O_1 than Q's did to O_2. I leave this aside, however, as not relevant to either The Strong or Weak Results.

5. Suppose we hear that Alfred caused a death. We may well think that shows Alfred was greatly to blame in that we think that shows Alfred was at a minimum negligent and perhaps worse. In the real world (as opposed to the world of carefully constructed hypothetical cases) he is likely to have been.

6. Once we learn that Alfred was not at fault, and that it was mere bad luck for him that he caused a death, we do not think Alfred to blame

at all. It is a plausible idea that that is why Smith inserted that qualifier "almost always". (His words were: "the actual consequences which happen to proceed from any action, have a very great effect upon our sentiments concerning its merit or demerit, and *almost always* either enhance or diminish our sense of both." My emphasis.) For it is not in the least plausible to suppose that the actual consequences of Alfred's backing his car out incline us to think him more to blame than we would otherwise have thought him—unless those consequences incline us to think he really was at fault.

7. To my knowledge, Bernard Williams is the first philosopher to have noticed and taken seriously the fact that we do feel terrible when we have caused a bad outcome, even if we were entirely without fault in causing it. (See his "Moral Luck", *op. cit.*) He calls this phenomenon "agent regret". Drawing attention to it was a valuable contribution to philosophy; the question what it issues from is much worth mulling over.

8. Some people so use "excuse" that by definition an excuse completely exonerates. I am using it here in such a way that an excuse may merely mitigate, so that only some excuses completely exonerate.

9. I take this to be one of the many lessons to be learned from P. F. Strawson's by now classic article "Freedom and Resentment", which is reprinted in his *Freedom and Resentment*, Methuen & Co., London, 1976.

10. Expanded versions of different parts of this paper were presented to several different groups, and I am very grateful to those present for their comments and criticism. I should in particular mention and thank those who invited me to give the Metaphilosophy Address (at the Graduate Center of the City University of New York), the Neibuhr Lectures (at Elmhurst College), and the Gramlich Lecture (at Darmouth College).

12

Luck and Moral Responsibility*

Michael J. Zimmerman

Considerable attention has recently been given to what has come to be called moral luck. It has been claimed that recognition of this phenomenon imperils the received conception of moral responsibility; some, indeed, have said that this conception must be revised in light of this recognition. The issue may be put in terms of a puzzle that revolves around the following argument:

1. A person P is morally responsible for an event *e*'s occurring only if *e*'s occurring was not a matter of luck.
2. No event is such that its occurring is not a matter of luck. Therefore
3. No event is such that P is morally responsible for its occurring.

The puzzle is supposed to reside in the fact that the premises seem true but the conclusion false. Reaction to the puzzle has been varied. Joel Feinberg, one of the first to pose the puzzle (though not exactly in these terms), seems prepared—at least provisionally—to accept the conclusion.[1] Thomas Nagel thinks that there is a genuine paradox here and seems prepared to accept both premises while denying the conclusion.[2] Bernard Williams, while arguing forcefully for the truth of the second

*This paper was completed in large part while I was attending an institute on human action funded by the National Endowment for the Humanities and directed by Robert Audi at the University of Nebraska at Lincoln in the summer of 1984. I wish to thank in particular George Agich, Robert Audi, Margaret Urban Coyne, Philip Devine, Eric Russert Kraemer, Peter McInerney, Thomas Moody, and Mark Strasser for helpful comments on an earlier version. I am grateful also for the comments of some anonymous referees. From *Ethics* 97 (1987): 374–86.

premise, appears to deny the first, claiming that such denial runs counter to the received conception of moral responsibility.[3] Judith Andre likewise denies the first premise but rejects the claim that this runs counter to the received conception of moral responsibility, contending that this conception has Aristotelian as well as Kantian elements and that the former, if not the latter, countenance luck.[4]

In this paper I shall critically evaluate the foregoing argument. I shall present two versions of it and argue that neither version is compelling. These versions will be presented in Section I. In Section II the first version will be criticized. The second version—far more interesting than the first—will be discussed in Sections III–VII.

I

The sort of moral responsibility with which I am concerned here is that familiar, even if elusive, brand of responsibility which is the focal point of discussions concerning freedom and determinism. Such responsibility is commonly thought to have some essential link to freedom of will or action—a link which I have no wish to deny. In this sense of "responsibility," if someone is responsible for some event, then he is worthy of praise or blame for that event. Such praise and blame are of a particular, inactive sort, consisting in a positive or negative evaluation of the agent in light of the event in question. An agent is worthy of such praise or blame just in case such an evaluation of him would be accurate or true to the facts. Now, just what the precise nature of such praise and blame is, and just what the precise conditions of someone's being worthy of such praise and blame are, are of course matters which I cannot try to spell out here. Nevertheless, it is very important to note that such praise and blame are *not* actions but merely judgments, judgments about a person's moral standing or moral worth in light of the event in question. Not being actions, such judgments of praise and blame are not subject to *moral* justification (although, as judgments, they are subject to *epistemic* justification). *Active* praising and blaming—actions which, typically, serve to express, and which thus *presuppose*, judgments of praise and blame—are, of course, subject to moral justification; that is, as actions, they may be morally right or morally wrong. There is thus a great difference between internal judgments of praise and blame and external or overt actions expressive of such judgments. It is solely with the former that I shall be concerned in this paper.[5]

Now what, more exactly, is the issue concerning luck and such responsibility? Nagel sets the scene well:

> Whether we succeed or fail in what we try to do nearly always depends to some extent on factors beyond our control. This is true of murder, altruism, revolution, the sacrifice of certain interests for the sake of others—almost any morally important act. What has been done, and what is morally judged, is partly determined by external factors. However jewel-like the good will may be in its own right, there is a morally significant difference between rescuing someone from a burning building and dropping him from a twelfth-storey window while trying to rescue him. Similarly, there is a morally significant difference between reckless driving and manslaughter. But whether a reckless driver hits a pedestrian depends on the presence of the pedestrian at the point where he recklessly passes a red light.[6]

Nagel goes on to distinguish a variety of types of luck. For present purposes, just two types may be distinguished. I shall call these *situational* and *resultant* luck. The former consists in luck with respect to the situations one faces, including the nature of one's character (inclinations, capacities, and so on) as so far formed. The latter consists in luck with respect to what results from one's decisions, actions, and omissions.[7]

Nagel explicitly ties the matter of luck in with the matter of control, and this seems right. Something which occurs as a matter of luck is something which occurs beyond anyone's control.[8] But we should distinguish two ways in which something may be beyond someone's control. Roughly, one may be said to enjoy *restricted* control with respect to some event just in case one can bring about its occurrence and can also prevent its occurrence. One may be said to enjoy *unrestricted* or *complete* control with respect to some event just in case one enjoys or enjoyed restricted control with respect both to it and to all those events on which its occurrence is contingent. Thus an event may be beyond someone's control either in the sense that it is not in his unrestricted control[9] or in the stronger sense that it is not even in his restricted control.

We thus arrive at two readings of the argument that constitutes the puzzle. First:

1a.   P is morally responsible for *e*'s occurring only if P was in restricted control of *e*.
2a.   No event is such that anyone is ever in restricted control of it.
      Therefore
3 .   No event is such that P is morally responsible for its occurring.

Second:

1b.   P is morally responsible for *e*'s occurring only if P was in unrestricted control of *e*.
2b.   No event is such that anyone is ever in unrestricted control of it.
      Therefore
3 .   No event is such that P is morally responsible for its occurring.

But now, it seems to me, the puzzle disappears. I shall argue that neither version of the argument is persuasive. Statement 3 is not forced upon us; nor is our received conception of moral responsibility in need of revision.

II

The first version of the argument is easily dismissed. Both premises are problematic. There is reason to think that *1a* is false, when "restricted control" is understood as just outlined.[10] But I shall not dwell on this, for two reasons. First, even if *1a* is false, some interesting modification of it (where "restricted control" is understood in a sense different from, but closely related to, that just outlined) may well be true. Second, *2a* is plainly false[11] (and seems likely to remain so no matter what reasonable construal is given to "restricted control"). For there are many things, it seems, of which I am in restricted control right now. For example: I now enjoy restricted control with respect to my thirst's being quenched (for there is a glass of water nearby).

III

The second version of the argument, while unsound, is more interesting; though easy to dismiss, it yet has undeniable force.

And I suspect that it is this version that Feinberg, Williams, Nagel, and others have had in mind. Certainly, 2b seems true; in this sense, it must be admitted, luck (whether situational or resultant) *is* an ineliminable part of existence. For example, I can now quench my thirst, but this appears to depend (causally) on all sorts of things that are beyond anyone's restricted control, such as: the world having come into existence (a situational matter), the world not ceasing to exist before my throat reacts appropriately to the introduction of water (a resultant matter), and so on.

But even if 2b is true, 1b is surely false (and would remain so on any reasonable interpretation of "restricted control" other than, but closely related to, that just outlined), although both Feinberg and Nagel appear at times to accept it. For instance, Feinberg writes: "If he [the champion of moral responsibility] is a rational man, he will admit that moral responsibility for external harm makes no sense and argue that moral responsibility is therefore restricted to the inner world of the mind, where the agent rules supreme and luck has no place. . . . Morals constitute a kind of internal law, governing those inner thoughts and volitions which are completely subject to the agent's control, and administered before the tribunal of conscience—the *forum internum*."[12] (Of course, Feinberg goes on to say, quite rightly, that even the inner domain of one's thought and volitions is not immune to luck, in that even it is not under one's complete, i.e., unrestricted, control.) And Nagel writes: "If the condition of control is consistently applied, it threatens to erode most of the moral assessments we find it natural to make. The things for which people are morally judged are determined in more ways than we at first realize by what is beyond their control. And when the seemingly natural requirement of fault or responsibility is applied in light of these facts, it leaves few pre-reflective moral judgments intact. Ultimately, nothing or almost nothing about what a person does seems to be under his control."[13] And again:

> How is it possible to be more or less culpable depending on whether a child gets into the path of one's car, or a bird into the path of one's bullet? Perhaps it is true that what is done depends on more than the agent's state of mind or intention. The problem then is, why is it not irrational to base moral assessment on what people do, in this broad sense? It amounts to holding them responsible for the contributions

of fate as well as for their own—provided they have made
some contribution to begin with. . . . If the object of moral
judgment is the *person*, then to hold him accountable for
what he has done in the broader sense is akin to strict liability, which may have its legal uses but seems irrational as
a moral position.[14]

Although there is, I think, an important element of truth in all of
this, it also seems to me, at bottom, importantly mistaken. After
all, *1b* is clearly false, if only because no one is in control of his
being born—an event on which all of his decisions, actions,
omissions, and the consequences thereof are contingent. And we
all recognize this. Why should anyone think that our received
conception of moral responsibility implies otherwise?

What Feinberg and the others have latched on to is an important fact, and that is that we tend, for example, to praise and
blame someone for a good or bad decision more than one who did
not make the decision, even though the one who did not failed to
do so only because he was distracted.[15] Similarly, we tend to
blame someone who collaborated with the Nazis more than someone who did not, even though the one who did not failed to do so
only because he did not have the opportunity to do so.[16] Or again,
we tend to praise someone who rescued a child from a burning
building more than someone who did not, even though the one
who did not failed to do so only because he did not have the opportunity to do so. These differential judgments, based on situational luck, have counterparts based on resultant luck. As Nagel
notes, we tend to blame the reckless driver who hits a pedestrian
more than the one who, through no merit of his own, avoids doing so; or again, we tend to praise the scientist who finds a cure
for the common cold more than his colleague who, though
equally dedicated to relieving the suffering of humanity, fails,
through no moral fault of his own, to do so.[17] Such differential
judgment seems hard to justify.

IV

Indeed, such differential judgment would appear impossible
to justify if the following principle were true:

4.   If (i)   P brought about *e*,
      (ii) P* would have brought about *e* if *e** had occurred, and

(iii) e^* was not in P^*'s restricted control,
then whatever credit or discredit accrues to P for bringing about e accrues also to P^*.[18]

If 4 were true, then, it seems, the Nazi collaborator would be no more blameworthy than the non-, but would-be, collaborator; the rescuer of the child would be no more praiseworthy than the non-, but would-be, rescuer; the successful scientist would be no more praiseworthy than the unsuccessful scientist; the "successful" reckless driver would be no more blameworthy than the "unsuccessful" reckless driver; and so on. And the principle need not be restricted to moral credit and discredit. The case of the two scientists, for example, can easily be recast so that its primary concern is intellectual credit. Similarly, if Arnold deserves athletic credit for hitting a round of 67, then so, it seems, does Arnold*, who would have done the same but for a splitting headache. (Of course, Arnold will win the prize and Arnold* will not, but there seems to be no good reason to attribute a degree of intrinsic athletic excellence, or skill, to Arnold and not to Arnold*.) Or again, if the Sex Pistols deserve musical discredit for the cacophony they produced, then so, it seems, do the Sex Pistols*, who would have done the same but for chancing on the occasional euphonious chord.

Perhaps it is something like 4 that Feinberg and others have in mind, and, indeed, its application to the foregoing cases seems to yield plausible judgments. But, of course, 4 is false; it is too broad, too strong. Let P be Mother Teresa and e be the action of succoring cripples in Calcutta; let P^* be me and e^* be the event of my acquiring the character of Mother Teresa. It seems plausible to think that, given these conditions, 4 yields the result that I deserve the same credit that accrues to Mother Teresa. Or again, let P be Hitler and e be the action of exterminating millions of innocents; let P^* be me and e^* be the event of my acquiring the character of Hitler. It seems plausible to think that, given these conditions, 4 yields the result that I deserve the same discredit that accrues to Hitler. These are preposterous results.

Still, we must be careful to point up just what it is that is preposterous about these results. To do this, I shall distinguish roughly between two senses of "character." First, there is one's "given character," that set of dispositions to feel, think, and act to which none of one's actions has contributed (and of which some may be innate). Then there is one's "character as so far formed," which comprises both one's given character and also those dispositions to feel, think, and act (if any) to which one has contributed by virtue of one's actions (and for which, therefore, one may bear some measure of moral responsibility; e.g., I may crave drugs now, but such a craving may well be of my own making in such a manner that I am responsible for it). Now, this is all very rough and is surely not without its problems. Nevertheless, it seems to me appropriate to point out that it is not obviously preposterous to praise (or blame) me as much as Mother Teresa (or Hitler) if I would have done what she (or he) did if only I had had her (or his) *given* character. What is preposterous is to accord me the same credit or discredit if I would have done what they did if, but only if, I had had their character *as so far formed* (insofar as this differs, as it presumably does, from their given character).

Even if 4 is false, there is, I submit, something intuitively appealing about it, and perhaps some modification of it, where its antecedent is restricted by further conditions, is acceptable. But it is very difficult to figure out just what modification this is. One must beware of the trivial. For instance, the necessity of not engaging in differential judgment regarding Arnold and Arnold* would clearly be yielded by a version of 4 whose antecedent included the condition that P and P* possess the same athletic skills; such a version would be uninformative, however. I suspect that any interesting modifications of 4 must be drawn up piecemeal: what is pertinent to athletic (dis)credit may not be pertinent to intellectual, musical, or moral (dis)credit, and so on. Henceforth, I shall concern myself solely with moral (dis)credit.

V

Rather than try to draw up a single version of 4 which pertains to all types of situation concerning the implications of moral luck on the ascription of moral (dis)credit, I shall divide the task into two segments: the drawing up of such a principle first where it is resultant luck that is at issue and then where it is situational luck that is at issue. This task will be facilitated by presupposing a certain rough (*very* rough) picture of action which I cannot seek to defend here.[19] The picture is this: action consists in an agent's making a decision and this decision's causing a certain event. Free action is simply action in which the decision is free. This is a very familiar and surely plausible picture, despite the attempts of Wittgenstein and his followers to ridicule it.

With this rough picture in mind, I propose the following two principles, drawn up in the spirit of 4 but more adequate than it, though doubtless still too rough and problematic. The first pertains to resultant luck:

5. If (i)   P made decision d in what be believed to be situation s,
    (ii) e resulted from P's making d,
    (iii) e's resulting from P's making d was not in P's restricted control (except insofar as P's making d was in P's restricted control),
    (iv) P* made the same decision d in what he believed to be the same situation s,
    (v) e did not result from P*'s making d, and
    (vi) e's resulting from P*'s making d was not in P*'s restricted control (except insofar as P*'s making d was in P*'s restricted control),
    then whatever moral credit or discredit accrues to P for bringing about e accrues also to P*.

The second principle pertains to situational luck:

6. If (i)   P made d in what he believed to be s,
    (ii) P* would have made d if he had been in a situation that he believed to be s, and
    (iii) P*'s being in a situation that he believed to be s was not in his restricted control,
    then whatever moral credit or discredit accrues to P for making d accrues also to P*.

Now, these principles are still vague; but I do not wish to argue for them here, although I do advocate acceptance of them (or of something like them). My purpose, rather, is to highlight an important limitation to 5 and 6, a limitation that they have despite their being expressly designed to neutralize—as, indeed, they do neutralize—the role of luck in the ascription or moral responsibility.

The point is simply this: 5 and 6, though very powerful in terms of the neutralization of luck, do *not* entail that 1b is true. And so we are still not constrained to accept 3, even if we accept 2b, 5, and 6. It is extremely important to distinguish the claim, for example, that the collaborator and the noncollaborator are equally to blame from the claim that neither deserves any blame.

The latter does not follow from the former without some further premise to the effect either that the collaborator deserves no blame or that the noncollaborator deserves no blame. Nagel, in his talk of strict liability, seems to embrace the claim that the noncollaborator deserves no blame and, from this together with the claim that differential judgment in this case is unjustified, infers that the collaborator also deserves no blame.[20] Feinberg seems prepared to accept this conclusion also. But I reject it; for I reject the claim that the noncollaborator deserves no blame. I would argue, on the contrary, that because differential judgment in this case seems unjustified, and because the collaborator deserves blame, therefore the noncollaborator deserves blame also. Analogous remarks pertain to the cases of the rescuer and the nonrescuer, the two scientists, and the two reckless drivers. If there is unfairness in the differential judgments which we commonly tend to make in such cases—as I believe there is and as, according to 5 and 6, there is—then, I believe, this unfairness does *not* consist in ascribing moral responsibility to one of the parties involved but, rather, in not ascribing it to the other.

The question arises, however: what is it that we are to hold the noncollaborator, the nonrescuer, the unsuccessful scientist, and the unsuccessful reckless driver responsible *for*? I shall answer this by stages, dealing first with resultant luck and then with situational luck.

VI

It has been noted that resultant luck in ineliminable. One is never in complete control of the consequences of one's actions and omissions. The successful reckless driver was not in restricted control of the pedestrian's decision to take a walk, and hence not in unrestricted control of the death that resulted from the accident. But I find nothing in this observation to prompt a retraction of any ascription of blame to the driver. *Why* blame the successful reckless driver for the pedestrian's death? Let us suppose that his recklessness is due to drunkenness. Then, we may suppose, he was free not to drink, and hence free not to drive drunkenly, and hence free not to run over the pedestrian. Surely this suffices, ceteris paribus, for blaming him for the death.[21] That is, the death serves as an indication that, it is a reflection of the fact that, the driver is to be evaluated negatively on this occasion. Now, of course, if the driver had luckily escaped hitting anyone, there would be no death to serve as an indication that he is to be evaluated negatively; he would not, in other words, be to blame for any death. But there would nevertheless be occasion to evaluate him negatively, and one event which would indicate this would be his *decision* to drink, knowing that he would subsequently drive. He would, in other words, be to blame for this decision, one that he was free not to make. (See clause iv of 5.) This, I submit, is perfectly in keeping with the received conception of moral responsibility.

But someone might object as follows. I have said that the successful driver is to blame for the pedestrian's death, while the unsuccessful one is not. I have said that the unsuccessful one is to blame for his decision to drink and drive. But surely the successful one is also to blame for *his* decision to drink and drive. Thus there is nothing for which the unsuccessful driver is to blame that the successful one is not, but there *is* something for which the successful driver is to blame that the unsuccessful one is not. Hence the successful driver is more to blame than the unsuccessful one after all. In response to this I need only point out the need to distinguish between "P is to blame for more events than P*" and "P is more to blame than P*." The successful driver is to blame for more events than the unsuccessful one—more events serve to indicate that he is to be evaluated negatively on this occasion—but this does not imply that he is to be evaluated negatively to a greater extent than is the unsuccessful driver.[22]

Of course, given that the successful driver is no more to blame than the unsuccessful driver, then it must be admitted that, from the point of view of ascribing moral responsibility, it does not matter whether or not the terrible event—the death—comes about as a result of the decision to drink and drive, as long as the decision itself occurs. But, again, this does not imply that the successful driver is not to blame for the death. The death indicates the need for a negative evaluation only indirectly, as it were, while the decision indicates it directly; but an indirect indication is still an indication. While the death that results is not itself the occasion of a fresh negative evaluation, it nevertheless reflects the fact that some negative evaluation is called for. Moreover, we may still say that the successful driver did something *wrong* that the unsuccessful driver did not do, namely, run over a pedestrian. For this reason we may accept that Nagel is *correct* in saying that there is something "morally significant" about the difference between reckless driving and manslaughter, while consistently cleaving to 5, that is, while consistently denying that this makes a difference with respect to moral *responsibility.*

VII

Similar remarks pertain to situational luck, although it requires somewhat different treatment. Such luck, again, is inelim- inable. One is never in complete control of the situations that one faces, either with respect to "external" matters such as being born, being of a certain physical constitution, being distracted by a loud noise, being in a certain geographical location, and so on, or with respect to "internal" matters such as being irascible, suf- fering from an Oedipus complex, having a kindly disposition, and so on. And all of these matters affect what one does. It is against them as a background that one makes the decisions that one does; indeed, without such a background, no decisions could be made. Nevertheless, as long as the decision, for example, to col- laborate is made freely, then one is surely, ceteris paribus, to blame for such collaboration.[23] But, if the noncollaborator is just as much to blame, what is he to blame *for?* Not collaboration, clearly; and in this case there is not even the *decision* to collab- orate. In this regard the noncollaborator is significantly different from the unsuccessful driver.[24] I am not sure what the answer to the question is. Perhaps we should say simply that the noncollab- orator is to blame but just not to blame *for* anything; or perhaps we should say that he is to blame for being such that he would have made the decision to collaborate had he been in a situation that he believed to be s (where s is the situation that the collab- orator believed himself to be in).

If we say the latter, the link that many have claimed to exist between moral responsibility and freedom of will or action be- comes quite problematic. Many seem to have supposed that, if P is morally responsible for e's occurring, then e was either a free action or a consequence of a free action of P's. But the noncollab- orator's being such that he would have made the decision to col- laborate under the conditions specified was clearly not an action of his and might very well not have been a consequence of an ac- tion of his; and, certainly, 6 does not require that this character- istic of the noncollaborator have been either of these things in order for him to be as much to blame as the collaborator. Is there then no essential link between freedom and moral responsibility? This, I think, would be too hasty a conclusion. The link can be restored, albeit in different guise, simply by altering clauses i and ii of 6 so that they read "freely made" instead of just "made" and by adding that P* had the capacity to act freely. I would support such emendation, although I shall not seek to defend it here (just as I have not sought to defend principles such as 4–6 in general), except to point out that it seems manifestly unfair to blame (and so, also, to praise) an object, even an agent, that lacks the capacity to act freely.[25]

It must of course be acknowledged that there is a further problem with 6, and that is its incorporation of the counterfactual in clause ii. The truth conditions of such counterfactuals are notoriously difficult to determine. This difficulty is due to one of two things: either such counterfactuals have no truth value, or empirical verification of them is very hard to come by. Of course, if the former is ever the case, then 6 is vitiated, or at least its scope is restricted to covering whatever counterfactuals (if any) are of the relevant form and do have a truth value. In such a case, Feinberg and the others are successfully rebutted simply in virtue of this fact, at least with respect to certain instances of situational luck, unless they can find an alternative to 6 that does not suffer from the same problem. But I am dubious whether any of the relevant counterfactuals are in fact without truth value; it seems much safer simply to say that their empirical verification is very hard to come by. After all, one can imagine setting up controlled laboratory conditions in order to test the noncollaborator's propensity to collaborate and being able to draw a fairly well founded conclusion as to the truth value of the relevant counterfactual.

VIII

In sum, I accept that freedom of decision is crucial to the ascription of moral responsibility and thus to the ascription of praise and blame. Even if we grant Feinberg and the others, as I am prepared to do, that it is unfair to engage in differential judgment in the cases cited earlier, still there is room for praise and blame. Insofar as what happens after one has made a free decision is, in a sense, up to nature, then these events, while perhaps serving as indirect indicators of praise and blame, are strictly dispensable in the assessment of moral responsibility. (Of course, these events might be quite relevant when trying to determine the moral justifiability of *active* praise and blame and of the meting out of rewards and punishments, but that is a separate matter entirely.)[26] But the decision itself is not at all irrelevant; on the contrary, it is, one might say, the fulcrum of such ascription. And this is true even in those cases where no decision was made (as with the noncollaborator) but where one would have been made but for some stroke of fate or fortune.

Thus my reaction to the puzzle posed at the outset of this paper differs from the reactions of others. In many ways, but not all, my position is a Kantian one, although this is not something that I wish to dwell on. Still, like Kant, I think that our received conception of moral responsibility requires both that the role of luck be neutralized and that it nevertheless be possible for someone to be morally responsible for an event's occurring. These requirements are, I believe, quite consistent with one another.[27] And so, unlike Feinberg, I unhesitatingly reject 3. Unlike Nagel, I do not believe both 1 and 2 to be acceptable (unless there is equivocation on "luck"). Unlike Williams, I do not think that any radical revision of our conception of moral responsibility is called for, even though I agree that the proper conception appears not to be a *purely* Kantian one.[28] And unlike Andre, I believe that this conception is not essentially Aristotelian, even though not purely Kantian.

Notes

1. At least, this seems to be the case in Joel Feinberg, *Doing and Deserving* (Princeton, N.J.: Princeton University Press, 1970), pp. 34–37. This is not to say that Feinberg now accepts this conclusion or that his other writings commit him to it.

2. Thomas Nagel, *Mortal Questions* [chapter three]. This is undoubtedly a simplistic and insensitive way of putting Nagel's point, but I am at a loss to understand the final two pages of an otherwise admirably lucid article. Compare the note on p. 30 of Richard B. Brandt, "Blameworthiness and Moral Obligation," in *Essays in Moral Philosophy*, ed. A. I. Melden (Seattle: University of Washington Press, 1958), pp. 3–39.

3. Bernard Williams, *Moral Luck* [chapter two], pp. 36ff., including n. 11 on p. 55. Williams is concerned, not just with moral responsibility but with morality in general; but I think that his view is not distorted by the present restriction of it. The restriction is important; I wish to allow for the possibility that what is to be said about the relation between luck and the moral responsibility of persons is not to be said

about the relation between luck and other aspects of morality (such as the rightness and wrongness of actions).

4. Judith Andre, "Nagel, Williams, and Moral Luck" [chapter 6] throughout, esp. pp. 128–9. Like Williams, Andre's concern is morality in general but, as with Williams, part of her concern is moral responsibility in particular.

5. The distinction between inactive and active (praise and) blame has affinities with the distinction between "censure" and "reproof" given in Elizabeth L. Beardsley, "A Plea for Deserts," *American Philosophical Quarterly* 6 (1969): 33–42.

6. Nagel, p. 58.

7. What I call situational luck comprises what in Nagel, p. 60, are called constitutive luck, luck in one's circumstances, and luck in how one is determined by antecedent circumstances. What I call resultant luck corresponds with what Nagel calls luck in the way one's actions and projects turn out.

8. More restrictively: something which occurs as a matter of luck with respect to someone P is something which occurs beyond P's control.

9. Note how tempting it often is to say that one is not "really" or "fully" in control of an event *e* unless one is or was also in control of all those events on which the occurrence of *e* is contingent. Compare Feinberg, p. 35.

10. See Harry G. Frankfurt, "Alternate Possibilities and Moral Responsibility," *Journal of Philosophy* 66 (1969): 829–39; and Michael J. Zimmerman, "Moral Responsibility, Freedom, and Alternate Possibilities," *Pacific Philosophical Quarterly* 63 (1982): 243–54.

11. Unless hard determinism is true—and I am assuming that it is not.

12. Feinberg, p. 33.

13. Nagel, p. 59.

14. Ibid., p. 63.

15. Feinberg, p. 35.

16. See Nagel, p. 66. Nagel says: "We judge people for what they actually do or fail to do, not just for what they would have done if circumstances had been different." If "judge" is understood as "tend to judge," I would agree. But there is some indication that Nagel means not just

"judge" but "ought to judge," and here I would disagree. See principle 6 below and the commentary on it. Again, cf. Brandt, p. 30n.

17. Nagel, p. 71, n. 11.

18. Recall, with respect to clause iii, that whatever is not in one's restricted control is ipso facto also not in one's unrestricted control.

19. It is defended in detail in Michael J. Zimmerman, *An Essay on Human Action* (New York: Peter Lang, 1984).

20. At the same time, Nagel seems to acknowledge the justifiability of blaming the collaborator. See n. 2 above.

21. The "ceteris paribus" clause is not unproblematic, but I shall not try to fill it in here. It includes such conditions as the driver not being a three-year-old, and so on. Note that if the driver were not free not to drink—if he were an alcoholic, say—there *might* be reason not to blame him for the death. But I am assuming that he is not an alcoholic.

22. Williams's interesting remarks concerning what he calls agent-regret need to be addressed here (see Williams, pp. 42–45). Contrary to what Williams seems to suggest, it is *not* morally appropriate for the successful driver to regret what he has done more than the unsuccessful driver regrets what he has done. (In our world, such unsuccessful drivers are all too ready not to feel the appropriate degree of regret.) At least, this is so for *intrinsic* appropriateness. We can, of course, admit that it can be *extrinsically* morally appropriate for a successful driver to feel a greater degree of regret than an unsuccessful one. Suppose that the successful driver had not been at fault in causing the pedestrian's death. If (in an intrinsically appropriate manner) he had shown no more regret than an unsuccessful driver would have done in similar circumstances, we might be warranted in being suspicious. For it is unlikely that anyone in such a position can turn regret off in a manner which is intrinsically appropriate to the circumstances; and thus the successful driver's showing no regret here would be an indication that he would have shown no regret in circumstances where it was intrinsically called for (cf. Nagel, p. 61).

23. Again, the "ceteris paribus" clause is not unproblematic. See n. 21 above.

24. Compare Feinberg, p. 35, where Feinberg says (of feelings rather than decisions), "[A person] can no more be responsible for a feeling he did not have than for a death that did not happen."

25. There is another sort of unfairness—not in judgment, but in fact—which seems to me to rest in the fact that an unfree object (whether animate or not) never has the opportunity to distinguish itself

(or to disgrace itself) in such a way as to deserve praise (or blame). In this sense, the world is unjust. Compare Joel Feinberg, *Rights, Justice, and the Bounds of Liberty* (Princeton, N.J.: Princeton University Press, 1980), pp. 276–77, n. 7, on a comparative conception of cosmic injustice. Compare also Nagel, pp. 65–66, including n. 9.

26. Compare Nagel, p. 61, where the matters are not kept separate. The matters are related, of course.

27. Still, see n. 25 above.

28. See Bernard Williams, *Problems of the Self* (Cambridge: Cambridge University Press, 1973), p. 228, where Williams accuses Kant of embracing absurdity when he (Kant) talks of a self which is not empirically conditioned. I agree that such talk is highly suspect, but none of what I have said in this paper commits me to such talk.

13

Moral Luck and the Virtues of Impure Agency*

Margaret Urban Walker

One's history as an agent is a web in which anything that is the product of the will is surrounded and held up and partly formed by things that are not, in such a way that reflection can go only in one of two directions: either in the direction of saying that responsible agency is a fairly superficial concept, which has a limited use in harmonizing what happens, or else that it is not a superficial concept, but that it cannot ultimately be purified—if one attaches importance to the sense of what one is in terms of what one has done and what in the world one is responsible for, one must accept much that makes its claim on that sense solely in virtue of its being actual.

—Bernard Williams, "Moral Luck" (pp. 44–45)

Moral luck consists in the apparent and allegedly problematic or even paradoxical fact that factors decisive for the moral standing of an agent are factors subject to luck. Although several variants have been noted,[1] the ones commanding most attention are luck in the ways our actions and projects turn out (sometimes called *resultant* luck), and luck in those circumstances we happen to encounter that provide opportunities for excellence or disgrace (*circumstantial* or situational luck). Favored examples of the former include the negligent driver who is unlucky enough to strike and kill a pedestrian, as opposed to the equally negligent driver who is lucky enough not to. In the latter category, we may consider the bad fortune of someone who has the opportunity to become a Nazi collaborator and the character that prompts her to

*From *Metaphilosophy* 22 (1991): 14–27.

do so; for one fit for heroic resistance, this same opportunity amounts to being luckily in just the spot for admirable moral achievement. In such cases someone winds up a killer or collaborator, someone else merely negligent or a moral heroine, and the substantial, even vast differences in the moral standings of such agents is due as much to luck as to anything these agents do.

Three positions on moral luck are recognizable in the contemporary literature: that moral luck is real, but constitutes a paradox in the context of other ordinary and central assumptions about morality; that moral luck is illusory, a misleading impression based on insufficiently fine analysis of belief and practice; and that moral luck is real and not paradoxical, even if wishfully distorted or simply inadequate views of the human condition make it appear so. In what follows I argue for the reality and deep importance of (resultant and circumstantial) moral luck in human life and against the view that assumptions which render moral luck paradoxical are truly ordinary or central to conceiving or conducting moral life. My view is thus a variant of the third sort of position. In Section I, I present an overview of the terrain of the discussion to date, identifying what is thought to constitute the problem. In Sections II and III, I defend the ways in which moral luck is in fact and indeed ought to be central to our conceptions of agency, responsibility, and our common good.

I

The "problem" of moral luck resides in a sense that persuasive general beliefs about the conditions for moral responsibility are at odds with our actual common practices of moral assessment in cases involving an element of luck. Common belief is said to endorse the principle—a "control condition"—that factors due to luck are "no proper object of moral assessment and no proper determinant of it, either" (Williams, p. 35) or, more simply, that people cannot be morally assessed for what is due to factors beyond their control (Nagel, p. 59). Yet common practice shows that uncontrolled happenstance indeed figures in the assessment of particular sorts of cases. For example, the negligent driver who cannot control the unlucky, untimely emergence of the child whom he strikes and kills is perceived as committing a greater offense than a merely, but equally negligent, nonkilling driver and is held to be worthy of greater blame. What is to be said about the differential moral assessment of cases where the difference is an element due to luck? What is to be done about the apparent persistent slip between persuasive principle and common practice?

Bernard Williams and Thomas Nagel, who introduced the problem into contemporary literature and baptised it so disconcertingly, held that moral luck, the determination of moral assessment in some cases by happy or unhappy contingency, is altogether *real* but constitutes a full blown *paradox* in "our conception" of morality (Williams, p. 37, 54) or "the ordinary idea of moral assessment" (Nagel, p. 59) when viewed in light of intuitive notions linking moral responsibility to the agent's control. A paradox requires a remedy that restores consistency, but neither Williams nor Nagel proposed one. Instead they suggested darkly that the reconstruction of principle required by practice might alter our understanding of ourselves or of the role of morality in our lives beyond recognition.

Others have argued, contrary to Williams and Nagel, that moral luck surely *cannot* be real; they find it deeply unfair, if not incoherent. The "control condition," the intuitive principle limiting moral assessment to just such factors as an agent controls, is held to be virtually self-evident. Further, its corollary, that "one cannot be more culpable or estimable for anything than one is for that fraction of it which is under one's control" (Nagel, p. 60), shows that differential assessments where the sole difference in cases is a factor due to luck cannot be correct. Hence, for example, the lucky and unlucky negligent drivers *are* both blameworthy, but can only be *equally* so; that one case resulted in a killing is a matter due to luck. Assuming that practice just cannot be so wildly at variance with self-evident truth, these critics adopt the strategy of explaining away the appearance of moral luck to restore consistency.

Henning Jensen [ch. 7] and Norvin Richards [ch. 9], in such attempts to show moral luck illusory, allow that we do *seem* often enough to allow matters of luck to figure in our moral assessments, but aim to show through closer scrutiny and additional distinctions that the control condition is not in fact violated. Unfortunately, the assumptions at work in their accounts are at least as counterintuitive as they take moral luck to be. Richards's account rests on the dubious assumption that we *in fact* consider only a person's character, and never acts or their results, worthy of praise or blame. Jensen's account requires us to accept the troubling assumption that actually causing the harm one risks merits no more blame than merely risking that harm without causing it.[2]

A third avenue is to take moral luck seriously enough to call into question theoretical principles that would not cohere with it. Martha Nussbaum's extensive and vivid study of moral luck as a defining theme of classical Greek thought demonstrates how long its recognition has been with us and how the *wish* to deny or contain moral vulnerability is a philosophical quest as old as the Western tradition [See ch. 4]. Judith Andre [ch. 7] reminds us that our long tradition of ethical thought makes for "hybrid" concepts, partaking of different (though not necessarily contradictory) strains; moral responsibility, for example, has more or less Kantian as well as rather Aristotelian applications and connections, the latter of which allow for the impact of luck in the sphere of moral value. If the recognition of moral luck is so deeply rooted, our theoretical pictures of moral value and responsibility should accommodate it. If they do not, the acceptability of those pictures needs defending.

From Nagel and Williams through Richards and Jensen, however, the control condition stands curiously undefended.[3] Yet the principle is not self-evident (and certainly not a tautology). It expresses a substantive view about the conditions under which we should see ourselves and others as responsible for actions and their outcomes. By consequence, it marks out the area in which various responses (owning up; assuming or accepting blame or liability; experiencing sorrow, anguish, shame, or guilt; offering reparative gestures) are appropriate for the actor, and various others (imputing responsibility to others or holding them blameworthy; experiencing indignation, outrage, disgust, or disappointment; expecting or demanding reparation, apology, or other fitting acknowledgment; developing or losing trust) are appropriate for others. The moral assessments at issue, then, in the contest between moral luck and the control condition are not only bare imputations of responsibility but evaluations of a full repertoire of perceptions, judgments, expectations, responses, attitudes, and demands with respect to ourselves and others in the matter of our conduct, its meaning, and its impact.

It is in light of this that I propose to defend the reality of moral luck and to reject the view that it generates an insoluble problem. Elsewhere I have argued that moral luck threatens paradox only in the context of a view of moral agents as noumenal, or virtually so (Coyne 1985). But we are human agents and as such are hopelessly "impure" in Williams's sense—agents of, rather than outside, the world of space, time, and causality; agents whose histories and actions belong to it. The beautifully simple regimentation of responsibility embodied in the control condition represents an alteration of our common life far more drastic than may at first be supposed. To accept it, I will argue, would rid us of far more than an alleged kink in our philosophical thinking.

In the following section I explore, albeit very briefly, some deep and extensive connections between our causal inextricability, which combines limited control with significant efficacy, and the moral significance of our response to it. I claim that the reality of moral luck alone makes sense of an important arena of assessment in which agents are found satisfactory or deficient, even admirable or base, to the extent that they understand their causal position and the appropriate responses to it. Judgments in this area center around the matter of an agent's *integrity*. In Section III I consider why certain responses *are* so widely considered appropriate: they are too valuable to us in our vulnerability and interdependence to dispense with. To show this I explore the disparity between an understanding of human agency that accommodates moral luck and one that refuses to accommodate it. Considering two pictures of agency polarized along the dimension central to the moral luck problem, the relation of control to accountability, I propose that the stakes in affirming one or the other of these pictures are high ones and that we have good reason to go with our luck.

II

How do we commonly regard and what do we expect of agents in actual situations of having "unluckily" caused serious harms or having "unluckily" confronted moral tests that their characters did not prevent them from failing miserably? Here only vivid and closely described cases could generate precise and specific results. It will matter whether a negligent killing driver drove knowingly with faulty brakes, drove 105 m.p.h. in a residential area, drove home in exhaustion to get to a dying parent's bedside, or refused friends' assistance and drove himself home very drunk. It will matter whether a woman with hungry children keeps a lost, money-filled wallet that contains identification, whether a child is caught up in a Nazi youth group at school or an adult informs on his Jewish neighbor for political advantage, whether someone lied out of humiliation or greed. These differences will matter for our judgments on the degree and type of wrong, and on the appropriateness of blame, its amount, and its nature. Yet in most, if not all, such cases of uncontrolled upshots or unchosen circumstances, there is one thing I think we will find at least faulty if not completely unacceptable: that the agent should *shrug it off.*

Suppose the agent says, in effect,

> It's really too bad about what happened and the damage that's been done, but my involvement was just a happenstance that it was my bad luck to suffer. I admit my negligence (dishonesty, cowardice, opportunism, etc.) and accept such blame as is due these common faults. But it would be totally unfair of you to judge, let alone blame me for unlucky results and situations I didn't totally control and stupid or masochistic of me to let you.

It is hard to imagine any variation on this sort of agent response not striking us as untoward. Given the nature of the case, it could be disappointing or irritating, shameful or indecent, shocking or outrageous. Even where we as third parties are disposed to be compassionate, fair-minded, and humane, we would be taken aback, and perhaps indignant. If our indignation were met by the agent with a cool reminder that we were conceptually befuddled about assessment and control, our estrangement would, I suggest, be aggravated rather than relieved. We would think there was something wrong with the agent that went deeper than the initial offense. What the agent's stance puts in question is how responsible or responsive he or she is. We might say that he is cavalier, or that she is kidding herself, or more simply and strongly, that this person lacks integrity. We might just experience the equivalents of these by feeling disgust, resentment, indignation, loss of trust.

Such responses are common phenomena of our moral lives together when we do not simply imagine ourselves as the ideal moral judiciary or as officers of the moral police, armed with sharp instruments of blame. When we do not restrict ourselves to thinking about this problem in the "juridical" mode—that of sitting in judgment and levying blame—we are more apt to remember the variety of assessments and considerations that will concern us, including ones about trust, confidence, and reliability and the responses that will express our grasp of these. The reality of moral luck renders these more varied phenomena intelligible, if we take moral luck for what it appears to be: a fact of our moral situation and our human kind of agency. The *fact* is our perfectly predictable entanglement in a causally complex world, with imperfectly predictable results. Part of the normal and required self-understanding of human agents is a *grasp* of that fact, of the loose and chancy fit between undertakings and impacts, and between where we would choose to find ourselves and where we actually do. This fact requires us to understand and respond to our actual situation of being at moral risk; that is, of being subject to assessment both for results of what we have (uncontroversially) done and for our actions under circumstances morally fraught, where these results and circumstances are determined in important part by luck. The truth of moral luck that the rational, responsive moral agent is expected to grasp is that *responsibilities outrun control,* although not in one single or simple way.

This truth in turn renders intelligible a distinctive field of assessments of ourselves and others, in terms of how we regard and respond to just this interplay between what we control and what befalls us; to, as Williams might say, the "impurity" of our agency. Here we expect ourselves and others to muster certain resources of character to meet the synergy of choice and fortune, which is especially burdensome in the case of bad moral luck. Here agents are found to have or lack such qualities as integrity, grace, or lucidity. These qualities might well be called *virtues of impure agency.* As is said of dispositions that are virtues, they issue in acceptable or even meritorious behavior that contributes "in extensive and fundamental ways" (Wallace 1978, p. 37) to our living well in concert with others a distinctively human life. They are corrective of temptations and deficiencies of sorts to which human beings are commonly susceptible with typically or overall undesirable results (Foot 1978, p. 8). They are constituted in important part by a reliable capacity to see things clearly, to take the proper moral measure of situations, so that a fitting response may be fashioned (McDowell 1979; Mackie 1977; Murdoch 1971).[4] While acceptance of responsibility, whether in excess of control or not, will often prompt reparative attempts that enlist various of the familiar virtues—courage, justice, benevolence—bad moral luck taxes agents in distinctive ways to which the qualities mentioned distinctively respond.

Integrity is a quality of character hard enough to describe in any case, but impossible to capture fully without reference to the

vicissitudes of moral luck. The "intactness" or "wholeness" that
are its core meanings imply freedom from corruption, spoilage,
shattering, or decay. What integrity so protects, however, is not
one's goals or goods or social standing, but one's *moral self*, that
center of moral commitments in oneself from which morally fitting and valuable responses flow in a sure and steady way. From
the viewpoint of others, the agent's firm moral center guarantees
dependability in the matter of morally responsible conduct not
just in the long run or in the sphere of the everyday, but more
especially in trying times where unwanted circumstance pro-
poses more severe tests. What integrity is a bulwark against is
not just lapses or simple wrongdoing, which are always possible,
but a deeper or more catastrophic loss or lack of moral center.

The conditions that most threaten us with this kind of loss
or most unequivocally reveal this lack are just those constituting
moral luck: the decisive moral tests one did not invite and that
may reveal one's moral competence or commitments as a pre-
tense; the faulty or horrifying results that one invited but did not
control and that one is expected to find resources to address or
redress without taking refuge in denial, demoralization, or paral-
ysis. People we know to have integrity are those who have been
challenged in just such ways; their integrity consists in the fact
that they are able to stand and respond in terms that embody ongoing moral commitments or such new ones as may be required.
They keep or make whole and well what might otherwise suffer
deformity, collapse, or desertion: a coherent and responsible
moral posture. Temptations to avoidance and denial are successfully countered.[5]

It is also true that integrity can be caricatured in an un-
seemly and narcissistic "heroism" or self-glorifying but ineffective
martyrdom (literal or symbolic). There are morally unlucky cases;
for example, where a life is lost or a deep human bond severed,
where there remains little place for meaningful reparation to others and where the self-reparative work of integrity seems a small
even if necessary response to an inexpungeable loss. Acceptance,
nonaggrandized daily "living with" unsupported by fantasies of
overcoming or restitution, may in its quiet way be as profoundly
admirable as integrity in those situations that permit no recon-
structive address. I would call this, simply, *grace;* it also has its
place in far less grievous situations, where it is one's good moral
luck to have received forgiveness or mercy and where one should
not succumb to self-absorbed or exhibitionistic contrition.

Further, integrity and grace depend critically on *lucidity*, a reasonable grasp of the nature and seriousness of one's morally unlucky plight and a cogent and sensitive estimate of repairs and self-correction in point. Temptations to self-deception, self-indulgence, and wishful thinking here must be overcome. As in the other cases, the capacities in question can be virtues only if they are relatively fixed dispositions; but their fixity may indeed be relative, varying concretely by degree or even, perhaps, with respect to contexts.

Perhaps *lucidity* is just a name for the reliable perceptual capacity that grounds integrity, as *grace* may refer to integrity's understanding of the limits of its own effectiveness. But whether these virtues are distinct or aspects of one thing, they are possible and necessary only for agents whose natural situation involves vulnerability to luck, and so part of whose distinctive achievement will rest on how well and truly they reckon with that. Virtue, James Wallace has said, "must tend to foster good human life in extensive and fundamental ways. It must be the perfection of a tendency or capacity that connects or interlocks with a variety of human goods in such a way that its removal from our lives would endanger the whole structure" (Wallace 1978, p. 153). If integrity is the capacity required to deal morally with the impurity of luck-ridden human agency, its general absence should be a disfiguring of human life in ways broad and deep. For the same reason, a way of conceiving agency that attempts to banish the impurity that gives integrity its point should produce under examination an alien and disturbing picture of moral life. And so it does. I turn to this now.

III

The "moral luck problem" is one about conceptions of agency and responsibility of the sort that morality requires. Moral luck is part of a picture of *impure agency:* agency situated within the causal order in such ways as to be variably conditioned by and conditioning parts of that order, without our being able to draw for *all* purposes a *unitary* boundary to its exercise at either end, nor always for *particular* purposes a *sharp* one. Such agents' accountabilities do not align precisely with their conscious or deliberate choices or undertakings and are not necessarily limited by them. Rather, the match between choice and action, on the one hand, and accountability and desert, on the other, is inexact

and conditional, and it is mediated by complex social understandings that these agents are expected to appreciate and
share.[6] To be sure, matters of control and faulty intention will be
elements in these understandings; but so will matters of fore-
seenness, forseeability, magnitude of adverse impacts, significance or conspicuousness of causal contribution, as well as (loose
or precise) appreciation of probabilities of different sorts. Part of
the complexity of these understandings consists in the fact that
there appears to be no single equation of responsibility in which
each or all of the elements play fixed roles. Still, an underlying assumption of these understandings is that responsibilities are apt
to outrun deliberate commitments, intentional choices, and even
their foreseen or foreseeable entailments. In this picture, we are
players within the complex causal set-up, where the price of our
often decisive participation is exposure to risk.

The view against which moral luck offends is that of *pure
agency:* agency neither diluted by nor implicated in the vagaries
of causality at all, or at least not by causality external to the
agent's will, itself understood as a causal power. This view is epit-
omized by Kant's conception of the moral agent as noumenally
free, so outside space, time, and causality entirely. But it also
comprehends nontranscendental pictures of agency that share
with Kant's just the feature of immunity to luck. Such views do
not need to withdraw agency entirely from the realm of causality
to secure this.[7] It is sufficient that the possibility of assessment
be allowed to stretch only so far as does that causality which may
be identified with the agent itself; for example, the causality of
character or of intention. Nagel has recently given striking expression to the ideal aspiration of pure agency: "What we hope for
is not only to do what we want given the circumstances, but also
to be as we want to be, to as deep a level as possible, and to find
ourselves faced with the choices we want to be faced with, in a
world that we can want to live in" (Nagel 1986, p. 136). It is, at
last, the drive "to be able to encompass ourselves completely, and
thus become the absolute source of what we do" (ibid., p. 118).[8]

It is characteristic of those who view moral luck as philosophically problematic or paradoxical to claim it is so in light of
"our" or "the ordinary" concept of agency, assessment, or moral
responsibility. Yet no one denies that facts of the matter *seem* to
resist. I have argued that they are indeed facts, that in some pre-
cincts especially our practice shows a grasp of our causal inextricability and some burdens we take it reasonably to impose. At the
same time, I do not mean to ignore the existence of some lively,

"principled" intuitions to the effect that such practices embody an unfortunate mistake. Rather than prolong indecisive proprietary disputes about intuitions, I turn instead to the question of what is at stake in the contest between the actual practices I have emphasized and some possible ones purified along lines provided by the control condition. We should ask, What is it *like* to live under the strict correlation of moral assessment and responsibility with control? What is it like to be, and to be among, pure agents?

First, pure agents will have far less to account for, and will bear, in total, far less responsibility than many of us think we and others currently do. No unforeseen results will place them at risk of assessment, let alone blame; even foreseen but uncontrolled upshots of their intentional performances will not properly place them in question. Presumably, no fewer damages, hurts, harms, deprivations, violations, cripplings, and killings will occur. Indeed, pure agents have fewer moral reasons to take care for these eventualities, even if they still have various social and practical ones. But these sufferings and misfortunes will go more often unattributed; they will be *other people's* hard luck.

Pure agents will not only be responsible for less, but will bear a special kind of relationship to their responsibilities: they will unilaterally control and constitute them. Pure agents are free, on their own, to determine what and how much they may be brought to account for by determining the intentional acts and commitments they will undertake, and recognizing the limits to their control beyond these. What will no longer be true, if it ever was properly thought to be so, is that the realities, potentials, needs, vulnerabilities, and sufferings of other things and people might be part of what constitutes their responsibilities. Relationships, situations, and encounters in which emerge uncontrolled and uninvited needs, demands, and opportunities to enable or harm will not be thought to ground morally legitimate claims upon us or in our behalf, in ways we might have thought or hoped. Even if we had invited these relationships, situations, or encounters, we would not have controlled all of the demanding possibilities they give rise to. I may have decided to have a child, but will probably not have decided to have a sickly and difficult one; I may have entered into a friendship, but surely will not have controlled the death of the friend's wife and the desperate neediness with which he turns to me. That legitimate moral claims can overreach deliberate commitments, that need or suffering can even sometimes *impose* responsibilities it would be indecent to ignore do not seem to be realities in the world of pure agents.

Being accountable and actually bearing responsibilities is burdensome. Being accountable means exposure to possibilities of criticism, rebuke, and punishment; to valid demands of reparation, restoration, or compensation; to proper expectations of regret, remorse, self-reproof, and self-correction. It would be nice to have to do and accept so much less of this, and pure agents enjoy such relief. Having conceptually divested themselves of much of their moral property, they have secured unusually favorable rates of moral taxation. In respect of any particular performance or default, they are rendered far less vulnerable to many burdens of these sorts that might have applied if features due to circumstantial and resultant luck had not been rendered morally unaccountable. Concomitantly, however, all other pure agents are thereby rendered a great deal more vulnerable. Their augmented burdens involve needs, pains, and frustrations deriving from various injuries and misfortunes that result from the actions of other, morally unburdened pure agents; the latter have achieved impunity in such respects, but the former can no longer rightfully propose or expect compensation or repair, nor even enjoy the mild satisfactions (or relief) of others' appropriate regret or fitting remorse.

Pure agents, in sum, are freer on the whole from responsibility; are freer to define for themselves what and how much responsibility they will bear; and hence are freer from the varieties of burden to which responsibility renders one subject. Pure agency is a model of *independence*. Unlike the Stoical independence of withdrawal from worldly, bodily, or common life, however, we see here independence of a more robust and worldly sort, reserving the full field of action while paring responsibilities to fit consent, commitment, and contract—the markers of voluntary control.[9] In pure agency we recognize the template of versions of the clearly bounded and rationally self-controlling agent of neo-Kantian and contractualist moral philosophies, and the socially discreet, rationally self-disposing self of liberal political theory.[10]

One cannot deny that pure agents are enviably free, in certain ways, of unhappy fate and of each other. Their enviable independence, however, cannot help being at the same time a worrisome and unpleasant *undependability*. Their unilateral control of responsibility and their exemption from reparative demands in all areas beyond strict control make clear that such agents may not reasonably be looked to for much. In particular, pure agents may not be depended on, much less morally required, to assume a share of the ongoing and massive human work of caring, healing, restoring, and cleaning-up on which each separate life and the collective one depend. That the very young and old, the weak, the sick, and the otherwise helpless—that is, all of us at some times—depend on the sense of moral responsibility of others unlucky enough to be stuck with the circumstance of their need will not be the pure agents' problem. It is alarming to anticipate life in a world where people routinely and with justification walk away from the harmful, cruel, or even disastrous results that their actions were critical, even if not sufficient, in bringing about. In a technologically advanced society in which some people's actions can have a disproportionate impact on huge numbers of unknown others, the prospect is worse than alarming. All these prospects are real ones in a world from which moral luck has been banished and agency purified.

Impure agents are saddled with weighty responsibilities and the open-ended possibility of acquiring more due to circumstances beyond their control. Yet agents who recognize their vulnerability to fortune are primed for dependability of humanly invaluable sorts. These are agents on whom we can depend, or at least to whom the presumption of dependability applies, and so whose undependability in many cases can be duly registered as failure. To the extent that these agents are people of integrity, they will not fail us, even under the blows of bad fortune or odd turns of fate that might otherwise prompt denial or opportunism; to the extent that we ourselves are such agents and possess integrity, we can depend, morally, on ourselves even in a bad spot.

Anyone may fail morally in the particular dimension of facing bad moral luck. There are also cases so trying as to be virtually beyond human endurance, circumstances or results so shattering that maintaining integrity would be supererogation. They are the stuff of tragedy. But the association of moral luck with tragedy should not obscure the fact that the tragic case is a rare one, whereas more pedestrian instances of moral luck are ubiquitous, and its common challenges are everyday matters. In a world where we need so much from each other so often, acceptance of our impurity is not the worst we can do.[11]

Notes

1. Nagel describes four types of moral luck: constitutive (luck in the kind of person one is); circumstantial (luck in the problems and sit

uations one faces); luck in how the will is determined by antecedent circumstances; and luck in the way one's actions and projects turn out (p. 60). The first and third types are often seen, correctly, as representing the metaphysical problem of freedom and determinism, whereas the second and fourth have drawn most interest as representing the problem of moral luck proper. Nagel's and Williams's discussions (the latter's "Gauguin problem" being of the fourth type) are the locus of the contemporary debate.

2. In a similar move, Michael Zimmerman [see ch. 12] claims that the killing driver's being to blame for a death just means that he is "to blame for more events" but not "more to blame." But being "to blame for a death" is here reduced to the death's being "an indicator" that one deserves a negative evaluation, the *same* negative evaluation one deserves for negligent driving alone (p. 227). This move appears to be a terminological maneuver; what is described is not "being to blame for the death" but is just being to blame *for negligence* in light of, or in view of, or because of a death.

Richards admits that his position looks more like a wholesale "utilitarian" revision of common understanding than an interpretation of it (pp. 177–178). Jensen elaborates a complex and interesting account of blaming to show how equally blameworthy persons might be in practice differentially blamed. But Jensen, although explaining why harmless negligent acts often escape active blame entirely and why malicious acts with or without harmful results typically receive blame, never does explain the specific case at issue, or propensity to actively blame (even punish) people for negligent acts with harmful but not completely controlled results (pp. 136–137). It is not clear to me that he can get the answer he needs. See Jonathan Adler (1987) for a strong reply to Richards.

3. In fairness to Williams, I should note that he does emphasize the role of immunity to luck (secured by limiting accountability to control) in rendering acceptable the idea that morality is ubiquitous in scope and supreme in authority. Williams thus locates the control condition in an ensemble of features of a certain vision of morality he argues cannot be right.

4. See also May (1984, pp. 248–249) on the importance of viewpoint, and not only action, in facing the "perennials" of human existence: birth, death, incapacitation, generational conflict, and I would add, moral luck.

5. This does not, of course, constitute a theory of integrity, but I believe it expresses the core of a plausible one. The central idea is that integrity is the capacity for reliably maintaining a coherent moral posture, and that this capacity is proven only under challenge. Whether the posture in play must meet some minimal standards of correctness or adequacy, and whether it must be in some way "authentic," that is, truly or

reflectively the agent's own, are questions a more complete discussion might address.

6. Joel Feinberg (1965) provides a useful discussion of the several senses of responsibility that may be distinguished in connection with human actions and the fact that just a bit of causal contribution suffices for some kinds of responsibility, whereas no causal contribution is even necessary for others. Robert Audi (1974) nicely analyzes a variety of conditions, including normative ones, that constitute, diminish, or cancel moral responsibility. For a probing conceptual examination of some intricacies in the legal understanding of connections among causal involvement, responsibility, and liability, see Judith Jarvis Thomson (1986).

7. Richards, Jensen, and Zimmerman are examples.

8. For Nagel these are expressions of what moral agency requires, even though the conditions set are impossible to attain, and so the appetite for autonomy is insatiable.

9. I thank Martha Nussbaum and Neil Delaney for suggesting to me that the Stoic approach to the neutralization of luck in human life deserves more thought. The contemporary discussion rather naturally tends to fix overmuch on Kant. A more just treatment would need to explore fundamental differences in meaning and motivation between the ideals of *autarkeia* and *autonomy*, as well as the important similarities.

10. The foregoing discussion of pure agency is not offered as a refutation of such moral or political views, but as a response to those who propose the control condition as limiting moral responsibilities. I do intend, however, to raise the question of the adequacy of an entirely constructivist or consensual view of responsibility to the role of contingency in our lives. An admirably concise and effective critique of attempts to ground all special moral responsibilities to particular persons or categories of persons on consent or agreement is found in Goodin (1985).

11. Two opportunities to present earlier versions of this paper were helpful to me: I thank the Vanderbilt University Philosophy Department Colloquium audience, especially Alasdair MacIntyre and John Post, for their comments; and those present at the University of Santa Clara conference on Agency, Causality, and Virtue (1987). Thanks to John Arthur, Robert Audi, Christopher Gowans, and Arthur Walker for helpful suggestions and criticisms. I am grateful to Fordham University for the Faculty Fellowship leave during which I wrote earlier drafts of this paper.

References

Adler, Jonathan. 1987. "Luckless Desert Is Different Desert." *Mind* 96:247–249.

Audi, Robert. 1974. "Moral Responsibility, Freedom, and Compulsion." *American Philosophical Quarterly* 11:1–14.

Coyne [Walker], Margaret Urban. 1985. "Moral Luck?" *The Journal of Value Inquiry* 19:319–325.

Feinberg, Joel. 1965. "Action and Responsibility." In *Philosophy in America*, ed. Max Black. Ithaca, N.Y.: Cornell University Press.

Foot, Philippa. 1978. "Virtues and Vices." In *Virtues and Vices.* Berkeley and Los Angeles: University of California Press.

Goodin, Robert. 1985. *Protecting the Vulnerable.* Chicago: University of Chicago Press.

Mackie, John. 1977. *Ethics.* New York: Penguin Books.

May, William. 1984. "The Virtues in a Professional Setting." *Soundings* 67:245–266.

McDowell, John. 1979. "Virtue and Reason." *The Monist* 62:331–350.

Murdoch, Iris. 1971. *The Sovereignty of Good.* New York: Schocken Books.

Nagel, Thomas. 1986. *The View from Nowhere.* New York: Oxford University Press.

Nussbaum, Martha. 1986. *The Fragility of Goodness.* Cambridge: Cambridge University Press.

Thomson, Judith Jarvis. 1986. "Causation and Liability." *Rights, Restitution, and Risk.* Cambridge, Mass.: Harvard University Press.

Wallace, James. 1978. *Virtues and Vices.* Ithaca, N.Y.: Cornell University Press.

14

Postscript

Bernard Williams

Daniel Statman has kindly given me the opportunity to add some remarks to my original article. It would not be appropriate for me to try to comment in detail on the papers collected here, but I would like to take up one or two points that are suggested in them or have come up in other work that has appeared since the article was first published.

When I introduced the expression *moral luck*, I expected it to suggest an oxymoron. There is something in our conception of morality, as Tom Nagel agreed, that arouses opposition to the idea that moral responsibility or moral merit or moral blame should be subject to luck. This is so, I still think, because the point of this conception of morality is, in part, to provide a shelter against luck, one realm of value (indeed, of supreme value) that is defended against contingency. However, there are some misunderstandings that I now think my formulations in *Moral Luck* may have encouraged.

One misunderstanding is fairly superficial. The conception of morality that has these associations is very well entrenched, with the result that if one says that there is a certain difficulty with (this conception of) morality, one may be taken to mean that the difficulty must arise with (any) morality; that is to say, with any scheme for regulating the relations between people that works through informal sanctions and internalized dispositions. One way of getting around this, which I have suggested more recently,[1] is to use the words *ethics* and *ethical* in the more general sense, reserving the term *morality* for the local system of ideas that particularly emphasizes a resistance to luck. (The emphasis that this system places on resisting luck is connected with other characteristics; it has, in particular, its insistence that the conclusions of moral reasoning should take the form of obliga-

tions.) The suggestion that we might use these words in this way
has hardly, as yet, swept all before it, and it no doubt has its own
powers to mislead, but I will follow it here. In these terms, morality does try to resist luck, in ways that my and Nagel's articles
bring out, but not every ethical outlook is equally devoted to doing so. I can entirely agree with Judith Andre that an Aristotelian
emphasis in ethics, for instance, would not run into the same
difficulties.

Morality, in the restricted sense in which I am now using the
term, is to some extent, of course, a theoretical construct, and
even those who agree that there is a special formation of this kind
may reasonably disagree about what exactly is central to it. It is
this kind of disagreement, I think, as well as the general distinction between morality and the ethical, that helps to sustain
controversy on the question of how significant or interesting morality's resistance to luck may be. About that controversy, it seems
to me that there is at any rate a fair dialectical point to be made:
critics who claim that morality is not so concerned about luck as
I suggested are at least matched in numbers and weight by those
who manifestly are concerned about luck and are anxious to
show that *moral* evaluations, properly understood, do not apply
to those aspects of a situation that are matters of luck.

The distinction between morality and the ethical may help
me to focus my view of Nagel's analogy with epistemological skepticism. I entirely agree with him, and indeed it is central to my
view, that the resistance to luck is not an ambition gratuitously
tacked on to morality: it is built into it, and that is why morality
is inevitably open to skeptical doubts about its capacity to fulfill
this ambition. In this respect, there is an analogy to the idea
(which I also accept) that there are intrinsic features of the concept of knowledge that invite skepticism. Indeed, I suggest in the
article that this is more than an analogy: the concept of knowledge is itself involved in discounting luck.[2] However, there is also
an important disanalogy. Everyone needs the concept of knowledge, but if morality is a local species of the ethical, and the resistance to luck is (at least in a strong form) one of its
idiosyncrasies, then not everyone is stuck with these skeptical
problems. Human beings have lived, do live, and doubtless will
live, by conceptions of the ethical that do not invite these problems, or invite them in a much less drastic form. For these problems to be endemic not just in morality (in the narrow sense) but

in our life, it would have to be the case that morality (in the narrow sense) was inevitably the form that ethical life took, and this is not so.

Nagel does suggest in his article, and has developed the idea in subsequent work,[3] that the general structure of these perplexities is inherent in the tension between a subjective and an objective view of action. Although I cannot argue it here, I do doubt whether it is simply the nature of action as a metaphysical problem that gives rise to these difficulties. It is reasonable to think that if we are to have the concept of an action, we must have the concept of a voluntary action; that is to say, very roughly speaking, the idea of an intended aspect of something done in a state of mind that is deliberatively normal. But we should recognize, and we can perfectly well recognize, that the idea of the voluntary is essentially superficial.[4] Stronger demands on the idea of the voluntary come not from the mere need to recognize human actions, but from ethical sources. We feel the need to exempt agents from (some) blame for (some) things done involuntarily and also, perhaps, to deepen the idea of the involuntary, because we think it unjust not to do so.

It can be readily pointed out that this idea, though it certainly expresses morality's concerns, can hardly be deployed to back them up: the notion of injustice at work here is morality's own. That is correct, but it is not very helpful. If these are our feelings and our dispositions of judgment, then that is what they are, and a historical or philosophical distinction between morality and a more general conception of the ethical is not, in itself, going to make them go away. We need, not that general formula, but insight into what the distinctions of the voluntary and the involuntary, and the other conceptions related to the avoidance of luck, mean to us. Among the questions raised here are the following. Because, necessarily, we cannot ultimately avoid luck, what do we actually do about it? Why do we mind more about it in some connections than in others? Among our reactions to things that are done wrongly or badly, what does blame, in particular, do? Does it apply in the same way to others and to one's own self?

We also need to understand the demands we make on the justice of public processes, in particular the criminal law. In framing these demands, we may suppose that we are being guided by an ideal of perfect justice, embodied in a notion of moral responsibility, and that what we are trying to do, in a necessarily imperfect way, is to make our institutions reflect that ideal. There is a striking phrase in Judith Andre's chapter that expresses this: she says that even an atheist who does not believe in an all-just, omniscient, judge "can ask what such a judge would do." My own view is that we have very little idea of what such a judge would or could do (the history of Christian belief, particularly of the doctrine of grace, perhaps bears me out on this) and that the very conception of somebody's knowing everything that bears on the judgment of a person's life or action, and giving indisputably the right weight to each element in it, is unintelligible. Atheists say that in forming ideas of divine judgment we have taken human notions of justice and projected them onto a mythical figure. But also, and worse, we have allowed the image of a mythical figure to shape our understanding of human justice.

Morality wants to understand everyday blame as a finite anticipation of a divine, perfect, judgment, but blame cannot be coherently understood in those terms. Granted this, we need to ask why blame should matter so much, why morality is disposed to make such a lot of it. This question has two sides to it, and they are equally important. On one side, we should ask why blame, just in itself, should be thought to be such a fearsome thing that, like weapons of destruction, it can be loosed only in circumstances that ultimately justify it. On the other side, we have to think of all those hostile and painful reactions, to oneself and others, that are not blame—or, at any rate, not blame as morality would wish it to be.

This second aspect raises a question that I still think needs to be pressed: what is the point of insisting that a certain reaction or attitude or judgment is or is not a *moral* one? What is it that this category is supposed to deliver? At several places in the course of the papers collected here, writers agree that an agent may reasonably feel bad about something that he or she has done, or indeed may reasonably attract negative reactions from others, but they go on to insist that these reactions do not belong to *morality*. Here I can only urge again the point that I have tried to make in various other places, that invoking this category achieves absolutely nothing, unless one has some account of the singular importance of morality in this restricted sense. I still cannot see what comfort it is supposed to give to me, or what instruction it offers to other people, if I am shunned, hated, unloved, and despised, not least by myself, but am told that these reactions are at any rate not *moral*.

The most important source of misunderstanding in *Moral Luck* was that I raised, as I now think, three different issues at once. One was the question that I have just mentioned: how important is morality in the narrow sense as contrasted with a wider sense of the ethical? The second question concerns the importance, for a given agent and for our view of certain agents, of the ethical even in the wider sense. Any conception of the ethical will include in some form a concern for people directly affected by one's actions, especially those to whom one owes special care: suppose that my fictional Gauguin offended against such a conception. The question remains of where we place our gratitude that he did so.

The points have been made that my Gauguin is not the real Gauguin, and that he (that is to say, my Gauguin) owes something to romantic conceptions of artistic creation. Both points are true. The first is uninteresting. The second is more interesting, but in itself does not contribute to understanding the problem: for it to do so, we will need to understand what values are involved in, or ignored by, a "romantic" conception of the artist. In any case, the question goes a long way beyond the example of Gauguin, however he is pictured. The question, as I would now express it, is directed to the placing of ethical concerns (even in the wider sense) among other values and, more broadly, among other human needs and projects. I discussed it in terms of an example that pictured, perhaps in "romantic" or bohemian terms, an artist's life. I took the case of artistic activity because the products of that activity, not least in a "romantic" or bohemian form, are things that people concerned about the ethical, or even about morality in the narrow sense, often take to be valuable; I took an individual life, even if a partly imaginary one, because I wanted to relate all these matters to personal decision, rationality, and regret. But this is just one application of two wider questions. What human activities have we reason to be grateful for? How can that gratitude be related to a concern with the ethical, or, more particularly, to a concern for morality in the narrow sense? Indeed, the question extends to a gratitude for morality itself. As Nietzsche constantly reminds us, morality owes a great deal, including its own existence, to the fact that it is not obeyed; it can seem to achieve closure on its own absolute kind of value only because the space in which it operates is created, historically, socially, and psychologically, by kinds of impulse that it rejects. *Moral Luck* does not explore these large issues, but pseudo-Gauguin does stand for more than a question about how far we can expect creative artists to be well-behaved.

The third question raised in the article is that of retrospective justification, and this is the widest, because it can arise beyond the ethical, in any application of practical rationality. It is the question of how far, and in what ways, the view that an agent retrospectively takes of himself or herself may be affected by results and not be directed simply to the ways in which he or she deliberated, or might have better deliberated, before the event. We may say that it is natural enough to be upset if things turn out badly, for oneself or others, as a result of one's action—in that sense, to regret the outcome—but that *self-criticism* rationally applies only to the extent that one might have avoided the outcome by taking greater thought or greater care in advance. Reflection will then naturally turn toward asking when it is true that one might have avoided the outcome; and this reflection may eventually lead to skepticism. But the question I wanted to press comes before that reflection. It questions, rather, a presupposition of dividing our concerns in this way. The presupposition can be put like this: as agents, we seek to be rational; to the extent that we are rational, we are concerned with our agency and its results to the extent that they can be shaped by our rational thought; to the extent that results of our agency could not be affected by greater rationality, we should rationally regard them as like the results of someone else's agency or like a natural event.

This idea seems to me very importantly wrong, and examples I have given in *Moral Luck* and elsewhere have sought to press the point that, in more than one way, my involvement in my action and its results goes beyond the relation I have to it as an ex ante rational deliberator. My discussion of this matter has no doubt not been helped by the fact that I put together the three questions that I would now distinguish as being about morality, about the ethical more broadly, and about rational agency. But although the questions must be distinguished, there are also reasons for eventually addressing them together. Morality in the narrow sense is formed, in part, by the attempt to shape the demands of the ethical to these conceptions of agency. In particular, morality's notion of guilt, of blame directed to oneself, is the notion of the rational self-criticism of a deliberator. This notion and others related to it support the powerful feeling that morality just is the ethical in a rational form. But, even leaving aside the standing invitation that it offers to skepticism, this conception of the ethical runs into impossible problems. In part this is because it is using what is in any case an inadequate idea of agency, which (as I just put it) effectively limits one's involvement in what one does to that of an ex ante rational decider. But further problems arise even if morality is granted this idea of agency. It cannot then meet all the demands of the ethical. Ethical beliefs express themselves, also, in rejection or hostility toward those (at least in the locality) who have the wrong ethical sentiments or none, and if morality is to limit genuinely moral comment to blame, and blame to what is available to the rational deliberator, it is faced with a vast epistemological demand, to show (as Kant appropriately thought) that the correct ethical demands are indeed available to any rational deliberator—as Kant was disposed to put it, "as such."

There are many ways in which the three questions are interrelated. This last argument traces one aspect of morality to its share in the more general idea of agency. Equally, it must be true that this idea of agency is itself formed by aspirations shared by morality, to escape as far as possible from contingency. Again, there are ways in which the demands of morality and rationality may resist being combined. Nagel in his paper made the good point that an agent may know in advance that if things turn out in one way he will have been guilty of an unforgivable wrong, and if in another, he will not. In Gauguin's case, this applies the theory of moral luck to yield an idea of moral hazard. This, in a sense, honors the demands of ex ante rationality, but it is not very acceptable to morality. Moral hazard is an idea that morality itself resists. If the downside risk involves a moral wrong, then (morality will say) one ought not to take that risk; if one ought, or may, take that risk, the downside cannot have those relations to morality. Rather similarly, morality resists the notion of a moral cost, in the sense of a moral wrong knowingly committed by an agent who is doing something that even from a moral point of view is better: in that case, it will say, the wrong cannot ultimately be a wrong, the cost cannot really be a moral cost.

To evaluate these replies, to assess the force of these invocations of the moral, we need to bring in another of the three questions: the placing of morality itself in relation to the ethical more broadly, and in relation to other human concerns. By pursuing such questions, we may be able to penetrate the misplaced reassurances that morality offers, and rid ourselves of some of the perplexities that it encourages. The oxymoron in "moral luck" shows up a fault line to which, I still think, it is worth applying the chisel.

Notes

1. In *Ethics and the Limits of Philosophy* (London and Cambridge, Mass., 1985).

2. But not for the same reasons. Edward Craig offers an illuminating approach to this and related aspects of knowledge in *Knowledge and the State of Nature* (Oxford, 1990).

3. *The View from Nowhere* (Oxford, 1986).

4. I have discussed this idea of the voluntary in "Voluntary Acts and Responsible Agents," *Oxford Journal of Legal Studies* 10 (1990), and have argued that it is both inherent in the concept of action, and essentially superficial, in chapter III of *Shame and Necessity* (Berkeley, 1992).